AFTER NEOLIBERALISM?

After Neoliberalism?

THE LEFT AND ECONOMIC REFORMS IN LATIN AMERICA

Gustavo A. Flores-Macías

OXFORD
UNIVERSITY PRESS

OXFORD
UNIVERSITY PRESS

Oxford University Press, Inc., publishes works that further
Oxford University's objective of excellence
in research, scholarship, and education.

Oxford   New York
Auckland   Cape Town   Dar es Salaam   Hong Kong   Karachi
Kuala Lumpur   Madrid   Melbourne   Mexico City   Nairobi
New Delhi   Shanghai   Taipei   Toronto

With offices in
Argentina   Austria   Brazil   Chile   Czech Republic   France   Greece
Guatemala   Hungary   Italy   Japan   Poland   Portugal   Singapore
South Korea   Switzerland   Thailand   Turkey   Ukraine   Vietnam

Published by Oxford University Press, Inc.
198 Madison Avenue, New York, New York 10016

www.oup.com

Library of Congress Cataloging-in-Publication Data
Flores-Macías, Gustavo
After neoliberalism? : the left and economic reforms in Latin America / Gustavo Flores-Macías.
    p.   cm.
Includes bibliographical references and index.
ISBN 978-0-19-989165-8 (hbk.)—ISBN 978-0-19-989167-2 (pbk.)
1. Latin America—Economic policy. 2. Neoliberalism—Latin America. 3. Political parties—Latin America.
4. Latin America—Politics and government—21st century. 5. Latin America—Politics and government—20th century. I. Title.
HC125.F529   2012
338.98—dc23   2011034943

Publication of this book was supported by The Hull Memerial Publication Fund of Cornell University.

9 8 7 6 5 4 3 2 1

Printed in the United States of America
on acid-free paper

A mi familia, por su cariño y por ser siempre mis mejores maestros.

Contents

List of Figures

List of Tables

Preface and Acknowledgments

ONE OF MY most vivid childhood memories growing up in Mexico was when my parents took me to a political rally in support of the leftist candidate in the 1988 elections. It was the first time in decades that an opposition candidate had a chance at challenging the 59-year-old regime. I was only 11 years old but was fully aware that, by joining in the demonstrations in Mexico City, I was participating in something big, something historic. In the midst of widespread fraud allegations, the government declared the incumbent the winner, but the close result landed a blow to the regime by showing it was not invincible. Although the election became a landmark in the country's push against authoritarianism, Mexico would have to wait another 12 years for an opposition candidate to reach the presidency—and it is still waiting for a leftist president. That election taught valuable lessons about the left and the opposition more generally, but for me, it instilled a desire to study politics and government.

Since, my interest in the left grew as a consequence of what happened in Mexico in the absence of a leftist government, juxtaposed against the rising prominence of leftist governments in other Latin American countries. In Mexico, the government that began in 1988 embraced in earnest a set of market-oriented policies that completely transformed the economic landscape of the country, at the same time modernizing it and worsening inequality and informality. Every subsequent government deepened these policies, and every time, the left categorically denounced them. Since the presidency has eluded the left since the transition to democracy, I could only wonder whether and how the Mexican left would have changed economic course as they claimed they would.

Elsewhere in Latin America, leftist opposition parties denounced the adoption of market-oriented policies with the same zeal, but their arrival to power in many countries resulted in an unexpected mosaic of economic policy courses. They ranged from those that maintained most of their predecessors' macroeconomic policies in place to those that significantly reversed market reforms. Given a shared rejection of market reforms, why leftist governments would follow such different policy courses was a question that puzzled me.

Since 2005, when I started writing the initial sketches of the book, I have accumulated a number of intellectual debts to family, friends, colleagues, and institutions. I am grateful to my graduate advisers, John Bailey, Marc Howard, and Chappell Lawson for their guidance, encouragement, and patience. Throughout the years they have been a source of inspiration and an example to follow for their generosity with their time.

I am also indebted to Francisco Flores-Macías, Sarah Kreps, Steven Levitsky, Raúl Madrid, Kenneth Roberts, and Kurt Weyland, who graciously read several drafts of the manuscript. Their feedback was not only invaluable for the completion of the book, but has shaped my work much beyond this project. My sincere gratitude goes as well to John Carey, Matthew Cleary, Javier Corrales, Jorge Domínguez, Oliver Kaplan, Michael Shifter, Eduardo Silva, and Nicolas van de Walle, who read all or parts of the manuscript and provided valuable comments.

I would like to thank Christopher Anderson, Moisés Arce, María Cook, Hernán Gómez Bruera, Kenneth Greene, Wendy Hunter, Peter Katzenstein, Margarita López Maya, Scott Mainwaring, Sean McGraw, Guillermo O'Donnell, Tom Pepinsky, Max Pfeffer, Pablo Pinto, Timothy Scully, Tige Stading, Susan Stokes, Sid Tarrow, Arturo Valenzuela, Wendy Wolford, and Brian Younger, who were very kind in sharing their perspectives and helping me think through major questions.

I also thank María Mercedes Agudelo, Carlos Arce Macías, Efrén García, Cassio Luiselli, and Fritz Mayer, who fostered my love for the study of politics and encouraged me to pursue a PhD. Bruno de Larragoiti, Don Leonard, Gabriel Rodrigues, Andrew Simon, and Kayla Strong provided stellar research assistance.

Three anonymous reviewers went above and beyond to provide detailed and constructive feedback. I really appreciate their thoughtful suggestions, which improved the book significantly. My gratitude goes as well to David McBride, OUP's editor-in-chief for the social sciences, and his team for skillfully shepherding the book to completion.

I also want to acknowledge Georgetown's Center for Latin American Studies, Harvard's Rockefeller Center for Latin American Studies, and Cornell's Polson

Institute for Global Development for providing financial support and an intellectual environment where many of the ideas reflected here took shape. Finally, I would like to recognize the many Brazilians, Chileans, Colombians, Mexicans, and Venezuelans, who kindly helped me conduct field research by sharing their perspectives and contacts. This project could not have been completed without their support.

Lastly, I am forever grateful to my family for their unconditional love and support from day one. My parents, Edna and Gustavo, instilled in me an appreciation for knowledge and have accompanied me in every step of the journey. My brother, Paco, has always been a true friend and a role model to me and has encouraged me to strive for excellence. My wife, Sarah, is not only the love of my life but also a relentless intellectual partner. Our sons, Luke and Sebastián, have brought unimaginable joy to our lives. With all my love and admiration, this book is dedicated to them.

Ithaca, New York

AFTER NEOLIBERALISM?

1 INTRODUCTION

The Left and the Challenge to Market Orthodoxy in Latin America

"THE PILLAGE OF our natural resources by foreign companies is over!" announced Bolivia's President Evo Morales on May 1, 2006—Labor Day in that country—as soldiers took control of facilities in the country's gas fields.[1] "Let it be nationalized. All that was privatized, let it be nationalized!" proclaimed Venezuelan President Hugo Chávez several months later as he unveiled plans to expropriate the country's telephone and power companies.[2] "Stop extorting the Argentinian people!" demanded Argentina's President Néstor Kirchner of the country's two largest supermarket chains after establishing price controls to ameliorate inflation.[3] Although the rhetoric may be common among Latin American politicians, these measures marked a sharp break from the market orthodoxy that prevailed in the region until left-of-center governments reached power at the turn of the 21st century. For the first time since the region adopted market-oriented reforms beginning in the 1980s, national governments introduced policies decisively increasing the state's intervention in the economy.

Left-of-center governments' responses to neoliberal reforms have not been uniform, however.[4] They have rolled back market reforms in different areas and to different extents. Some have aimed to reverse liberalization across several areas of the economy, as in Bolivia, Ecuador, and Venezuela. Others have opted for preserving market reforms while compensating with redistributive policies—social provisioning and broad-based safety nets as complements to neoliberal reforms—as in Argentina, Brazil, and Nicaragua. In Chile and Uruguay, socialist governments continued many of the policies of previous administrations, which aimed to reduce inequalities within a decidedly market-oriented economy.

This book is about those economic policy changes conducted by leftist governments in Latin America at the turn of the century and the factors that have made such changes possible. It speaks to a fundamental question of comparative political economy: what are the conditions that make the initiation and maintenance of economic transformations more likely? I address this question in the context of the region's leftist governments and the degree to which they have reversed market-oriented reforms, taking into account nationalizations, price controls, foreign exchange controls, tax reform, and government spending. Beyond the broad question of what makes economic transformation more likely, I answer two additional, more specific questions: What explains why some governments have moved more aggressively than others to reverse pro-market reforms? Which aspects have they rolled back and why?

This book tackles those questions with a theoretical and empirical study of economic transformations in Latin America. The analysis produces two central findings. First, the rise of the left to power in the region was not a unified movement with coherent economic policies. Rather, it was a succession of victories for leftist candidates whose policies occupy a broad swath of the economic spectrum. Thus, in contrast to the warnings of a "leftist tsunami" across Latin America,[5] or the concerns that Ricardo Lagos's economic policies in Chile would represent a return to Allende's socialism,[6] that Lula's presidency in Brazil would constitute a "workers' government,"[7] or that Evo Morales would follow through on his promises to "defeat the Colonial state and the neoliberal order" in Bolivia,[8] the left in government's record shows that not all leftist projects were diametrically opposed to the Washington Consensus. Instead, economic pluralism is the currency of leftist governments in the region. While some have been markedly statist, others have adhered to the pro-market trend that prevailed in the region during the 1980s and 1990s.

Second, regarding the factors that explain differences across leftist governments' economic policies, I argue that a key factor in these governments' ability to undertake drastic economic policy transformations is the degree of institutionalization of the party system. Countries with an institutionalized party system—those with a predictable, structured political process, a wide sense of legitimacy among the population, and a well-rooted tradition of playing by the rules of the game—are likely to preserve the pro-market status quo and conduct moderate economic transformations. Conversely, countries with a disjointed party system—those where party identities are weak among the population, party discipline is low, and the parties' internal life is loosely organized—tend to depart from the status quo and carry out drastic, unpredictable reforms.

The different outcomes attributed to the two types of party systems result from differences in: (1) the type of candidate likely to reach power, and (2) the parties' ability to influence the executive's policies. On the one hand, incentives and constraints characteristic of institutionalized party politics make it harder for outsider candidates without a stake in the system to reach the presidency and carry out drastic economic transformations. On the other hand, those incentives and constraints facilitate interparty and interbranch cooperation, making it easier for the different political forces to influence the president's policies. In contrast, centrifugal incentives characteristic of party systems in disarray make it likely for anti-system candidates to reach power, and undermine political parties' ability to prevent the president from conducting drastic changes to the status quo. This relationship between party systems and policy outcomes is not peculiar to the left or the right—indeed, weak party systems do not necessarily result in policies associated with a particular ideology or group but in extreme policy positions away from the prevailing order.

However, the arrival of leftist candidates to power at the end of the 20th century in Latin America offers a range of cases—from the generalized adherence to pro-market policies to the adoption of significant statist policy transformations—to test this relationship while holding several cultural, institutional, and historical factors constant.[9] As the book discusses at length, the evidence regarding the type of leftist governments' economic policies provides empirical support for this causal relationship. Leftist governments that resulted from elections in party systems with low levels of institutionalization—Bolivia, Ecuador, and Venezuela—have carried out policies significantly altering the prevailing model. As the level of institutionalization of the party system increases, as in Argentina, Brazil, or Nicaragua, so does policy moderation. Those leftist governments that came to power in countries with higher levels of party system institutionalization—Chile and Uruguay—are those where the pro-market status quo has generally remained unchanged. In short, in the context of the arrival of the left to power at a time when market orthodoxy was the dominant paradigm, the less institutionalized the party system, the more statist the policies and the greater the departure from the pro-market baseline. In other words, it is the interaction between party systems in disarray and the executive's leftist ideology that is likely to lead to drastic statist transformations.

A Study of the Left, Economic Reforms, and Party Systems

This book combines the study of three main topics, namely the left, economic reforms, and party systems. It advances our understanding of how the left has governed, what policy changes it has carried out, and the determinants of those transformations. Compared to previous studies, this book breaks new ground in each topic as follows:

THE LEFT IN GOVERNMENT

To date, most studies of the left in Latin America have focused on political or social dimensions. For example, some scholars working at the intersection of the left and politics have focused on the political parties that brought leftist candidates to power.[10] Others have sought to explain the factors conducive to the arrival of the left to power and the timing of this arrival, emphasizing as key explanatory factors the region's unaddressed income inequality and the erosion of the military's veto power[11] or declining public enthusiasm for market reforms.[12] Others have emphasized classification issues, highlighting the variety of leftist projects and the inadequacy of monolithic or dichotomous classifications of the left.[13] Still others have grappled with the relationship between the rise of the left and democracy[14] and the expansion of citizenship rights.[15]

While these studies of the left have offered valuable insights regarding electoral, taxonomical, and political issues, they have virtually ignored the left in government in general and its economic policies in particular.[16] Little attention has been paid in scholarly work to systematically documenting and analyzing the coincidences and disparities in the type of economic policy transformations conducted by these governments across the region. This is an important oversight given that leftist governments relied mainly on the condemnation of pro-market reforms as a way to define their political platforms and give meaning to their political projects. Often it was precisely the repudiation of pro-market policies that became their raison d'être as opposition candidates. In particular, the striking differences in economic policies followed by leftist governments—in spite of their shared commitment to social justice and wealth distribution—remain understudied.

Furthermore, the study of *how* the left governs should be a central concern for scholars, since leftist governments' policies affect the lives of hundreds of millions of people. In 2009 roughly 330 million people—or two thirds of Latin America's total population—living in Argentina, Bolivia, Brazil, Chile, Ecuador, Nicaragua, Uruguay, and Venezuela were governed by the left at the national level. Similarly, leftist presidents were stewards of approximately 62 percent of the region's gross domestic product (GDP).[17] This study addresses a substantive slice of the policies conducted by these leftist governments, namely their economic policies.

PARTY SYSTEMS

A second contribution is that this study reconsiders the relationship between party systems and economic policy reform, and contributes to its theoretical development. Thus far, most of the theoretical development of party systems has focused on its effects on democracy[18] rather than economic policy making. The existing studies on the importance of party systems in explaining economic reforms have overlooked the role of institutionalization in favor of fragmentation and polarization and have failed to generate a plausible causal logic. For example, in their seminal work on dual transitions, Stephan Haggard and Robert Kaufman study the determinants of economic reforms during the 1980s and early 1990s in 12 middle-income developing countries[19] and suggest that party systems played an important role in the consolidation of market reforms.[20] This work constitutes a valuable first step in identifying the role of party systems in shaping economic policy transformations, but the mechanism is underdeveloped and systematic testing is lacking. As one scholar observed, Haggard and Kaufman's claims about the effect of party systems on economic transformations "are more an assertion than an argument about how things are" and the exact role that these institutions play for economic reform "is still up for grabs."[21] As the authors readily admit, their work "only begins to explore this issue."[22]

This book differs from Haggard and Kaufman's approach in a number of respects. While they are interested in the factors that "determine the capacity of governments to manage the economy effectively,"[23] the argument presented here makes no assumption as to what constitutes effective or desirable economic policy (or any normative considerations). Instead, this book's main concern is the factors that determine governments' ability to effect economic transformations in general, regardless of whether such changes are sound economic policy. Moreover, while Haggard and Kaufman emphasize the role of party system *fragmentation* and *polarization* as key determinant factors, this book underscores the role of party system *institutionalization*. As I show, party system fragmentation and polarization do not provide much explanatory leverage to account for variation across leftist governments' economic policy changes in the region. In addition, while Haggard and Kaufman point to the role of the party system as an important factor in "understanding the *consolidation* of reforms,"[24] this book points to the role of party systems both in determining the type of candidates likely to reach power and in *initiating* economic reforms.[25] It takes a step back to account for the arrival of certain leaders with agendas for drastic transformations in some cases and moderate reform in others, as well as leaders' ability to carry out reform once they are in office. Lastly, and most importantly, Haggard and Kaufman posit a relationship in which centrifugal forces result in policy paralysis, thus making reforms more difficult, while centripetal forces reduce the power of actors opposed to reform, thus making reforms more likely.[26] Conversely, this book finds that centrifugal dynamics in the party system facilitate the election of antisystem candidates advocating drastic change, and then encourage the executive's circumvention of the legislature in order to carry out significant transformations by decree. Centripetal dynamics, in contrast, tend to facilitate the election of moderate leaders and the adoption of piecemeal reforms through a policy process where intra- and interparty deliberation shapes the executive's economic policies in meaningful ways.

ECONOMIC POLICY TRANSFORMATIONS

This book also advances our understanding of the determinants of economic reform more generally. In the context of leftist governments, the explanation I advance based on party system institutionalization challenges alternative explanations frequently invoked as key determinants of economic transformations. First, it runs counter to widely held views that leftist radicalism is mainly due to the availability of natural resources or the resource curse.[27] This account suggests that statist economic policies in countries governed by the left are a consequence of these countries' dependence on commodity exports because natural resource abundance generates the illusion that fiscal and monetary stringency are unnecessary. While this goes some way toward accounting for governments' additional room for maneuver, I show that fluctuations in commodity prices alone cannot account for governments' ability to carry out statist economic transformations across countries.

Second, this argument also challenges accounts that point to economic crises as the cause of economic transformation.[28] The economic crises view suggests that such events determine how drastically governments will tend to implement corrective measures. The logic rests on the notion that crises make economic transformations more palatable and even desirable to the public, whereas the same reforms would encounter considerably more opposition in the absence of extreme hardship. However, although I find that financial instability played a role in motivating caution in economic policy making, severe economic crises before leftist governments took office failed to generate a pattern of significant reform across the region.

Third, the party institutionalization argument runs counter to the view that executive powers are crucial in carrying out policies that significantly depart from the status quo.[29] Instead, some of the weakest presidents by regional standards carried out significant economic transformations. Although new constitutions gave executives considerable power vis-à-vis the legislature in some cases, important economic changes were conducted before the new powers were granted. Most importantly, the presidents' ability to alter executive-legislative relations rests on the type of party system, which determines the extent to which parties represent meaningful actors in the policy process.

Fourth, this book's findings challenge the claim that governments' ability to carry out significant economic transformations is contingent on the degree to which the previous economic model was established. This view implies that a country's past policies play an important role in the government's ability to modify them in the present.[30] However, while I find that the extent to which the market model is ingrained in society plays a role in one case, this explanation fails to account for important statist reforms in countries that adopted deep and early market reforms before the left arrived to power.

Lastly, a fifth contested explanation focuses on the relative strength of interest groups to account for economic reforms.[31] This view argues that organized labor has been one of the groups most affected by market reforms and one of the main champions of statist policies.[32] However, I find that organized labor was not one of the main determinants of statist transformations and that in some cases it even became an obstacle to such reforms.

As this book will show, some of these factors have played a role in explaining economic policies in specific countries, from unprecedented oil windfalls in Venezuela, to economic instability in Brazil, to the depth of market reforms in Chile. Thus, for any given country, party system institutionalization is not alone in explaining why a leftist government conducted statist or pro-market policies.

However, although different configurations of factors help account for economic transformations depending on the country, party system institutionalization is the explanatory factor that best accounts for differences across the region in a systematic way. Other factors are less useful in explaining the type of economic transformations when evaluated in comparative perspective.

Leftist Governments' Economic Policies in Historical Perspective

In order to situate historically the leftist governments in Latin America and understand the scope and timing of their economic policy changes, the next section introduces the prevailing context in which leftist candidates reached power at the turn of the 21st century.

THE REVERSAL OF A GREAT TRANSFORMATION? MARKET ORTHODOXY AS THE DOMINANT PARADIGM

Over the course of the 1980s and 1990s, Latin America undertook what Barbara Stallings described as the "most significant transformation of economic policy since World War II."[33] During this period, the region's economies increasingly moved toward an open, market-oriented model of development and moved away from the state-interventionist, import-substitution industrialization (ISI) model that had characterized them for decades. Sometimes gradually and other times suddenly, Latin American governments conducted a series of reforms toward liberalizing their economies. Beginning with Chile's economic liberalization shortly after Augusto Pinochet's military coup in 1973,[34] one after another, countries in the region followed in the adoption of different sets of market-oriented policies to reduce the role of the state in the economy.

The ISI model had been Latin America's predominant paradigm following the Great Depression until the debt crisis in the early 1980s. ISI consisted of a government-led industrialization policy based on the replacement of imports with the domestic production of goods.[35] It relied on the protection of infant industries through fiscal policy tools such as subsidies and trade barriers in the form of tariffs and quotas. In addition, it was characterized by the proliferation of state-owned enterprises and state-funded development banks "entrusted with the promotion of specific ventures."[36] The quick success of the ISI process during the 1940s and 1950s led observers to describe the economic growth in some Latin American countries as true "developmental miracles"—with Brazil and Mexico experiencing annual growth rates hovering around 6 percent, for example. As a result, the Latin American social landscape was transformed from a predominantly rural to an industrializing urban society, with emerging domestic markets, business sectors, and a middle class.

The debt crisis of the 1980s, however, marked the end of the ISI model and the beginning of the "lost decade" for Latin America. Although scholars pointed out initial signs of the model's exhaustion—such as the national industries' inability to generate backward linkages, declining competitiveness, and the poor quality of products—as early as the 1960s,[37] the crisis that ensued after Mexico's default in 1982 became the ISI model's coup de grace and accelerated the adoption of market-oriented reforms. Fostered by Latin America's worst recession since the 1930s, the adoption of market-oriented reforms quickly gained traction in the rest of the region. Reforms included the reduction or elimination of trade barriers, government subsidies, state-owned enterprises, price and exchange rate controls, and public deficits.

Toward the late 1990s, virtually all countries in the region had adopted some or most of the market-oriented model. Following Chile's early embrace of market orthodoxy, the rest of the region, with the exception of Cuba,[38] began a transition by first adopting stabilization measures—to contain balance of payment, debt, and inflation emergencies—and then conducting structural changes aimed at reorienting the economy away from state intervention.[39] Among the early movers were Bolivia and Mexico. A second wave followed, including Costa Rica and Uruguay. Some of the late adopters were Argentina, Brazil, Peru, and Venezuela.[40]

The adoption of the new model has had a mixed record of success and failure. It was successful in shoring up government finances, keeping inflation at bay, and bringing macroeconomic stability to the region.[41] Trade liberalization introduced more and better products for consumers, and privatizations improved the quality of services. The elimination of subsidies and tariffs forced firms to become competitive in order to survive in the global marketplace.

But the "most significant transformation since WWII" came with important costs as well. Entire industries—unable to compete with the sudden exposure to foreign competition—disappeared. The thinning of state bureaucracies augmented the ranks of informality and unemployment. Firms had to reduce their production costs in order to compete, often at the expense of workers' social security contributions. By and large, the new model was unsuccessful in keeping the countries' increasing inequality in check.[42]

As with any measure with significant redistributive consequences, there were those who favored market reforms—generally the capital-intensive business sectors—and those who opposed them—largely labor and labor-intensive industries. The reforms, however, appeared to be omnipresent and irreversible. The Washington Consensus permeated most policy and academic circles as the dominant paradigm.[43] International financial organizations staunchly championed market reforms and conditioned monetary and technical assistance on adherence to the neoliberal canons. Courses emphasizing supply-side economics took a prominent place in the most prestigious universities in the United States and the developed world. In several Latin American countries, US-educated government elites were firm believers in the benefits of the neoliberal model and went to great lengths to apply its principles to their countries.[44]

Several aspects of the global economy appeared to make market reforms permanent. Financial liberalization created incentives for governments to maintain orthodox policies in an effort to attract and retain much-needed foreign investment. Otherwise—whenever a country's macroeconomic stability presented signs of weakness, for example—technology and communications made it easy for investors to remove funds from a country in seconds. Moreover, a web of bilateral and multilateral international commitments, such as trade agreements and investment promotion accords, made it particularly difficult for future governments to reverse market reforms.

Not surprisingly, and in line with Francis Fukuyama's proclamation of the death of alternative developmental paradigms in "The End of History?,"[45] market reforms were considered "nearly ubiquitous"[46] and "the norm in virtually every Latin American nation."[47] Opposition to market orthodoxy was "voiced but not well-articulated, broadly considered, or able to appeal to voting majorities."[48] Dani Rodrik wrote about the remarkable "convergence" on what constitutes good economic policy.[49] In the words of Sebastian Edwards, macroeconomic populism in Latin America—as distributive policies are often referred to—was dead.[50] Without a doubt, market orthodoxy reigned supreme in Latin America.

At the turn of this century, however, a wave of leftist electoral victories took neoliberal hegemony by surprise. Assisted by the ghost of *fracasomanía*—the certainty that grips Latin Americans that yet another model of development has failed them[51]—leftist political projects advocating a change of developmental model became increasingly popular among broad sectors of the electorate in different countries. One by one, the same leftist projects that had been proscribed or had received little electoral support during the 1980s and 1990s began to gain traction at the ballot box, winning local, regional, and, eventually, national elections. More often than not, the rejection of market orthodoxy was at the center of their political campaigns.

Beginning in 1998 with the election of Hugo Chávez as president of Venezuela, governments headed by left-of-center presidents conducted a series of economic policy changes aimed at modifying the prevailing economic model. Although most presidents campaigned on an anti-neoliberal platform, the extent of the reversal of market reforms has been varied. At times, the changes in economic policy have been moderate—preserving the market as the core of the model of development but trying to correct some of its failures through increased government intervention. Other times, economic policy changes have been drastic—significantly reversing market reforms and giving the state a prominent role as an agent of economic development. As a result, some statist policies that had fallen out of grace after the failure of ISI reappeared. To varying degrees, countries governed by the left turned to nationalizations, trade barriers, price controls, foreign exchange restrictions, and land reform in an effort to deliver on the promise of economic prosperity made during the campaigns. In short, the "most important economic transformation since WWII" was being transformed again.

AN ADVERSE CONTEXT FOR THE RISE OF THE LEFT

Between 1998 and 2008, leftist presidents came to power through the ballot in Venezuela (1998), Chile (2000), Brazil (2002), Argentina (2003), Uruguay (2005), Bolivia (2005), Nicaragua (2006), and Ecuador (2007). For the first time in history, incumbent leftist parties have been reelected in Venezuela (2000 and 2006), Brazil (2006 and 2010), Chile (2006), Argentina (2007 and 2011), Bolivia (2009), Ecuador (2009), and Nicaragua (2011). Matthew Cleary describes the recent arrival of leftist governments to power as:

> a stunning turn of events for a region in which previous leftist victories (such as Salvador Allende's in Chile in 1970, or Alan García's in Peru in 1985) occurred so rarely and ended so disastrously. And it comes as a surprise to most observers, who had interpreted the dearth of leftist victories in the 1980s and 1990s as evidence that the left was permanently hamstrung by "pacted" transitions, which tilted the electoral playing field to the right, and by the hegemony of neoliberal economics, which constrained the possibilities for redistributive policy-making and decimated labor and other mass organizations. Leftist electoral victories in such a context seemed impossible.[52]

To be sure, the left's prospects of reaching power—both peacefully and violently—during the last quarter of the century were severely undermined by a series of setbacks on military, political, and economic fronts.[53] Beyond the hard blows landed by adverse events, including Ernesto "Che" Guevara's military defeat and death in Bolivia in 1967, the death of Salvador Allende in the 1973 military coup, and the electoral defeat of the Sandinistas in the 1990 election in Nicaragua, several more enduring obstacles stood in the way of the left's transformation into a real electoral force in Latin America.

First, the proscription and persecution of the left during Latin America's military dictatorships severely undermined the left's ability to continue—let alone strengthen—its political institutional life.[54] To different extents, depending on the country, leftist leaders were persecuted, exiled, tortured, and assassinated by the military regimes. Although some parties maintained certain continuity through clandestine meetings and communication with leaders in exile, their inability to participate openly in politics undermined their organizational ability and popular support.

Second, when the right-wing dictatorships turned over power to civilian governments, several institutional constraints remained as important obstacles for the left's arrival to power. Several "pacted" transitions—negotiated compromises between an authoritarian regime and a democratic opposition—that took place across Latin America gave the right an advantage in the new democratic playing field.[55] In the case of Chile, for example, the dictatorship's institutional legacy remained in place long after Pinochet turned over power to elected President Patricio Aylwin.[56] In Brazil, the military was able to maintain important prerogatives including designated cabinet posts, control over the intelligence agency, and implicit veto power over key policy decisions.[57] In Uruguay, the leader of the leftist National Front and up to 5,000 politicians were banned from participating in elections in the aftermath of the Naval Club Pact.[58] In places where the left was not openly forbidden, such as Mexico, the old regime frequently sabotaged leftist candidates during campaigns.[59]

Third, the military remained an important veto player across the region.[60] Even after military governments turned over power to civilian rule, the armed forces in Latin America remained as the guardians of the nation's values and the permanent interest of the nation. The military returned to the barracks, but took with it its historical mission of upholding the constitutional order and remaining "the last bulwark of nationality."[61] Throughout the 1980s and 1990s, the threat of the armed forces intervening to correct civilian imprudence or to protect the nation's permanent interests and the institutions left behind by the authoritarian regimes was ever-present in the background. Several prominent examples of the armed forces' directly confronting civilian rule served as a constant reminder that the military was willing to leave the barracks if civilians overstepped their restricted mandate.[62]

Fourth, the left's prospects of reaching power also suffered from the disrepute of its economic projects—from socialism (which the left had historically advocated) to ISI (which the left often reluctantly embraced as second best alternative). Two major events contributed to the left's discredit: the debt crisis of the early 1980s and the collapse of the Soviet Union.[63] The debt crisis contributed to a generalized perception of failure of the ISI model and statist policies advocated by the left. Lax monetary policies, tolerance for high fiscal deficits, and trade protectionism became the culprits responsible for the economic debacle that marked the beginning of Latin America's lost decade. Government intervention in the economy became synonymous with inefficiency, corruption, and bureaucracy. Similarly, the collapse of the Soviet Union demonstrated the economic vicissitudes of centrally planned economies and the vices and inconsistencies of the Soviet system. It heralded the universalization of the market economy as the only feasible mode of organizing economic relations.

Fifth, the neoliberal reforms that followed weakened the organized labor movements that constituted one of the left's main bases of support.[64] Several factors contributed to the weakening of labor. The reduction in government spending and the privatization of state enterprise translated into the massive dismissal of formerly unionized government bureaucrats and the elimination of special privileges. Also, trade liberalization sharpened the differences among workers of different industries, undermining their horizontal solidarity.[65] Moreover, the exposure of a previously protected domestic industry to foreign competition resulted in layoffs particularly affecting highly unionized industries.[66] Finally, the adoption of stabilization policies that relied on wage restraints to enhance productivity and competitiveness further eroded labor's ability to negotiate.[67]

Overcoming these obstacles seemed an impossible task for leftist parties in the region. In describing its general disarray in the early 1990s, Steve Ellner characterized the left as "more disoriented and lacking in credible options than ever before."[68] For Jorge Castañeda, the left was "on the run and on the ropes."[69]

OFF "THE ROPES" AND ON TO POWER IN A POST-SOVIET WORLD

Much has changed in the region since the early 1990s. The post-Soviet world presented a completely different—and unexpected—panorama for the left in Latin America. Paradoxically, the collapse of the Soviet Union resulted in conditions that benefited the left's rise. The left dropped the burden of the link with the Soviet Union.[70] Soviet rhetoric and policies no longer affected the dynamics of leftist parties. This gave room to other forms of left, including social democracy and the "new left," to jump to the political arena without the stigma of being labeled as agents of international communism.

Moreover, the democratic norm gained traction both domestically and internationally after the end of the Cold War. Internally, after a series of peaceful turnovers of power through elections, countries gradually became more habituated to democracy. Civilian governments steadily pushed back on institutional restrictions inherited from military governments. Democratically elected governments began to hold the armed forces accountable for atrocities committed during the military dictatorships.[71] As a consequence, a breach in the constitutional order of a country became more difficult to justify before domestic audiences.

Internationally, a change in US foreign policy from anticommunist to democratic activism contributed to the spread of the democracy norm and the preservation of the constitutional order in the region.[72] US foreign policy shifted from supporting anticommunist governments in the region at all costs—regardless of their respect for democracy and human rights—to promoting democracy abroad as a central foreign policy objective. In turn, the European Union also contributed to buttress the democratic norm by including "democratic clauses" in trade agreements with Latin American countries, for example.

Lastly, the process of economic interdependence and the margins established by international financial institutions left governments with little room to maneuver outside the market economy. Capital mobility and the facility with which much-needed foreign investment could leave a country appeared to reduce the possible options available for any government, regardless of ideological affinity. To some extent, these restrictions forced the left to operate within certain parameters—effectively bringing the extremes of the political spectrum closer to the middle—and reduced the fear of the left radically transforming the economy. This gave voters confidence to vote for an economically constrained left that often focused more on human rights and the environment rather than a dramatic economic return to communism.

As conditions changed, the left also adapted to the new reality. It had to renounce violence if it was to dispute power through elections. Thus, democracy and human rights became two core issues in the left's agenda.[73] It also had to reject communism, embrace a minimum of market orthodoxy, and commit to the respect of private property in order to appeal to broader sectors of the population and win a national election. These two transformations did not resolve the left's ensuing identity crisis, but they allowed the left to both enter the institutional arena and differentiate its project from the rest of the democratic actors. In short, they provided a sense of direction if not destination. The currency of the left's historical demands for social justice helped it endure the test of the transformation. The severe economic inequality affecting Latin America made the left's project increasingly popular following the generalized adoption of market reforms.

Conceptual Clarifications

The study of the economic policy transformations conducted by leftist governments in Latin America requires that three central terms be defined clearly, namely *the left*, *pro-market policies*, and *statist policies*. Defining them early on is important because they may carry multiple connotations and are often normatively charged. For some, for example, the left evokes disregard for private property, the obesity and inefficiency of the welfare state, and economic recklessness in the form of public deficits, debt, and inflation. It invokes the specter of a return to the statist model of development that led to the region's economic catastrophe during the "lost decade" of the 1980s. For others, the left represents valiantly resisting the injustices of savage capitalism, striving to achieve social justice, and advocating respect for human rights and the environment.[74] It conjures up the struggle to ameliorate poverty.

The same is true for pro-market and statist policies. For some, pro-market policies have become synonymous with a system of economic domination imposed by the "center" onto the "periphery," whereby multinational corporations and the "masters of the private economy dominate policy formulation as well as the structuring of thought and opinion."[75] For others, it represents a system conducive to economic freedom and decentralization that promotes growth by unleashing the commercial energy of the private sector.[76] In the next paragraphs I set out my use of these terms throughout the rest of the book.

DEFINITION OF THE LEFT

Defining *the left* is an elusive task, but having a working definition is important. Former Brazilian President Fernando Henrique Cardoso offers a general definition, regarding the left as being against the established social order, and the right as being for preserving it: "being a Leftist is to be in favor of progress."[77] Although useful as a first step toward providing conceptual clarity, several elements in this definition remain problematic: what constitutes progress and what is the established social order, for example? A more specific definition is provided by Castañeda, who defines *the left* as "parties, movements, groups, and political leaders who privilege democracy and human rights over domestic security, social justice over economic performance, income distribution over well-functioning markets, social spending over controlling inflation, and the need to spend over healthy government finances."[78] However, this definition would overlook the experiences of governments that emerged from parties historically identified with the popular sectors but that have privileged orthodox economic policies, economic performance, and healthy government finances.

A more current definition is presented by Cleary:

> a political movement with historical antecedents in communist and socialist political parties, grassroots social movements, populist social organizations, or other political forces that traditionally have had anti-systemic, revolutionary, or transformative objectives. The mobilization form and degree of radicalism may vary across countries. But in all cases the left shares (at least rhetorically, and usually substantively) a concern with redistribution and social justice, and it finds mass support among segments of the population that are severely disadvantaged under the current economic order.[79]

I rely on this broad conception of the left for the purposes of this study, because it recognizes a central concern—social justice—at the heart of the political movement's objectives, but it also acknowledges variation in the ways through which this objective is achieved. Thus, when I use the term *leftist governments*, I refer to those governments that reached power through the nomination of one of the political parties belonging to the political movement described above. I do not mean, however, that every government resulting from such parties will implement a coherent or unified set of policies. Indeed, one of the motivations of this study is that these governments have often implemented policies that do not cohere around a unified program.

DEFINITION OF PRO-MARKET AND STATIST POLICIES

I use the term *pro-market* to refer to the set of free-market economic policies implemented as a response to the import-substitution industrialization in Latin America. These policies, sometimes generally referred to as neoliberalism or the Washington Consensus, include undistorted market prices, fiscal discipline, market-determined exchange rates, trade liberalization, and privatizations.[80] In essence, it refers to those stabilization and structural reform measures aimed at reducing government intervention in the economy and facilitating freer market activity.

Conversely, I use the term *statist* to refer to those policies that seek to increase the level of government intervention in the economy. Such policies include nationalizations, price controls, foreign exchange controls, barriers to trade, and lax fiscal discipline. Thus, when I refer to the reversal of pro-market reforms, I am speaking of economic policy changes aimed at replacing market-oriented policies with those favoring state intervention in the economy, and vice versa.

It is worth noting that a normative evaluation of the desirability of a particular set of economic policies—whether pro-market or pro-statist—is well beyond the scope of this study. Each country is unique in its particular economic situation and requires a different mix of policies depending on its specific characteristics and needs. Regardless of the passion that the debate between advocates of pro-market and pro-statist policies arouses, it is not the objective of this study to evaluate the appropriateness of these policies in general or the suitability of leftist government policies in particular.

Research Design and Plan of the Book

I make the case for the importance of party systems for economic reform through a combination of *small-n* qualitative methods. First, I document leftist governments' economic policy transformations, which constitute the dependent variable of this study. Next, I advance an explanation for differences among leftist economic policies based on the type of party system and evaluate it cross-nationally alongside five alternative hypotheses explaining economic reforms, including institutional, economic, structural, interest-group-based, and path dependence factors. Finally, through case studies on Brazil, Chile, and Venezuela, I provide detailed accounts of the relationship between party system institutionalization and the type of economic policies observed in each country, as well as the role that other factors play in explaining these policies.

Methodologically, these cases were selected because they fully span the variables of interest—in this case, leftist governments' economic policies and party system institutionalization—known as the diverse case method. According to Jason Seawright and John Gerring, this case selection, "has stronger claims to representativeness than any other *small-n* sample."[81] Venezuela and Chile constitute extreme cases—along both the type of party system and the type of economic policies—and Brazil constitutes a middle value. These three cases perform a (dis)confirmatory role of the nexus between party system institutionalization and the type of economic policies at different values of these dimensions.

In order to achieve this goal, I follow a focused, structured, case comparison approach.[82] It is focused in that the explanatory factors explored cross-nationally also guide the analysis of events in each case study. It is structured because the same aspects are studied in every case, allowing for cross-case comparisons. These two features are useful in "eliminat[ing] some alternative explanations and increasing our confidence in others."[83]

Throughout the book, I rely on a number of primary and secondary sources to support my findings. During field research in Brazil, Chile, Colombia, Mexico, and Venezuela, I conducted 50 elite interviews with relevant actors, including government officials, legislators, party leaders, and journalists.[84] In doing so, I sought to incorporate views from a variety of perspectives, including the government and opposition. Additionally, the book draws on government documents, congressional transcripts, political party platforms, local newspaper articles, and other scholars' work.

Chapter 2 documents the type of leftist governments' economic reforms—the dependent variable. I organize governments' economic transformations along a pro-market/statist continuum reflecting the extent to which they departed from the market orthodoxy that prevailed at the time they reached power. On the statist end of the spectrum, Venezuela experienced increased intervention through a series of changes in several sectors of the economy. Conversely, leftist governments in Chile generally adhered to the trend of pro-market reforms. Having followed a mix of reversal in some areas but continuity in others, the rest of the leftist governments falls somewhere in between these extremes.

In measuring the leftist governments' reforms, I rely on five indicators to capture the main areas in which economic transformations have taken place in Latin America, namely (1) privatizations/nationalizations, (2) taxation, (3) government spending, (4) trade, financial, and monetary liberalization, and (5) poverty alleviation. These dimensions or arenas of reform allow for a systematic cross-national analysis of the region's economic policies. They are particularly helpful in identifying whether changes have occurred—i.e., policies running counter to the pro-market trend—and in which policy spheres.

In addition, this chapter contrasts leftist reforms with those of right-of-center governments in the region. By and large, governments from both the left and the right have preserved a model of development based on the market economy. However, while right-of-center governments have maintained a strict adherence to promarket policies, their left-of-center counterparts have tried out statist alternatives in several areas of reform. By identifying the differences in economic policy between governments from the left and the right, this chapter contributes to the understanding of the relationship between ideology and the spectrum of alternatives available for economic policy making.

Chapter 3 introduces the causal logic behind party system institutionalization as a determinant of economic reform and tests the logic empirically. It explains how certain features of party systems, including continuity of parties across time, routinization of internal procedures, strong roots in society, and generalized sense of legitimacy, are conducive to gradual, piecemeal reform. It also contrasts explanations based on party system institutionalization, fragmentation, and polarization.

Drawing on the main explanations put forth to account for the adoption of market-oriented reforms during the 1980s and 1990s, Chapter 3 also evaluates alternative hypotheses based on their ability to account for economic transformations carried out by leftist governments across Latin America. Other explanations are less parsimonious and show a weaker ability to account for differences in economic policies at the regional level. The evaluation is accomplished in three steps. First, I introduce the most relevant theoretical considerations for each explanatory factor and formulate corresponding hypotheses. Second, I operationalize each factor with empirical evidence from the region. Finally, I compare the extent to which different factors are correlated with the type of economic reaction—i.e., whether the explanatory factors covary with the dependent variable.

The relationship between party systems and alternative explanations on the one hand and the type of economic reforms on the other is further explored through case studies in the following three chapters. Chapter 4 studies the case of Venezuela. The government of Hugo Chávez in Venezuela has defied the prevailing view that pro-market policies had emerged unchallenged. He has become the standard-bearer of many of the leftist claims of the 1960s and 1970s, and many characterize him as Fidel Castro's heir in the region. Unrivaled in the extent to which he has carried out statist reforms, the study of Chávez's "21st Century Socialist Revolution" presents an opportunity to evaluate the factors that have allowed him to conduct the most drastic transformations among leftist governments to date in the post–Cold War period. While it appreciates the importance of resource rents in providing governments with additional means to carry out their agendas, this chapter shows how the party system's disarray made likely the election to power of an outsider, antisystem candidate like Chávez. It then goes on to explain his ability to carry out drastic transformations in the form of nationalizations, price controls, foreign exchange controls, and increased levels of taxation—to name a few—based on the political parties' inability to shape these policies in any meaningful way.

Chapter 5 draws on Brazil's experience to show how this country's increasingly institutionalized party system played a role in conducting moderate economic transformations. It underscores how the progressive institutionalization of party politics contributed to moderating Lula and the Workers' Party's (*Partido dos Trabalhadores*—PT) economic agenda before the 2002 election, and shows how his government faced meaningful opposition in Congress, which resulted in the watering down of economic policies in order to appeal to a semi-fluid working majority. It also shows how financial instability on the eve of Lula's election and the president's reliance on executive decrees contribute to explain Brazil's leftist government's economic moderation.

Chapter 6 analyzes the role of Chile's highly institutionalized party system in economic policy making. Chile has long been considered a poster child for economic orthodoxy and moderation, and its economic policies have influenced the rest of the region for decades. As this chapter shows, Chile's adherence to pro-market policies results from a process of intra- and intercoalition accommodation. This chapter also illustrates how the deep roots of the neoliberal model and a solid economic performance have provided incentives to maintain the prevailing pro-market model.

I conclude the book in Chapter 7 by addressing the broader implications of the study's findings. First, I discuss theoretical implications for study of the left, party systems, and economic reforms. Next, I evaluate the left's economic performance and its consequences for market orthodoxy and democracy in the region. In the final section, I address the implications of the type of party system for long-term sustainability and horizontal accountability.

2 ECONOMIC REFORMS
The Dependent Variable

"BRAZIL IS CHANGING peacefully, and hope prevailed over fear!" shouted Lula as he addressed his supporters on election night in his first speech as president elect. That evening, the first socialist to become president of Brazil called "on all of Brazilian society to build a more equal and fraternal country."[1] The following morning, as the country and the world woke up to the news, the stock market in São Paulo fell by 4 percent. The dramatic fall was testimony to the generalized uncertainty that had characterized the months leading to the election. Between January and October of 2002, as Lula's candidacy gained steam and his victory became more likely, the Brazilian stock market lost 30 percent of its value.[2] Brazil's currency—the real—had depreciated by 40 percent since April, and the spread between Brazilian and other emerging market bonds doubled during that period.[3] Although a majority of Brazilian voters had overcome the fear to elect a socialist candidate as president, what Lula's government would look like was anybody's guess.

The uncertainty surrounding Lula's economic policies exemplifies the mood that prevailed in every country following the election of a leftist president. In Venezuela, where Hugo Chávez campaigned openly against market orthodoxy, an op-ed in *El Universal* warned that, "in the best of cases, Chávez's government would look like Allende's, and, in the worst of cases, it would resemble a Stalinist/Castroist revolution."[4] Even in

Chile, where Ricardo Lagos had been part of President Patricio Aylwin's and President Eduardo Frei's cabinets, there were concerns that a Lagos presidency would return to Allende-style socialism. After all, as a Chilean economist warned in his newspaper column, "Lagos cannot deny his association with the Allende administration in the 1970s. During that period, the banking sector was nationalized and government controls became pervasive, choking the economy, creating generalized chaos and runaway inflation."[5] Even though Lagos's campaign focused on assuaging these concerns, the Socialist Party's red flag flying over his campaign headquarters, posters of Salvador Allende as part of his campaign paraphernalia, and the presence of Allende's widow as one of Lagos's guests of honor in a televised presidential debate greatly contributed to keeping these concerns alive.

Across the region, the left's radical record—whether previously in a government coalition as in Chile, in the opposition as in Brazil, or emerging from a failed military coup as in Venezuela—remained a cause for concern. Would these concerns prove to be warranted? Have leftist governments dismantled the orthodox policies that prevailed in the 1980s and 1990s? If so, how drastically and in which areas? Have all leftist governments embarked on this enterprise? If not, what are the main differences and coincidences across countries? Has the left followed a different path than the right? In sum, what changes in economic policy have occurred in the region since leftist governments came to power?

In answering these questions, this chapter seeks to fill a gap in the scholarly literature: little attention has been paid to systematically documenting and analyzing the coincidences and disparities in the left's economic transformations across countries. This oversight is particularly surprising given that many leftist presidents relied mainly on the condemnation of market orthodoxy as a way to define their political platforms and give meaning to their electoral campaigns. In many cases the repudiation of neoliberal policies became their main demand as opposition candidates.

Most existing studies on leftist governments have focused on a limited number of cases and placed special emphasis on political aspects of leftist governments.[6] For example, they tend to concentrate on whether leftist governments have dismantled the legislature, encroached on the judiciary, undermined freedom of speech, or attacked the United States in international fora.[7] This chapter addresses the need for systematic and comprehensive analysis of the left's economic policies in Latin America.

With this objective in mind, the chapter is divided into three main sections. First, I break down reforms into five indicators to provide for the nuance that the systematic cross-country comparison of such a complex issue requires. Second, I document and analyze economic policy changes—both in the statist and pro-market directions—along these dimensions for each country. Third, I classify countries based on the degree to which they carried out statist or pro-market policies, and assess the state of economic reforms in the region.

I find that, although remaining within the margins of a market economy, leftist governments are more likely to depart from market orthodoxy and pursue statist reforms than their right-of-center counterparts, and that there is considerable variation among leftist governments' policies—from pursuing government intervention in most areas, as in Venezuela, to preserving the pro-market trend in most areas, as in Chile. I also find that statist policies were introduced in different countries along the five indicators under study, with nationalizations, taxation, and trade, financial, and monetary liberalization being the areas that experienced the most intervention in the economy.

It is important to note that the discussion presented in this chapter does not intend to assess how "leftist" each government is, or the extent to which a particular type of policy or policy mix deserves such a label. Many more dimensions other than an economic policy perspective must be taken into account to determine what constitutes *left*.[8] Based on Cleary's definition—introduced in Chapter 1—I consider these governments' leftist bona fides as a given.[9] Instead, the goal is to document leftist governments' policies and determine whether they have departed from the status quo—the market orthodoxy prevailing at the time—and if so, how drastically.

Five Indicators of Reform

By way of defining the dependent variable, I present an account of the different types of economic policy changes. No government is purely pro-market or purely statist. In reality, we find that different governments implement policy combinations of these ideal types. Consequently, and in order to avoid broad generalizations and contribute to taxonomical clarity, the type of reaction is measured along the five indicators introduced in Chapter 1, which capture the main areas in which reforms have taken place: (1) privatizations/nationalizations, (2) taxation, (3) government spending, (4) trade, financial, and monetary liberalization, and (5) poverty alleviation. These indicators were selected because they correspond roughly with those employed by the United Nations Economic Commission on Latin America and the Caribbean as well as other authors to distinguish between the different dimensions during the adoption of market reforms in the 1980s and 1990s.[10] The exception is poverty alleviation policies, which were included here in order to capture some of the changes along a dimension with important distributional consequences and which have historically been one of the main priorities of the left in the region.

There are several advantages to using these indicators. First, on a methodological level, these dimensions allow us to compare apples with apples. Changes in economic policies can be comprehensive or limited. They may take place across the board to alter the model of development, or they may occur only in targeted areas preserving the general economic model. By studying economic reforms along each of the five dimensions or spheres, we can isolate changes in different aspects of the economy and compare them across countries. In this way, a government's economic changes can be assessed based not on the salience of a particular event—the sudden nationalization of oil fields, for example—but on the aggregate changes along the five indicators.

Second, mapping changes in economic policy along the five dimensions allows us to determine which areas have been the most prone to reversal and which the most resistant. Some aspects of market reforms—privatizations in the energy sector, for instance—have been particularly vulnerable to reversal, while others, such as government spending, have experienced little change. Thus, this chapter takes stock of leftist governments' changes to market reforms in Latin America.

The third advantage to using this approach lies in the ability to identify where the different governments stand with regard to each other. Since no government is purely market-oriented or purely state-interventionist, focusing on each indicator allows us to flesh out fine differences across countries. The diagnosis along the five indicators enables us to both assess the extent to which each government has rolled back or furthered pro-market reforms, and classify governments accordingly. The degree to which governments have departed from the market-orthodox status quo constitutes the dependent variable of this study.

These indicators are not exhaustive means by which to study reactions to market reform. Other gauges could be used, such as GDP growth, inflation, and unemployment rates, or an index such as the Heritage Foundation Index of Economic Freedom.[11] However, these measures are less useful for our purposes for several reasons. Measures of GDP growth, inflation, and employment reflect macroeconomic outcomes that are more distant from the executive's direct policy making reach.[12] They constitute measures of *performance* or effectiveness rather than indicators of a *policy course*. It is therefore difficult to determine exactly to which policies such outcomes correspond and whether they correspond to a government policy at all instead of factors beyond the government's reach, such as international business cycles or a global economic recession.

A case in point is GDP growth, which may be the result of both structural and conjunctural factors—often unrelated to a president's tenure. Likewise, in the case of inflation, the executive may have had little to do with the monetary policy conducted by an independent central bank—as is the case in many countries under study. Another challenge would be to determine the extent of a lag between policies and outcomes.

Similarly, using the Heritage Foundation Index of Economic Freedom is problematic in identifying an administration's policy course for three main reasons. First, there is a two-year lag for most indicators, so the 2010 Index refers to 2008 (and sometimes even to 2007 depending on the indicator). For leftist governments inaugurated in 2007, such as those in Ecuador and Nicaragua, this lag provides a brief window in office. This makes it particularly difficult to rely on the index for any meaningful comparisons between leftist administrations and their predecessors.

Second, not only does the index incorporate measures of performance, such as inflation, but it also includes elements that are extraneous to the economic policy process. For example, its fiscal freedom component takes into account the share of GDP raised in taxes by the government, which is often determined by a government's capacity to extract resources from the population regardless of whether policies are statist or pro-market. Similarly, its property freedom index takes into account corruption.

Third, several indicators are fully qualitative (e.g., financial freedom) or partially qualitative (e.g., monetary freedom), which makes the index dependent on many judgment calls that are not made public. Naturally, the index of reform presented in the following pages also involves judgment calls in many cases; however, an important difference is that the steps in constructing the index presented in this chapter are transparent—which allows the reader to agree or disagree with particular coding decisions and build on them for future research.

In contrast, the five dimensions of reform in this chapter have the advantage of presenting a general picture of the executive's policy course. Nationalizing a private company, signing a free trade agreement, defaulting on sovereign debt, and implementing price and exchange controls require direct executive action. Other initiatives, such as setting the government's level of spending or the maximum marginal tax rates, or ratifying a Free Trade Agreement (FTA), require legislative approval and the original project may look different from the approved version of the bill depending on the president's ability to navigate the legislative waters. In both cases, however, there is a clear connection between the executive and the policies in question. In the next paragraphs I describe the five indicators and justify their use.

1. PRIVATIZATIONS/NATIONALIZATIONS

Privatizations are the most emblematic of the neoliberal measures in the region,[13] with more than 800 public enterprises privatized in Latin America during the 1990s.[14] Advocates of this measure claimed that, as a result of competition, the private sector could produce goods and deliver services more efficiently than the government, which in turn would translate into lower prices, a wider range of consumer choices, better quality, and reduced corruption and waste.[15] Moreover, privatizations brought liquidity to governments trying to exit fiscal hardship and freed up limited government resources to spend on other, more pressing needs.

Privatizations were also the most contentious neoliberal reform in the region.[16] Detractors argued that privatizations led to the concentration of wealth in a few privileged hands, generalized layoffs, increased corruption in the form of opaque bidding processes, foregone revenues from previously state-owned enterprises, and the erosion of state capacity. Critics also claimed that privatizations represented a direct loss of sovereignty by means of the transfer of the nation's resources from public to private ownership, particularly in the case of nonrenewable resources.

In Latin America, the process of privatization was characterized by the full or partial sale of government enterprises, mostly in the utilities, telecommunications, energy, banking, construction, and aeronautics industries. Some of the most representative privatization cases were Argentina's energy company (Yacimientos Petrolíferos Fiscales), railroad company (Ferrocarriles Argentinos), and telephone company (Entel); Mexico's telephone company (Telmex); Brazil's aircraft manufacturer (Embraer) and telephone company (Telebrás); Venezuela's telecommunications company (CANTV); and Bolivia's hydrocarbons company (Yacimientos Petrolíferos Fiscales Bolivianos).[17]

In order to assess how leftist governments responded to this trend, this indicator focuses on privatizations and nationalizations. It classifies governments as pro-market if they continued with the sale of state-owned enterprises, neutral if they interrupted this policy, or statist if they nationalized companies.

2. GOVERNMENT SPENDING

Neoclassical thought advocates the reduction of government intervention in the economy as much as possible.[18] It deems governments as inefficient, bureaucratic, and detrimental to efficient economic activity. It understands government spending as justified whenever it is aimed at providing truly public goods and correcting for negative market externalities.[19] According to this view, there are three main drawbacks associated with maintaining budget deficits. First, servicing the debt absorbs resources that could be spent otherwise. Second, government borrowing can crowd-out the savings pool available to the private sector, hindering private investment. Third, government spending can distort prices and generate inflationary pressures on the economy.

Accordingly, governments across the region began to tighten their government spending to reduce their budget deficits during the 1980s and 1990s. They eliminated government subsidies and reduced excessive government bureaucracies. These measures resulted in a decline of government spending during the 1980s and 1990s compared to the rapid increase observed during the 1970s.[20]

To determine whether leftist governments have departed from this trend, changes in government spending across time are measured as changes in the magnitude of the public deficit/surplus as a proportion of GDP with respect to the previous administration. Governments are coded as pro-market if their average primary fiscal balance—i.e., the balance before interest payments on debt[21]—increased by at least one percentage point, statist if it decreased by at least one percentage point, and neutral if it remained within this range. While this threshold is necessarily arbitrary, interviews with ministers and vice ministers of finance and the economy pointed to a change of one percentage point in the primary balance over the course of a presidency as a good indicator that an inflection point had taken place.[22]

3. TAX REFORM

One of the main objectives of fiscal reform during the 1980s and 1990s was the reduction of marginal tax rates to foster private sector activity.[23] The neoclassical view sustained that an obese and wasteful government apparatus encouraged excessive taxation. In turn, high levels of taxation stifled business activity. Domestic entrepreneurs found it too onerous to start up new enterprises, and foreign investors were discouraged by the high cost of doing business. At the same time, advocates of market reforms understood the reduction of marginal tax rates as a solution to Latin America's low levels of tax collection. By decreasing tax rates, tax evasion would decline and revenues would increase. With these objectives in mind, governments across the region reduced the maximum marginal tax rates in an attempt to foster private economic activity, attract investment, and reduce evasion.[24]

In order to assess whether leftist governments' reversal of this trend has occurred, this indicator focuses on changes—increase or decrease—in marginal tax rates. Focusing instead on tax revenue collected by the government as a share of GDP is problematic since this indicator does not necessarily reflect changes in tax policy. There may be changes in the share across time, without any modifications of the tax structure. A more effective tax collection system may account for the change, for example. Instead, I look at changes in the tax structure itself, identifying change whenever a rate is increased or decreased, or a type of tax is introduced or scrapped. While this procedure sacrifices the quantitative indicator provided by the tax share of GDP, it directly establishes a connection with the actual policy changes. Tax rate increases are coded as statist, decreases as pro-market, and the absence of change as neutral.

4. TRADE, FINANCIAL, AND MONETARY LIBERALIZATION

At the heart of neoclassical thought is the market as the self-regulating mechanism for the allocation of resources and the establishment of relative prices.[25] During the 1980s and 1990s Latin American governments adopted reforms aimed at liberalizing trade, capital flows, and monetary policy. These reforms included relinquishing control of monetary policy to an autonomous central bank, guaranteeing the free flow of capital, eliminating tariffs and nontariff barriers to trade, and removing investment restrictions and price controls.[26] Free trade agreements became a popular instrument for trade liberalization in the region, beginning with Mexico's signing of the North American Free Trade Agreement (NAFTA) with the United States and Canada.[27] Other countries quickly followed suit, entering webs of agreements decreasing tariffs and nontariff barriers to trade, including the General Agreement on Tariffs and Trade (GATT)—which later became the World Trade Organization (WTO)—and Chile and Central America's FTAs with the United States.

Moreover, financial liberalization was aimed at attracting flows of foreign investment to compensate for the low levels of domestic savings that characterized the region and to facilitate technological transfer from capital-intensive countries. Similarly, the region experienced a trend toward the liberalization of the exchange rate systems during the 1980s and 1990s.[28] Pegs or crawling pegs, which were the norm during the 1970s, transitioned toward managed floats during the 1980s. Following Mexico's adoption of a floating exchange rate as a result of the 1994 crisis, other countries, such as Brazil, Chile, and Colombia, further liberalized their exchange rate regime. By 2002 most countries had adopted either a floating or a managed floating exchange rate regime, and Ecuador, El Salvador, and Panama even adopted the US dollar as their currency.

A number of leftist governments have reversed liberalization in these areas, sometimes reinstituting price controls, returning to fixed exchange rate systems, or rejecting trade opening. Changes in issues such as central bank independence, free trade agreements, and currency and price controls are coded as pro-market if governments increase the role of the market, statist if they increase the role of the government, and neutral if there is no change.

5. POVERTY ALLEVIATION

The fifth indicator reflects changes in poverty alleviation programs implemented across the region. The main rationale for including this indicator is threefold: addressing poverty remains as one of the left's historic demands; efforts to provide a minimum, decent standard of living to the poor have become a defining feature of the left in government; and poverty alleviation programs that reflect different approaches to redistribution proliferated during the period under study.

Classifying governments' poverty alleviation efforts as pro-market or statist is a challenging task, however. During the 1990s, poverty alleviation strategies that did not discriminate based on need fell out of favor. Instead, means-tested programs reducing the role of the state were preferred. Some of the most prominent examples were the creation of such programs as *Pronasol/Oportunidades/Progresa* in Mexico or *Bolsa Escola* and *Bolsa Alimentação* in Brazil.[29]

Therefore, in order to classify poverty alleviation efforts, I rely on the following decision rule. If a government introduces a means-tested program, I classify it as pro-market. If a government introduces a program that is not means-tested, I classify it as statist. If a government maintains the previous administration's poverty alleviation programs or reorganizes existing programs into a new one, I classify this effort as neutral. It is important to note, however, that this classification does not intend to determine whether conditional cash transfer programs are a "leftist" or "rightist" policy tool.[30]

In short, for every country, I use three values to code for each of the five indicators, namely statist, neutral, and pro-market. *Statist* implies that the government has expanded its role in the economy within the scope of that indicator. For instance, conducting nationalizations, establishing price controls, carrying out land reform, or implementing unconditional poverty alleviation represent examples of increased state intervention in the economy. *Pro-market* expresses the retrenchment of the role of the state and the furthering of the role of the market. A decrease in corporate tax rates, continuation of privatizations, and the signing of free trade agreements are cases in point. *Neutral* expresses no change in either direction.

Taken together, these five indicators present a more nuanced account of the left's economic policies than the conventional dichotomous classifications that characterize governments as either right or wrong,[31] reformist or bourbon,[32] moderate or radical,[33] moderate or contestatary,[34] social democratic or populist.[35] Although imperfect in that they do not cover every single sphere related to economic policy, these indicators allow us to conduct a systematic comparison across countries.[36] They show which areas have been more prone to reform and which governments have most significantly altered the status quo. The resulting classification of governments' economic reforms will become the dependent variable of this study.

It is worth noting that these indicators are not intended to establish a normative evaluation of whether change in a particular direction—pro-market or pro-statist—is desirable. Regardless of the passion that the debate between advocates of pro-market and pro-statist policies generates, it is not the objective of this project to evaluate the appropriateness of these policies in general or the suitability of leftist government policies in particular.

Cross-National Analysis of Economic Policy Changes

The following pages analyze the leftist countries' government policies along the five dimensions discussed before. The analysis focuses on the eight countries with a leftist government in office at the time of writing—Argentina, Bolivia, Brazil, Chile, Ecuador, Nicaragua, Uruguay, and Venezuela. I also analyze two countries with right-of-center governments—Colombia and Mexico—that serve as a control group in order to identify whether the government's ideology—rightist or leftist—makes a difference in the type of reaction.

The assessment along the five indicators of reform for each country is summarized in Table 2.1. Reforms that increase the level of state intervention in the economy are coded (-1). Reforms that further the role of the market are coded (+1). Policies that remained unchanged are coded (0). Each country's score represents the algebraic sum of the five indicators. The analysis reveals that leftist governments' reactions have been varied in the region, ranging from state intervention in all areas—as in Venezuela—to the adherence to pro-market policies in most areas—as in Chile. Bolivia, Ecuador, Argentina, Nicaragua, Brazil, and Uruguay lie between these extremes. Following each country's discussion, I present a brief table summarizing the policy changes conducted as well as the coding along every indicator.

VENEZUELA: HUGO CHÁVEZ'S ECONOMIC POLICIES

Hugo Chávez became president of Venezuela on February 2, 1999, running with the Patriotic Pole (*Polo Patriótico*), an electoral alliance including his own party, the Fifth Republic Movement (*Movimiento V República*—MVR), along with other leftist parties such as the Movement toward Socialism (*Movimiento al Socialismo*—MAS) and the Venezuelan Communist Party (*Partido Comunista de Venezuela*—PCV). A former lieutenant colonel, he gained national prominence after leading a failed coup in 1992. Pardoned after two years in prison, Chávez became a symbol of discontent with the political order. In the 1998 presidential election, he defeated Henrique Salas Römer with 56.2 to 39.9 percent of the vote.[37] Since, Chávez has stood for reelection twice following the approval of a new Constitution in 1999. He was reelected in July 2000 with 60 percent of the vote and again in December 2006 with 63 percent.[38] He is scheduled to govern until 2013.[39]

Dubbed the "Bolivarian Revolution," or "21st Century Socialism,"[40] Chávez's project has been the most statist in the region. Although still far from a centrally planned economy, his economic program increased state intervention in each of the five economic dimensions. First, the Chávez administration not only interrupted privatizations that were underway—such as that of the health system[41]—but also conducted

TABLE 2.1

Dimensions of Economic Reform: Evaluating Governments' Economic Policy Changes

Country and Administration	Privatizations/ Nationalizations	Taxation	Government Spending	Trade/Financial/Monetary Liberalization	Poverty Alleviation	Score	Type of Policies
Venezuela / Chávez (1999–)	Statist (-1)	Statist (-1)	Statist (-1)	Statist (-1)	Statist (-1)	-5	Statist
Ecuador / Correa (2007–)	Statist (-1)	Statist (-1)	Statist (-1)	Statist (-1)	Neutral (0)	-4	
Bolivia / Morales (2006–)	Statist (-1)	Statist (-1)	Pro-market (+1)	Statist (-1)	Statist (-1)	-3	
Argentina / Kirchner (2003–2007)	Statist (-1)	Neutral (0)	Pro-market (+1)	Statist (-1)	Neutral (0)	-1	
Nicaragua / Ortega (2007–)	Neutral (0)	Statist (-1)	Pro-market (+1)	Pro-market (+1)	Neutral (0)	1	
Brazil / Lula (2002–2010)	Neutral (0)	Neutral (0)	Pro-market (+1)	Neutral (0)	Neutral (0)	1	
Uruguay / Vázquez (2005–2010)	Neutral (0)	Neutral (0)	Neutral (0)	Pro-market (+1)	Pro-market (+1)	2	
Chile / Lagos (2000–2006)	Pro-market (+1)	Neutral (0)	Neutral (0)	Pro-market (+1)	Pro-market (+1)	3	
Mexico / Fox (2000–2006)	Pro-market (+1)	Neutral (0)	Pro-market (+1)	Pro-market (+1)	Neutral (0)	3	
Colombia / Uribe (2002–2010)	Pro-market (+1)	Pro-market (+1)	Pro-market (+1)	Pro-market (+1)	Neutral (0)	4	Pro-market

nationalizations in a variety of industries, including oil extraction and refining, telecommunications, utilities, steel, and cement. The 2001 Hydrocarbons Law—one of the earliest and most salient of the Chávez Presidency—drastically increased the government's control over the oil industry.[42] This legislation reserved for the state the majority shareholding in any new ventures for exploration and production.[43] As a result, all oil production and distribution activities became domain of the Venezuelan state, with the exception of joint private-public ventures extracting extra heavy crude oil.

In addition to the modification established in the Hydrocarbons Law, the Chávez administration unilaterally modified agreements between the government and the oil companies. By March 2006 the government had converted the private investments in all marginal oil fields into joint ventures with Petróleos de Venezuela's (PDVSA) majority ownership between 60 and 80 percent. Of the 32 marginal or low yielding operating agreements, five were voluntarily turned over to PDVSA and two were confiscated from France's Total and Italy's ENI after these companies rejected the government's new terms.[44] On May 1, 2007, Chávez announced the nationalization of 60 percent of four refineries in the Orinoco Belt.[45]

Nationalizations took place in other industries as well. Shortly after his reelection in December 2006, Chávez announced the nationalizations of telecommunications company CANTV and power company Electricidad de Caracas. On April 4, 2008, he decreed the nationalization of Mexican cement maker CEMEX,[46] and on May 1, 2008, announced the nationalization of Argentine steel maker Ternium Sidor and the rest of the steel industry.[47] Six months later, Chávez nationalized Santander's Banco de Venezuela. In 2009 his government nationalized the coffee producers Fama de Américas and Café Madrid,[48] the sardine processing plant La Gaviota,[49] a rice mill owned by US company Cargill,[50] and the Hilton Hotel in Isla Margarita.[51]

Chávez also carried out nationalizations through a land reform program meant to establish limits on land ownership and to tax and redistribute land considered inactive.[52] In addition to establishing limits to property size and introducing taxes on idle land, the 2001 Land Law allowed confiscation of the land by the government. According to the legislation, landowners would be compensated for their lands at market value. This provision has been enforced by the Chávez administration through the National Land Institute (*Instituto Nacional de Tierras*), created in January 2002. For example, the government distributed more than 1.5 million hectares to about 130,000 families organized as cooperatives in 2003.[53] In 2005 the government nationalized almost half the British-owned "El Charcote," a 13,000-hectare cattle ranch in the state of Cojedes.[54]

Second, the Chávez administration increased state intervention in the economy by raising taxes on oil companies. Following the 2001 Hydrocarbons Law, Chávez increased royalties from 16.7 percent to 30 percent on the extraction of oil from conventional oil fields.[55] In 2004 the government raised the income tax rate for strategic associations to extract heavy crude oil from the Orinoco River from 1 to 16.67 percent.[56] In 2006 income taxes were increased again for oil corporations, from 34 to 50 percent. The increase was made retroactive to 2001.[57]

Third, regarding government spending, the Chávez administration was characterized by fiscal deficits in spite of the government's increased oil revenues. On average, Chávez's fiscal deficits amount to -2.39 percent of GDP. This primary balance is considerably lower than Caldera's average government surplus of 0.08 percent.[58]

Fourth, regarding trade, financial, and monetary liberalization, Chávez conducted statist policies related to currency controls, price controls, and trade. The Law Governing the Foreign Exchange System in Venezuela enables the executive to intervene in the foreign exchange market whenever it is a matter of national interest.[59] Following the sharp devaluation of the bolivar after the strike that brought PDVSA to a standstill, the central bank stopped trading local currency on January 22, 2003. Shortly thereafter, Chávez decreed the creation of an exchange administration board (*Comisión de Administración de Divisas*—CADIVI) to regulate foreign exchange transactions.[60]

Moreover, President Chávez announced the establishment of price controls in a nationally televised address on February 5, 2005. The government introduced price controls for 400 leading consumer products, including food, medicines, raw materials, and basic services. As a result, the Ministry of Production began monitoring prices for these goods and enforcing the decree as an attempt to control inflation. The government justified this measure as necessary to keep speculators in line.[61]

Venezuela also exited trade agreements that the Chávez government deemed inconvenient, such as the G-3 with Mexico and Colombia and the Andean Community.[62] Instead, it has made efforts to join Argentina, Brazil, Paraguay, and Uruguay in Mercosur.[63] Chávez also announced his intention to withdraw from multilateral financial organizations such as the World Bank and the International Monetary Fund (IMF),[64] but this course of action had not formally materialized.

Lastly, Chávez relied on oil revenue to finance a host of social programs dubbed as *Misiones*, or Missions. Prominent examples are Misión Robinson, which taught literacy in both urban and rural communities and benefited more than one million Venezuelans; Misión Barrio Adentro, which provided health care in shantytowns with the assistance of thousands of Cuban doctors and benefited more than 4 million people; and Misión Mercal, which provided subsidized food for the poor

TABLE 2.2

Chávez's Economic Policy Changes

Privatizations/ Nationalizations	Taxation	Government Spending	Trade/Financial/ Monetary Liberalization	Poverty Alleviation
- Interruption of privatizations - Nationalization of several industries - Land Reform	- Increase in oil royalties and corporate income taxes	- Lax fiscal discipline led to large government deficits	- Exchange controls - Price controls - Increased central bank subordination - Left G-3; joined Mercosur	- Misiones Bolivarianas
Statist	Statist	Statist	Statist	Statist

through government-run convenience stores and benefited more than 9 million people. Such programs were financed through oil revenue transfers from PDVSA to a special fund managed by the president.[65] The fund's 5.5 billion dollars, representing almost 5 percent of the country's GDP, constitutes "one of the largest social fund experiments administered in Latin America in the last decade."[66] Table 2.2 presents a summary of Chávez's main economic policy transformations along the five indicators of reform.

Ecuador: Rafael Correa's Economic Policies

Rafael Correa became president of Ecuador on January 15, 2007, after campaigning on an antisystem, anti-neoliberal message. In his inauguration speech, he denounced the Washington Consensus as a set of "disastrous policy prescriptions" and criticized free-trade agreements, dollarization,[67] the autonomy of the central bank, and "other similar insanities."[68] A PhD graduate in economics from the University of Illinois at Urbana-Champaign, he gained national prominence after a brief tenure as President Alfredo Palacios's (2005–2007) finance minister. During this period he embraced a nationalistic stance, which led to his resignation in August 2005 due to a disagreement with Palacios over financial policy and debt management. In February 2006 he created the "Alliance for a Proud and Sovereign

Fatherland" (*Alianza para una Patria Altiva y Soberana*—Alianza PAÍS) in order to run for the presidency.[69] Without nominating a single candidate for the country's unicameral congress, Alianza PAÍS became more an ad hoc electoral vehicle than a political party.

Correa's government program expressed severe discontent with the status quo. His campaign's underlying tone was one expressing the need for a "radical change" with the previous governments and the rejection of the neoliberal economic model. Correa promoted the renegotiation of all oil contracts to ensure a larger participation for the state, rejected the Free Trade Agreement with the United States as "an imposition on the country," and promised "no more structural adjustment and no more submission to the IMF and the World Bank."[70]

On October 15, 2006, Rafael Correa lost to National Action Institutional Renewal Partido (*Renovador Institucional Acción Nacional*—PRIAN) candidate Álvaro Noboa 26.8 to 22.8 percent of the vote in the first round of the presidential election. However, Correa became president of Ecuador after defeating Noboa 50.5 to 38.6 percent in a runoff held in November of that year.[71] After a new Constitution was approved in 2008 and early elections held in April 2009, Correa was reelected president with 52 percent of the vote, and Alianza PAÍS won almost half of the seats in the legislature. Correa's term is scheduled to end in 2013.

Among the most statist in the region, Rafael Correa's administration has carried out such measures as nationalizations, price controls, sovereign debt default, and the elimination of central bank autonomy. In none of the five spheres has he followed a pro-market orientation, although his administration remained neutral in poverty alleviation by maintaining the existing conditional cash transfer program Bono de Desarrollo Humano.

First, regarding nationalizations, Correa significantly increased state ownership in the energy sector.[72] Following reforms to the law governing hydrocarbons that came into effect on July 27, 2010, the state acquired ownership of the oil industry and forced private companies to operate as service providers or leave the country. As Wilson Pástor, Ecuador's natural resources minister put it, "the entire oil production will be owned by the state and commercialized by state-owned PetroEcuador."[73] The 2010 Hydrocarbons Law establishes that at least 25 percent of the revenue of the companies that remain as service providers must go to the state regardless of fluctuations in oil prices, and that 12 percent of profits must be destined toward social programs.[74]

Nationalizations have also taken place in the hydroelectric industry, with Ecuador's expropriation of four infrastructure projects conducted by Brazilian firm Odebrecht. Following Executive Decree 1348, Correa sent the military to take over the hydroelectric complex San Francisco, two irrigation projects, and an airport.[75]

Second, Correa's administration has carried out a series of tax reforms increasing the tax burden. His government raised taxes on oil companies, from 50 percent of excess revenues to 70 percent in October 2007.[76] Most companies agreed to the increase, including Brazil's Petrobras, Spain's Repsol YPF, China's Andes Petroleum, and US-owned City Oriente. The French company Perenco, however, was an exception, with its assets being seized by the government and transferred to state-owned Petroecuador and Petroamazonas in July 2009.[77] Additionally, his administration established a 2-percent tax on capital outflows and included dividends in the calculation for personal income tax. It also incorporated previously exempt goods—such as newspapers and magazines—to the value-added tax of 12 percent.[78]

Third, regarding trade, financial, and monetary liberalization, the Correa administration eliminated the central bank's autonomy from the executive, introduced price controls, and defaulted on its sovereign debt. In July 2009 Ecuador ended the autonomy of its central bank.[79] Arguing that an independent central bank was unnecessary under dollarization, Correa pushed for the change of status to be included in the country's 2008 Constitution.[80] The change was approved by an interim legislature—*El Congresillo*—through changes to the Law of the Monetary Regime and the Bank of the State on July 30, 2009.[81] The change gave Correa the ability to conduct monetary, interest rate, and exchange rate policy directly.

In April 2008 Correa's administration implemented price controls on a variety of goods and services. It introduced price ceilings in consumer products, utilities, and government services.[82] In December 2008 Correa announced that a government commission had found roughly a third of the country's total foreign debt illegal and illegitimate, and that his administration refused to pay it.[83] It estimated that the "2012 and 2030 Global Bonds," which replaced the Brady Bonds in 2000, were negotiated 70 percent above their fair value.[84] In July 2009 the government successfully carried out a buyback, offering 35 cents on the dollar.[85]

Fourth, the Correa administration has also decreased fiscal stringency.[86] Correa's primary balance has averaged 1.09 percent of GDP, compared with a surplus of 4.23 percent that preceded him.[87] The significant decrease is noteworthy in the context of high commodity prices.

Finally, regarding poverty alleviation, the Correa administration maintained the existing conditional cash transfer program *Bono de Desarrollo Humano* with some modifications. Based on the poverty alleviation program *Bono Solidario* created in 1998 during the Jamil Mahuad presidency (1998–2000), *Bono de Desarrollo Humano* adopted its conditional features and current name in 2003

TABLE 2.3

Correa's Economic Policy Changes

Privatizations/ Nationalizations	Taxation	Government Spending	Trade/Financial/ Monetary Liberalization	Poverty Alleviation
- Interruption of privatizations - Nationalizations in energy and hydroelectric industries	- Increase in royalties and corporate taxes - 2 percent tax on capital outflows - 2 percent tax on capital outflows	- Decrease in fiscal stringency	- Price controls in utilities, consumer goods, and government services - End of central bank autonomy - Debt default	- Continued with Bono de Desarrollo Humano
Statist	Statist	Statist	Statist	Neutral

during Lucio Gutiérrez's presidency (2003–2005).[88] Correa's modifications include an increase in the allowance of the conditional cash transfer program, from US$15 to US$35, and reorganization of the program to grant a pension for adults over the age of 65.[89] Table 2.3 summarizes Rafael Correa's main economic reforms.

Bolivia: Evo Morales's Economic Policies

An Aymara leader of the coca growers' union, Evo Morales became president of Bolivia on January 22, 2006. The candidate of the Movement toward Socialism (*Movimiento al Socialismo – MAS*), he pledged to empower the poor, transform the prevailing economic model, and renovate the country's traditional political elites. His platform became an extremely popular political alternative for the Amerindian population that predominates in the *Altiplano*—as Bolivia's impoverished highlands are known. Morales called for the refoundation of the Bolivian state through the establishment of a new constitutional assembly.[90] Throughout his campaign, he urged to dismantle the existing political order, which he claimed had "only brought hunger and misery, plundering and privatization."[91]

Morales defeated Social Democratic Power (*Poder Democrático y Social—*PODEMOS) candidate Jorge Quiroga with 53.7 to 28.6 percent of the vote in the presidential election held in December 2005.[92] With legislative elections held concurrently, the MAS gained a majority of the Chamber of Deputies but fell short of reaching one in the Senate. Although Morales's constitutional term was due to end in 2010, the country's new Constitution, approved in 2009, allowed him to win the presidency again in December of that year and potentially seek reelection in 2015.

Under Morales's leadership, Bolivia has pursued statist reforms in four of the five areas of interest. Nationalizations, tax increases, price controls, and the creation and expansion of poverty alleviation programs are examples of the breadth of his government's intervention in the economy. The notable exception is government spending, where the Morales administration drastically increased the fiscal balance to achieve surpluses.

First, regarding privatizations, Morales reversed the liberalizing trend of his predecessors and expropriated several industries, including: energy, telecommunications, hydroelectric, and pensions. On May 1, 2006, he issued a presidential decree effectively nationalizing Bolivia's energy sector by reducing the role of private companies to gas field operators.[93] As a result of the decree, ownership of all the natural gas produced in the country was transferred to the government's Yacimientos Petrolíferos Fiscales Bolivianos (YPFB). This decision directly affected production in Bolivia's two main gas fields, San Alberto and San Antonio.[94] The foreign firms affected by this measure were Brazil's Petrobras, France's Total, and Spain's Repsol YPF.[95]

On May 1, 2008, exactly two years after Morales's first nationalizations, the government issued another series of expropriations. This time, the government expropriated three energy companies: British Petroleum's natural gas producer Chaco, the pipeline company Transredes, and the storage company Compañía Logística de Hidrocarburos Boliviana.[96] The decree also mandated the nationalization of the telecommunications industry through the purchase of Entel, which had been privatized in 1996 and was owned mostly by Telecom Italia and two public pension funds administered by Zurich Financial Services and BBVA.[97]

In January of 2009, Morales expropriated Chaco Energy Company, a subsidiary of Pan-American Energy,[98] and in May of that year he nationalized Air BP, a subsidiary of British Petroleum that supplied jet fuel at Bolivia's airports.[99] The following year, Morales nationalized the hydroelectric sector. On May 1, 2010, Morales expropriated the Empresa Eléctrica Guaracachi SA, controlled by Rurelec PLC of Britain; Empresa Corani SA, operated by France's GDF Suez; Valle

Hermoso Company; and the Empresa de Luz y Fuerza de Cochabamba.[100] The state-owned Empresa Nacional de Electricidad (ENDE) took over operations on that day.

On December 10, 2010, Evo Morales signed a law nationalizing the pensions system.[101] The Pensions Law transferred ownership of the privately run funds from Zurich Financial Services and BBVA to the state and reduced the retirement age from 65 to 58 with some exceptions.[102] The measure included the creation of a Solidarity Fund as a redistributive mechanism from high to low-income retirees.

Additionally, Morales enacted the land reform law, one of the government's most trumpeted initiatives, aimed at the redistribution of some 77,000 square miles—20 million hectares—of unused land, in addition to the 8,500 square miles of government land given to poor farming communities.[103] The two mechanisms contemplated to this end are the expropriation of private land considered unproductive or fraudulently obtained, and the distribution of titles to government-owned land.

Second, regarding taxation, the Morales administration has also followed a statist orientation. Morales opted for increasing corporate taxes for energy corporations rather than altering the value-added tax or personal income taxes. As a result of Decree 28701, the government collects 82 percent of production revenues from private energy companies, up from the previous rate of 50 percent.[104]

Third, the Morales administration implemented price controls in several sectors, including water, electricity, hydrocarbons, and government services.[105] Price controls had remained absent from the Bolivian economy since President Víctor Paz Estenssoro's planning minister—and later president—Gonzalo Sánchez de Lozada conducted a "shock therapy style" liberalization program between 1985 and 1989.[106]

Fourth, regarding poverty alleviation efforts, Evo Morales renamed an existing program with some modifications and created a new allowance. On February 1, 2008, the Morales government ended *Bonosol*, an allowance program put in place in 1997 by President Gonzalo Sánchez de Lozada (1993–1997 and 2002–2003). Bonosol, which granted Bolivians 65 and over a yearly transfer of $1,800 bolivianos,[107] was replaced by Dignity Allowance (*Renta Dignidad*), which granted all Bolivians over the age of 60 a yearly transfer of $2,400 bolivianos—about US$330—regardless of their socioeconomic status.[108] The program cost US$205 million and benefited 700,000 Bolivians.[109]

Additionally, on October 26, 2006, the Morales administration created a non-means-tested allowance "Juancito Pinto" (*Bono Juancito Pinto*) to encourage school attendance.[110] Initially, the program granted $200 bolivianos—about US$27—every year to families with children in grades one through six.[111] In October 2007 Juancito Pinto incorporated grades seven and eight, which expanded the number of beneficiaries from 1.4 million to 1.9 million students.[112] The program costs the government US$54 million each year.[113]

In contrast to the four previous policy spheres, government spending was the sole indicator in which the Morales administration adhered to market canons. Contrary to expectations, Morales reversed the trend of severe fiscal deficits that characterized his predecessors. Between 2002 and 2005, during the administrations of Sánchez de Lozada, Carlos Mesa, and Eduardo Rodríguez, the government's deficit averaged -3.4 percent annually. Conversely, the Morales administration has maintained substantial surpluses every year, averaging 3.9 percent of GDP.[114] The main economic policies conducted by President Evo Morales are summarized in Table 2.4.

Argentina: Néstor Kirchner's Economic Policies

Néstor Kirchner became president of Argentina on May 23, 2003, with an ambiguous economic agenda and a precarious electoral mandate. A former governor of the southern province of Santa Cruz, Kirchner ran with the Front for Victory (*Frente para la Victoria*—FPV), a faction within the Peronist Party (*Partido Justicialista*—PJ). Kirchner came in second behind Carlos Menem after the first round of the presidential elections held on April 27, 2003. Before the second round was held, however, Menem withdrew from the race due to an imminent Kirchner landslide victory forecasted for the runoff.[115] Menem's withdrawal obviated the

TABLE 2.4

Morales's Economic Policy Changes

Privatizations/ Nationalizations	Taxation	Government Spending	Trade/Financial/ Monetary Liberalization	Poverty Alleviation
- Interruption of privatizations - Nationalization of energy, telecommunications, pensions - Land reform	- Increase in royalties and corporate taxes	- Government budget balance from deficits to high surpluses	- Price controls in utilities, hydrocarbons, and government services	- Maintained Renta Dignidad (former Bonosol) - Created Juancito Pinto
Statist	Statist	Pro-market	Statist	Statist

need for a second round and allowed Kirchner to become president with only 22 percent of the vote in the first round.[116] Kirchner governed until 2007, when he turned over power to his wife, Cristina Fernández de Kirchner, who won the presidential election held in that year.

Argentina's leftist government's reaction toward neoliberalism was mixed during Néstor Kirchner's administration, with statist policies in some areas and pro-market policies in others. On the one hand, Kirchner's government conducted nationalizations, defaulted on its sovereign debt, and established price controls on utilities and food. It did not hesitate to rescind concessions based on claims of poor performance or national security, impose export bans, or defy the IMF prescriptions to solve the country's solvency problems, for example. On the other hand, it adhered to market orthodoxy by maintaining tax rates unchanged and substantially increasing government fiscal surpluses as a proportion of GDP.

First, the Kirchner administration reversed the privatizing trend of the 1990s by creating new state-owned enterprises and nationalizing existing ones. In the first case, the government started two state-owned corporations in the airline and energy industries. In August 2003 Kirchner signed a decree creating the Líneas Aéreas Federales, a state-owned airline that would take over the two moribund private airlines LAPA and Dinar.[117] In 2004 Kirchner created Energía Argentina Sociedad Anónima (Enarsa) for the exploitation of oil and natural gas and generation of electricity.[118] The energy sector had been privatized during the Menem years, following the high-profile sale of the government's Yacimientos Petrolíferos Fiscales to the Spanish Repsol.

Additionally, Kirchner expropriated five companies that had been previously privatized during the Menem years. Shortly after his inauguration in May 2003, the government nationalized the postal service.[119] The leftist government also reversed the privatization of the operator of the airwaves used by cellular phone companies. In 1997 the Menem administration granted the operation of the airwaves to Thales Spectrum, a subsidiary of a European defense contractor. Kirchner rescinded the concession in 2004, arguing that the operation of the airwaves was a task that corresponded solely to the state and could not be conceded to the private sector.[120]

Furthermore, his government rescinded the concession of Suez, the French water company that administered Aguas Argentinas and provided potable water to the Buenos Aires metropolitan area. In March 2006 the government created Aguas y Saneamiento Argentinas and took control of Aguas Argentinas's operations, alleging poor service.[121] A similar case is the nationalization of the passenger train route San Martín, from Buenos Aires to the capital's suburb of El Pilar, operated by the Argentine-owned Tasseli Group until 2004. The government argued that accidents were too frequent and investment inadequate, so the concession was rescinded.[122] Lastly, a few months before leaving office in 2007, Kirchner issued a decree nationalizing the navy shipyard Talleres Dársena Norte (Tandanor). The government justified this nationalization in the name of national security.[123]

Second, regarding trade, financial, and monetary liberalization, Kirchner earned a reputation in economic heterodoxy after defaulting on Argentina's sovereign debt, establishing price controls, and meddling in the procedure to measure inflation. In December 2001 he declared a debt moratorium on Argentina's foreign debt and took a strong stance against the IMF and international creditors. As a consequence of the 2001–2002 financial crisis, the IMF wanted Argentina to pay $95 billion to defaulted bondholders, follow stringent austerity measures, and correct for the economic imbalances that ended the convertibility regime.[124] Instead, Kirchner achieved interest rate cuts, longer terms for repayment, and a reduction of the debt. In the final restructuring toward the end of 2004, the value of the debt amounted to about 25 percent of the original amount.[125]

Kirchner also implemented price controls aimed at managing inflation and providing relief to the poor. His government established price freezes mostly in utilities, natural gas—cases in which the nationalizations proved to be useful to set price controls—and food.[126] Price controls in utilities, for instance, made Argentina's public services among the cheapest in Latin America, and a ban on beef and wheat exports forced producers to sell these goods in the domestic market at prices set by the government in order to fight inflation.[127]

Additionally, Kirchner was severely criticized for tampering with the methodology to measure inflation in order to appease concerns about yearly price increases hovering around 25 percent. In February 2007, a few months before Kirchner left office, his administration altered the National Institute of Statistics and Census's (*Instituto Nacional de Estadísticas y Censos*—INDEC) methodology employed to measure the consumer price index. This practice was denounced by the opposition and academics as an attempt to underreport inflation.[128]

In contrast to the changes in the statist direction in the aforementioned areas, the Kirchner administration's policies remained neutral regarding tax rates and poverty alleviation programs. Concerning taxation, the Kirchner government maintained personal and corporate income taxes unchanged. His administration preserved the country's maximum marginal income tax rates for individuals and corporations at 35 percent.[129] Although the rates date from Menem's presidency, they are high by international standards.[130]

Regarding social programs, in 2004 the Kirchner administration announced the creation of Plan Families (*Plan Familias*),[131] a conditional cash transfer program that replaced the existing Plan Heads of Family (*Plan Jefes y Jefas*), which had been founded in 2002 as a national response to the country's financial crisis.[132] By 2007 Plan Familias benefited more than 500,000 families—roughly the same as Plan Jefes y Jefas—through a monthly allowance of US$49 for the first child, and a supplementary US$8 per additional child. Its objectives were to improve the education and health levels of the population by encouraging parents to make sure their children attend school and receive all of the necessary vaccines. Participation in the program required proof of vaccinations records and school enrollment and report cards.[133] The program's budget amounted to 1 percent of the country's total GDP in 2007.[134]

In contrast, government spending is the only sphere in which the Kirchner administration followed a pro-market orientation. The leftist government adopted a more stringent fiscal policy than its predecessors. The government's primary fiscal surplus as a share of GDP increased substantially during Kirchner's tenure. In contrast to the average surplus of 0.9 percent of GDP observed during the Menem administration,[135] Kirchner's presidency averaged a surplus of 3.3 percent.[136]

A summary of President Néstor Kirchner's main economic transformations is presented in Table 2.5.

TABLE 2.5

Kirchner's Economic Policy Changes

Privatizations/ Nationalizations	Taxation	Government Spending	Trade/Financial/ Monetary Liberalization	Poverty Alleviation
- Nationalization of postal service and water company and creation of state-owned airline and energy companies	- Unchanged	- Decrease in government spending resulting in higher surpluses	- Price controls in utilities, natural gas, and food - Debt default - Change in inflation measurement	- Replaced Plan Jefes y Jefas with Plan Familias
Statist	Neutral	Pro-market	Statist	Neutral

Nicaragua: Daniel Ortega's Economic Policies

Daniel Ortega became president on January 10, 2007, running with the Sandinista National Liberation Front (*Frente Sandinista de Liberación Nacional*—FSLN). After helping overthrow Anastasio Somoza's regime in 1979, Ortega was a member of the revolutionary junta that ruled the country until elections were held in 1984. Upon the FSLN's electoral victory, he became president of Nicaragua between 1985 and 1990. During his tenure in office, he headed a government characterized by Marxist discourse, moves toward a centrally planned economy, and close ties with Cuba and the Soviet Union. He was unable to win reelection in the 1990 presidential race and turned over power to Violeta Chamorro. Ortega remained active in politics after his electoral defeat, holding office as a deputy and running unsuccessfully for president in 1996 and 2001.

Running with a former "Contra" spokesperson as his vice presidential candidate,[137] Ortega defeated Eduardo Montealegre, the candidate of the Nicaraguan Liberal Alliance (*Alianza Liberal Nicaragüense* — ALN), 38 to 27.1 percent of the vote on November 5, 2006.[138] A former finance minister with an MBA from Harvard who based his campaign on the continuation of market orthodoxy with an emphasis on education,[139] Montealegre was unable to finish within the five-point difference required by a new electoral rule in order to warrant a runoff. However, his party's second place prevented the FSLN from reaching a majority in Congress. In 2011 Ortega comfortably won reelection by defeating Independent Liberal Party's (*Partido Liberal Independiente* — PLI) candidate Fabio Gadea 63 to 31 percent of the vote. Ortega is scheduled to govern until 2017.

Daniel Ortega's government in Nicaragua has implemented a combination of pro-market and statist policies. On the pro-market side, his administration has pursued free-trade agreements with several countries and decreased the government's deficit. On the statist side, Ortega has increased the tax burden. Other spheres, including privatizations and poverty alleviation, remained unchanged.

First, regarding pro-market reforms, Ortega's government has actively promoted trade liberalization. Shortly after taking office, Ortega began negotiations toward a free-trade agreement with the Caribbean Community and Common Market (CARICOM) in May 2007.[140] On July 1, 2009, Nicaragua approved a free-trade agreement with Panama. The agreement came into force on November 23, 2009.[141] Ortega has also taken important steps toward signing a free-trade agreement with Canada,[142] and has successfully closed negotiations with Chile[143] and the European Union.[144] Regarding monetary policy, Ortega has maintained the crawling peg for currency exchange at a 5-percent depreciation rate.

Additionally, Ortega's administration has reduced the government's budget deficit compared to his predecessor's administration. During the presidency of Enrique Bolaños, the deficit averaged -8.6 percent of GDP. In contrast, the Ortega administration has brought down the deficit to an average of -2.17 percent.[145]

Conversely, the leftist government in Nicaragua has followed a statist orientation regarding taxation. Ortega raised taxes on corporations, requiring companies to pay 1 percent of their gross sales, 10-percent tax on interest from bank deposits, dividends, and capital gains, and a 10-percent tax on interests from loans. The reform was approved by the National Assembly on December 3, 2009.[146]

Additionally, Ortega's administration has remained neutral in the spheres of nationalizations/privatizations and poverty alleviation. Ortega brought privatizations to a halt in Nicaragua, and no nationalizations have taken place during his administration. Regarding the country's efforts to fight poverty, Ortega's administration replaced the existing Social Protection Network (*Red de Protección Social*) with the Food Productive Program (*Programa Productivo Alimentario*), or "Zero Hunger" ("*Hambre Cero*"), a poverty alleviation effort that distributes about US$2,000 worth of goods to low-income female heads of household. Goods include livestock, seeds, and construction materials and are intended to help families in rural areas generate sustainable nourishment and income. The program benefited 40,000 families between 2007 and 2009.[147] Daniel Ortega's main economic transformations are summarized in Table 2.6.

TABLE 2.6

Ortega's Economic Policy Changes

Privatizations/ Nationalizations	Taxation	Government Spending	Trade/Financial/ Monetary Liberalization	Poverty Alleviation
- Ended privatizations	- Raised corporate taxes	- Decrease in government spending resulting in lower deficits	- Signed FTA with Panama and began negotiations with Chile, Canada, and the European Union. - Currency peg unchanged	- Replaced Red de Protección Social with Hambre Cero
Neutral	Statist	Pro-market	Pro-market	Neutral

Brazil: Lula da Silva's Economic Policies

Following three unsuccessful attempts to become Brazil's first leftist president, Luiz Inácio "Lula" da Silva was inaugurated on January 1, 2003. Shining shoes as a child and with little formal schooling, Lula first gained political prominence as a union leader organizing national strikes against the military dictatorship. He was one of the founders of the Workers' Party (*Partido dos Trabalhadores*—PT) in 1980 and of Brazil's Workers' Confederation (*Central Única dos Trabalhadores*—CUT) in 1983, and was part of the leadership of the *Diretas Já* movement, which pushed the military dictatorship to organize direct presidential elections.

The experience accumulated in four presidential races and the progressive moderation of his rhetoric allowed Lula to beat José Serra, Fernando Henrique Cardoso's health minister and the candidate of the Party of Brazilian Social Democracy (*Partido da Social Democracia Brasileira*—PSDB), with 46.4 percent of the total vote in the first round.[148] Vowing to continue with Cardoso's economic policies, Serra was able to garner only 23.2 percent of the national vote.[149] Lula easily won the runoff election, obtaining 61.3 percent of the total vote compared to Serra's 38.7 percent. In October 2006 Lula was reelected to a second term by beating PSDB candidate Geraldo Alckmin. His second presidential period ended in 2010.[150]

Lula's government preserved the status quo in most areas, with the exception of government spending. His administration's fiscal policy was even more stringent than that of his predecessor, maintaining higher primary government surpluses than those set by the IMF. Two of Lula's first economic measures were to raise the target for the government's primary surplus from 3.75 to 4.25 percent and to increase interest rates in order to meet the new target.[151] Shortly after his appointment as the head of Brazil's central bank in 2003, for example, Meirelles increased Brazil's interest rates by 100 base points in the first two meetings to 26.5 percent to show his commitment to fighting inflation.[152] The government also signed a 15-month extension of its standby agreement with the IMF.[153] The Lula administration's primary fiscal surplus averaged 3.74 percent of GDP, which was higher than the Cardoso government's average of 1.75 percent.[154]

In contrast, Lula's government maintained continuity in the areas of privatizations, taxation, trade, financial, and monetary liberalization, and poverty alleviation. Lula halted the privatizing impulse, but did not nationalize any of the state-owned companies that were fully or partially privatized during the Fernando Collor (1990–1992), Itamar Franco (1992–1994), and Fernando Henrique Cardoso (1995–2002) administrations. Such companies include the steel giant Usinas Siderúrgicas de Minas Gerais—Usiminas, the aeronautics company Empresa Brasileira Aeronáutica—Embraer, or the oil company Petróleo Brasileiro—Petrobras.[155]

Continuity has also characterized trade, financial, and monetary liberalization in Brazil. A notable case is that related to the autonomy of the country's central bank. Although granting formal autonomy to the central bank was outlined as one of Lula's main objectives,[156] this goal remained unfulfilled during Lula's presidency. Instead, Lula's government maintained the central bank's de facto autonomy, retaining the prerogative of government manipulation of monetary policy but without exercising it.[157]

Similarly, Brazil's fiscal structure has remained unchanged throughout the Lula administration. The maximum marginal tax rates continued at 25 percent for corporations and 27.5 for individuals, the same level that characterized Cardoso's presidency.[158] Although the Lula administration attempted to push for a fiscal reform along the lines of what the Cardoso administration had outlined,[159] this effort met considerable resistance in Congress.[160]

Finally, regarding social programs, Lula's government consolidated programs administered by four different ministries during the Cardoso presidency—*Bolsa Escola* from the Ministry of Education; *Bolsa Alimentação* from the Ministry of Health; *Cartão Alimentação* from an extraordinary Ministry to Combat Hunger; and *Auxílio Gás* from the Ministry of Energy and Mines—into *Bolsa Família*, its flagship social assistance program.[161] Run by the Ministry of Social Development, the program's goals included increasing school attendance rates, improving the quality of diets, fostering local economic activity, and making government assistance efforts more efficient.[162] By 2009, the number of beneficiary families had reached 11.4 million (approximately 44 million people) and spending on the project represented 0.5 percent of GDP.[163] The cash transfer ranged between US$5 and US$33 per month, with an average payment of US$24 for a family of four, and the program's disbursements increased as goals and conditional milestones were met.[164] Table 2.7 summarizes the discussion of President Lula's economic policies presented above.

Uruguay: Tabaré Vázquez's Economic Policies

The first president to come from outside Uruguay's traditional Blanco and Colorado parties, Tabaré Vázquez was inaugurated on March 1, 2005. Although an oncologist by training, Vázquez had a long history of party politics by the time he reached the presidency. In 1990 he became the first mayor of Montevideo to run with the Broad Front (*Frente Amplio*—FA), a broad coalition of left-of-center parties including Uruguay's Socialist and Communist parties, and the Tupamaros, a former guerrilla group. He was the president of the Frente Amplio between 1996 and 2004 when he reached the presidency in his third bid. Constitutionally unable to run for reelection, Vázquez's government ended in 2010.[165]

Lastly, Lagos's average primary fiscal balance was similar to the average balance reported during his predecessor's administration. Lagos's budget balance averaged 1.9 percent of GDP, compared to Frei's 2.4 percent.[195] Table 2.9 summarizes the economic policy changes conducted during the Ricardo Lagos presidency.

Non-Leftist Governments' Economic Reforms

The following pages analyze whether non-leftist governments have rolled back any of the market reforms previously implemented in their countries. The objective is to determine whether left-of-center governments acted differently from the rest of the region or whether the pursuit of statist reforms became a generalized phenomenon transcending ideology. If, for example, right-of-center governments also reversed privatizations, increased marginal tax rates, became more protectionist, and curtailed central bank independence, what was thought to be a leftist trend would in reality be a regional trend. The analysis of the following countries therefore provides evidence to determine whether leftist governments are different from rightist governments in the first place. At the time of the left's rise to power, eight countries in Latin America had a right-of-center government, namely Colombia, Costa Rica, El Salvador, Guatemala, Honduras, Mexico, Panama, and Paraguay. I rely on the cases of Mexico and Colombia as representative for the analysis of right-of-center economic reforms because of their regional importance in terms of economic and political weight.

TABLE 2.9

Lagos's Economic Policy Changes

Privatizations/ Nationalizations	Taxation	Government Spending	Trade/Financial/ Monetary Liberalization	Poverty Alleviation
- Privatizations in the transportation, infrastructure, water and sanitation, and energy sectors	- Income and corporate tax rates unchanged	- Maintained fiscal surpluses unchanged	- Eliminated capital controls - FTAs with the US, South Korea, the EU, and China	- Created Chile Solidario
Pro-market	Neutral	Neutral	Pro-market	Pro-market

MEXICO: VICENTE FOX'S ECONOMIC POLICIES

The Fox administration furthered pro-market measures implemented by the preceding administrations of presidents Miguel de la Madrid (1982–1988), Carlos Salinas de Gortari (1988–1994), and Ernesto Zedillo (1994–2000). Fox privatized state-owned enterprises, reduced corporate taxes, and continued with the trade liberalization observed since 1982. The two areas that remained unchanged were government spending and poverty alleviation, where Fox maintained similar surpluses as his predecessor and changed the name of the existing conditional cash transfer program, from *Progresa* to *Oportunidades*.[196]

First, in contrast with most leftist governments, the Fox administration in Mexico continued with the trend of privatizations. Although the state-owned enterprises sold by the government were not as significant as those in previous administrations, the Fox government turned over important infrastructure projects, such as highways, ports, airports, and an airline to the private sector.[197] These transactions included the highway between Tepic and Villa Unión in Nayarit, the airport consortium Grupo Aeroportuario del Centro-Norte, the container terminal in the port of Progreso, Yucatán, and the airline Mexicana de Aviación.[198]

Second, the maximum marginal corporate tax rate in Mexico declined gradually during the Fox administration. Although the federal government was unable to get Congress to approve a comprehensive tax reform early in the presidential term, a compromise version was passed in the second half of Fox's tenure. The reform slightly reduced the oil company's—Pemex—fiscal burden, and gradually decreased corporate tax rates by 2 percent every year to reach a floor of 25 percent.

Third, regarding trade and financial liberalization, the Fox administration was an avid free-trade promoter. It launched an FTA with Japan and an economic complementation agreement with Colombia, and initiated negotiations for FTAs with India, Panama, and Trinidad and Tobago.[199] These agreements show a clear continuation of the trade openness that has characterized Mexican governments since the signature of NAFTA.[200]

In contrast, the Fox administration left the areas of government spending and poverty alleviation unchanged. Regarding government spending, Fox presided over similar levels of primary budget balance as his predecessor. During his six years in office, Fox averaged a 2.5 percent surplus as a share of GDP, comparable to Zedillo's 2.9 percent.[201]

Finally, the Fox administration's poverty alleviation programs maintained continuity with existing efforts.[202] The Salinas government's flagship conditional cash transfer program *Solidaridad* was renamed *Progresa* during the Zedillo administration and experienced an important decentralization process.[203] The Fox administration changed the name again to Oportunidades but without any major transformations.[204] Oportunidades continued to provide a minimum level of income to poor families in exchange for compliance with school attendance and health visits. This program's expenditures amount roughly to 0.4 percent of total GDP.[205] Table 2.10 summarizes the main economic policy transformations carried out by the Vicente Fox administration.

COLOMBIA: ÁLVARO URIBE'S ECONOMIC POLICIES

Álvaro Uribe's right-of-center government conducted pro-market reforms across most policy areas. His administration privatized several industries, reduced tax rates, decreased government spending, and expanded the country's network of free-trade agreements. Social programs constitute the only area where he maintained continuity with President Andrés Pastrana's (1998–2002) policies.

First, in line with presidents César Gaviria's (1990–1994), Ernesto Samper's (1994–1998), and Andrés Pastrana's privatization efforts, the Uribe government sold a series of state-owned companies to the private sector in the energy, telecommunications, and financial industries. The privatized enterprises include Granahorrar, Banco Aliadas, and Bancafé in the banking sector; Central Hidroeléctrica de Caldas, Empresa de Energía del Quindío, and Minercol in the energy sector; and Empresa Nacional de Telecomunicaciones (Colombia Telecomunicaciones) in the telecommunications sector.[206] In July 2006 Uribe announced his intention to sell 20 percent of Ecopetrol, the state-owned oil company.[207] This sale—floating equity in the local capital markets—was approved by Congress in December 2006 in an effort to finance exploration and extraction operations.[208]

TABLE 2.10

Fox's Economic Policy Changes

Privatizations/ Nationalizations	Taxation	Government Spending	Trade/Financial/ Monetary Liberalization	Poverty Alleviation
- Privatized airports, highways, ports, airline	- Gradual reduction of corporate taxes, 2% annually	- Maintained government surplus	- Economic complementation agreement with Colombia - FTA with Japan	- Unchanged
Pro-market	Pro-market	Neutral	Pro-market	Neutral

Second, the Uribe administration reduced corporate and personal income taxes. In 2006 Uribe submitted to Congress a comprehensive tax reform package aimed at simplifying the tax code and reduction of corporate and income tax rates from 38.5 to 30 percent.[209] Approved by the Colombian Congress in December of that year, the reform decreased the corporate and income taxes from 38.5 to 34 percent in 2007 and 33 percent in 2008.[210] The reform also eliminated a remittance tax that foreign corporations paid when repatriating profits from Colombia.

Third, regarding government spending, Uribe substantively increased the government's primary surplus from the beginning of his presidency,[211] averaging a budget balance surplus of 3 percent of GDP. This balance was considerably higher than his predecessor's average of 0.02 percent.[212]

Fourth, the Uribe administration continued with the promotion of FTAs that characterized his predecessor's government. His efforts to promote trade liberalization included an economic complementation agreement with Mexico and a free-trade agreement with the United States.[213] The FTA with the United States, ratified by the Colombian Congress in June 2007 and by the United States Congress in October 2011, attempted to further liberalize the existing trade prerogatives between the two countries under the Andean Trade Promotion Agreement.[214] The Uribe administration also revised and expanded its Economic Cooperation Agreement with Chile and began negotiations for an FTA with El Salvador, Honduras, and Guatemala in 2006.[215] In 2008 the Uribe administration began negotiations toward FTAs with the European Free Trade Association (EFTA), formed by Iceland, Liechtenstein, Norway, and Switzerland.[216]

Finally, regarding social programs, the Uribe administration maintained in place President Andrés Pastrana's conditional cash transfer program Families in Action (*Familias en Acción*), launched in 2000. Providing monthly allowances between US$5 and US$17 to poor households with children, the program reaches about 600,000 people and focuses on education and nutrition. The program's annual budget is US$140 million, which represents 0.08 percent of the country's GDP.[217] Table 2.11 summarizes the Álvaro Uribe administration's main economic policy changes along our five indicators.

Conclusion

Several important findings stem from the cross-national analysis of reactions to neoliberalism in Latin America. First, there is considerable variation, from statist policies in each of the five policy spheres to pro-market policies in most areas. Rather than fitting a clear dichotomous classification, the extent to which governments

TABLE 2.11

Uribe's Economic Policy Changes

Privatizations/ Nationalizations	Taxation	Government Spending	Trade/Financial/ Monetary Liberalization	Poverty Alleviation
- Privatizations in energy, infrastructure, and financial sectors	- Decreased income tax rates	- Increased government budget surplus	- Economic complementation agreement with Mexico - FTAs with the US, Central America, and EFTA	- Maintained Familias en Acción
Pro-market	Pro-market	Pro-market	Pro-market	Neutral

have departed from market orthodoxy is better reflected along a continuum. The most statist leftist government, Venezuela, underwent significant state intervention across policy spheres. At the other end of the spectrum of leftist governments, Chile implemented the most pro-market policies. The rest of the leftist governments lie somewhere between Chile and Venezuela, with Argentina, Bolivia, and Ecuador close to Venezuela on the statist side, and Brazil and Uruguay close to Chile on the pro-market side. Contrary to concerns that Daniel Ortega's administration in Nicaragua would follow a statist path in line with that of Chávez in Venezuela,[218] his administration has followed a moderate pro-market orientation.

Second, there is a distinction between the type of policies carried out by left-of-center governments and those observed in governments identified with the right. Right-of-center governments are found in the pro-market end of the spectrum, not only preserving the orthodox status quo prevailing at the turn of the century, but even furthering it in several areas. Conversely, although spanning a broad range along the continuum, leftist governments are less pro-market than their right-of-center counterparts. This suggests that, contrary to what Susan Stokes has found regarding the previous wave of reform in Latin America,[219] ideology is a first general indicator of the direction of economic transformations in the region.

Third, although spanning the statist/pro-market spectrum, all cases have remained within the boundaries of a market economy. In this sense, leftist governments' reactions to neoliberalism run counter to warnings that the region would be swept by a leftist tsunami ushering in socialist experiments from the past. Despite a shared emphasis on poverty alleviation across leftist governments, most of them have made fiscal discipline a priority.

However, no policy area under study remained untouched. From the most contentious of market reforms—privatizations—to the least visible—government budgets—different leftist governments implemented policies departing from market orthodoxy. Regarding privatizations, leftist governments mostly interrupted the sale of state-owned enterprises, with the notable exception of Chile. In Argentina, Bolivia, and Venezuela, leftist governments reversed privatizations—by either completely taking over or reacquiring a majority ownership—in some cases and created state-owned enterprises to coexist with the private sector. Most of the state's intervention in this sphere has taken place in the energy and telecommunications industries. These transformations have been characterized for sharing the same visibility that distinguished the privatization process during the period of neoliberal reform.

With respect to taxation, leftist governments left personal income taxes entirely unchanged, with the exception of Uruguay's introduction of a two-tier income tax. Instead, corporate tax rates were their preferred instrument. Bolivia, Ecuador, Nicaragua, and Venezuela increased corporate tax rates, while Uruguay lowered the maximum marginal income tax rate for corporations.

In the sphere of government spending, most leftist governments have either maintained or tightened fiscal discipline. In Argentina, Bolivia, Brazil, and Chile, reductions in government spending resulted in substantial fiscal surpluses. In Uruguay, general continuity in the government's balance was maintained, continuing with yearly surpluses. Even in Nicaragua, where fiscal surpluses have been absent, fiscal stringency has increased significantly. The exceptions are Ecuador and Venezuela, where greater budget imbalances have been the norm in spite of unprecedented commodity revenues.

Regarding trade liberalization, the search for commercial opportunities in the form of new trade agreements slowed down among leftist governments, although trade liberalization achieved during the 1980s and 1990s has not been reversed. Chile, Nicaragua, and Uruguay actively promoted free trade by signing multiple investment protection and free-trade agreements. Venezuela abandoned the G-3 and the Andean Community but took steps to join Mercosur as a full member. Financial liberalization also remained mostly unchanged, except for the countries at the extremes of the spectrum: Chávez instituted foreign exchange controls—which has been a recurrent measure in Venezuela to avoid capital flight—while Chile removed capital controls mandating foreign investment to remain in the country for a period of time before leaving. Regarding monetary liberalization, price controls were implemented in Argentina, Bolivia, and Venezuela.

Poverty alleviation is an area where there was considerable variation across leftist governments. In Chile and Uruguay, leftist governments introduced means-tested conditional cash transfer programs. In Bolivia and Venezuela, leftist administrations adopted programs without restrictions based on need. In the rest of the cases, governments maintained existing efforts or reorganized their predecessors' programs into a consolidated program.

In short, a coherent leftist economic project failed to emerge across the region. Although leftist governments remained within the boundaries of a market economy, there are significant differences regarding the extent to which they have preserved the status quo. Conversely, right-of-center governments opted for deepening the pro-market reforms prevailing in the region before the left reached power. The natural question that follows is what explains these differences? In the following chapter, I advance an explanation based on party system institutionalization, revise existing institutional accounts based on fragmentation and polarization, and evaluate alternative explanations seeking to account for differences in leftist reactions to market reforms.

3 PARTY SYSTEMS AND LEFTIST GOVERNMENTS' ECONOMIC POLICIES

THE ANALYSIS OF the leftist governments' economic reforms revealed that there is considerable variation in Latin America. The differences in these reactions across countries raise some critical questions. What accounts for the variation? Which factors allowed some presidents to implement significant economic policy transformations departing from the prevailing market orthodoxy?

This chapter's objective is to answer these questions by accounting for the different factors behind leftist governments' statist policies that deviate from the status quo. As a starting point, I advance an explanation of how the type of economic policy conducted by leftist governments in the region is best explained by the degree to which the party system is institutionalized. In contrast to previous work on party systems that has only tangentially focused on the formulation of economic policy, or that has remained relatively cursory and exploratory—mainly at the level of "provocative ideas with some fairly anecdotic evidence," as one observer put it[1]—this chapter contributes to theory building by developing the causal logic behind the relationship between party system institutionalization and economic policy changes. It then offers a macro-level, systematic test of the logic and alternative explanations using empirical evidence of leftist governments in the region.

Building on insights from the literature on the importance of party systems for democracy and economic transitions, I find that centripetal dynamics characteristic of institutionalized party systems make piecemeal reforms and the preservation of the status quo more likely. In contrast, centrifugal dynamics typical of party systems in disarray are conducive to significant economic transformations.[2] This is due to differences in both the type of candidate who is likely to reach power and the parties' ability to influence the executive's policies.

As this chapter and subsequent case studies show, the empirical evidence from Latin America provides strong support for this relationship. The most significant statist reforms took place in those countries with the lowest levels of party system institutionalization, whereas policies in line with the prevailing pro-market trend were conducted in the countries with the highest levels of party system institutionalization. This relationship is observed across cases: as party system institutionalization increases, the departure from the prevailing trend of pro-market policies becomes less drastic.

This explanation refines prevailing views on the role of party systems in economic reform. It suggests that the number of parties in the system and the ideological distance among them tend to be relevant determinants of reform whenever party systems are institutionalized. Otherwise, lacking the ability to translate society's views into legislative muscle, parties are unable to meaningfully shape the executive's policies.

In addition to advancing the party system explanation, I assess five alternative accounts that occupy a prominent place in the literature on economic reforms—(1) natural resources, (2) prevailing economic conditions, (3) depth of market reforms (4) interest groups, and (5) executive power—for their ability to explain differences in the left's economic policies across Latin America. Overall, these explanations span the main institutional, economic, class-based, structural, and path dependence factors found in the literature on economic reforms in general[3] and the adoption of leftist governments' economic policies in Latin America in particular.[4]

After considering each of them closely in comparative perspective, I find that they provide less explanatory leverage than the party system institutionalization account. This does not mean, of course, that party systems are the only factor at play in determining the type of economic policies carried out in each country. Quite the contrary, these alternative explanations are considered precisely because there is evidence they have played an important role in shaping the type of government policies in various geographical and historical contexts. However, although they may play an undeniably important role in *particular* cases, as case studies on Venezuela, Brazil, and Chile will show, they are less helpful in accounting for variation *systematically* across all cases.

Party System Institutionalization and Governments' Economic Reforms

The features of highly and poorly institutionalized party systems have been studied by a variety of scholars.[5] For the purposes of the argument presented in the following paragraphs, I rely on Scott Mainwaring and Timothy Scully's influential work on party systems in Latin America, where they identify institutionalized party systems as those where parties present stable patterns of continuity across time, have strong roots in society, enjoy a generalized sense of legitimacy among the population, and have party organizations with established rules and structures.[6]

Although research on party systems has focused mostly on their consequences for democracy, the features of institutionalized party politics also have important implications for the type of policies carried out by governments. Their consequences hinge on two factors: (1) the type of candidate—insider versus antisystem—that is likely to reach the presidency; and (2) the type of dynamics—consensual versus contentious politics—affecting whether parties are able to shape the president's policies. I argue that centripetal incentives characteristic of institutionalized party systems make it more difficult for outsider candidates without a stake in the system to reach the presidency and carry out drastic economic transformations. Additionally, such incentives facilitate interparty and interbranch cooperation, making it easier for the different political forces to influence such changes. In contrast, centrifugal incentives characteristic of party systems in disarray make it likely for antisystem candidates to reach power, and undermine political parties' ability to shape the executive's reforms and prevent the president from conducting drastic transformations to the prevailing order (see Table 3.1).

INSIDER VS. ANTISYSTEM CANDIDATES

In party systems with a strong institutional life there are several constraints that come with participating in party politics. First, candidates are unlikely to run for president unless they have followed a certain institutional path—often local, then regional, then national politics—with the party.[7] This process forces politicians to accommodate different party sectors behind their campaign and generates experience and negotiation skills. Thus, their support is more a product of their ability to rally other party members behind their campaign—for programmatic or compromise reasons—than exclusive charismatic appeal.[8] Moreover, participation in party politics establishes a record of discipline, and a reputation of honoring commitments with supporters throughout the process. In highly institutionalized party systems, parties' policies tend to be moderate and consistent with the party's historical program. Political leaders strive to protect not only the party brand, but also the

TABLE 3.1

Institutionalization of the Party System and Type of Economic Policies

Type of Party System	Type of Incentives	Type of Dynamics	Economic Policy
Institutionalized	Centripetal	Insider candidates and consensus-building politics	Status quo
Disarray	Centrifugal	Antisystem candidates and contentious politics	Drastic transformations

Source: Gustavo A. Flores-Macías, "Statist vs. Pro-Market: Explaining Leftist Governments' Economic Policies in Latin America," *Comparative Politics* 42:4 (July 2010).

system in which they play a prominent role in checking the president's power and shaping his or her policies.

In contrast, in disjointed party systems, newcomers are able to rise to power without the preelectoral alliances, broad consensus building, and political record. There are few incentives for interest accommodation and the incorporation of differing views behind a common government program. Owing their power to charismatic stardom, programmatic coherence and reputation become secondary concerns, and being associated with the party establishment becomes an electoral liability.[9] Thus, lacking the political commitments that party politics requires, outsider politicians without a stake in the system are more likely to adopt drastic measures to alter the status quo than rank-and-file politicians.[10]

THE POLITICS OF CONTENTION VS. CONSENSUS

In addition to the type of candidate likely to reach power, party systems also play a role in determining whether moderate or extreme policies are likely to take place.[11] Institutionalized party systems generate centripetal incentives that facilitate finding common ground among political forces and enable parties to shape the executive's economic policies. First, the continuity of parties across time results in longer time horizons, which generates incentives for negotiation and intertemporal cooperation.[12] As has been underscored in the game theory literature on iterative games, the expectation of repeated interactions across time increases tolerance for dissenting views and encourages consensus seeking.[13] The prospect of dealing with the same political parties—and sometimes even the same people—in future legislatures involves legislators' personal and party reputations and makes them relevant. All-or-nothing situations are eschewed because politicians expect to have many future interactions with their political opponents, alternating between majority and minority positions. This dynamic favors negotiation and is therefore conducive to compromise solutions. Repeated interactions create certain boundaries for conduct that tend to be absent when time horizons are short.

Additionally, complex rules and organizational structure result in parties with wide-ranging, collective interests that become more important than particularistic views. As highlighted in the overlapping generations literature, parties function as a network of overlapping interests and cohorts resulting in policy moderation, or what Alesina and Spear call "far sighted policies."[14] Since the policy positions of an office holder affect the political prospects of other members of the party—both office holders and non-officeholders—it is in everybody's interest to rein in maverick candidates and office holders. Complex selection mechanisms—those involving several layers of membership (e.g., geographical or group-based) in the process, such as primaries or assemblies—are particularly important because they tend to bring members' policy positions closer to a common ground acceptable to the party's core.

Further, strong roots among the population enable parties to acquire and mobilize resources, and consolidate a consistent base of supporters. Strong ties to the electorate tend to supply the party with a reliable block of votes, resources, activists, and cadres. The more socially embedded parties are, the more likely they are to consistently articulate constituents' demands in the legislative process. Finally, and significantly, a generalized sense of legitimacy gives parties the necessary traction to shape the president's policies. In institutionalized party systems, parties are able to translate popular support into the legislative leverage that makes them relevant political actors worth taking into account.

These incentives play a crucial role in shaping the executive's policies to a common denominator acceptable to a working majority. Although agreement is not guaranteed on every issue, predictable, established, and legitimate patterns of competition encourage negotiation among the different forces because political parties matter.[15] Since common ground is found among a narrow range of policy alternatives acceptable to a working majority, the result is piecemeal reform rather than drastic transformations.[16]

Conversely, party systems in disarray generate centrifugal incentives that discourage cooperation and are conducive to extreme, unpredictable positions. In such systems, lack of party continuity results in the shortening of the different actors' time horizons and encourages extreme positions in order to acquire fast, short-term gains. The prevalence of ephemeral electoral vehicles diminishes the incentives for negotiation and raises the stakes of policy decisions, given the high uncertainty that concessions today will be paid back in the future. Also, often lacking complex rules and organizational structure, parties in these systems forego the process of interest accommodation and negotiation that comes with the formation of cadres and the participation in local, regional, or national governments. Instead, the particularistic concerns of a charismatic leader become the law of the land, and collective reputations become secondary matters.

Moreover, without strong roots in society, parties are more likely to be malleable in their policy positions.[17] Often without a clear government program, it becomes easier to switch back and forth between opposite ends of the spectrum. Lastly, the generalized discredit of parties undermines their legislative muscle, which leads to street politics rather than legislative bargaining. Due to low levels of legitimacy in the eyes of the population, the president lacks incentives to incorporate them in the decision making process. Instead, executives will tend to sideline political parties and appeal directly to the public to carry out their government program.

Thus, these centrifugal incentives contribute to the adoption of extreme positions away from the status quo. They discourage legislative bargaining and interbranch cooperation, and favor the politics of confrontation and street mobilizations. Confrontation among the different political forces in turn raises the stakes of adopting a particular policy course and contributes to the radicalization of positions. In this context, the president has every incentive to circumvent opposition to his or her project and push for extreme transformations by decree.[18]

It is worth emphasizing that party systems in disarray do not lead to statist policies per se, nor do institutionalized party systems necessarily result in the adherence to pro-market policies. Instead, party systems in disarray make the election of revisionist candidates more likely and enable governments to carry out extreme, less predictable policies that severely depart from the status quo, regardless of whether such policies are statist or pro-market. Whether a particular candidate wins a given election is contingent upon a variety of factors, from how well they run their campaign,[19] to their policy positions,[20] and even their looks.[21] However, insider candidates are more likely than their antisystem counterparts to reach power in an institutionalized party system, because parties in these systems constitute socially legitimate barriers to entry for outsiders and provide the infrastructure, resources, and organizational capacity often required to win a national election. This selection mechanism is effective, since parties in such systems are regarded by the population as decisive in determining who governs. Thus, outsider candidates may reach power in institutionalized party systems, but the odds are against them. The same logic holds for the parties' ability to shape the executive's policies. Although a consensus may not be reached on every policy initiative, institutionalized party systems tend to generate incentives to take into account the perspectives of the main congressional forces, for whom reputation and compromise matter. Such incentives obviate the president's need to circumvent the legislature and govern by decree, and make legislative bargaining, rather than the politics of street confrontation, the norm.

Ideology is thus expected to play an important role in determining whether significant economic transformations are likely to follow a statist or a pro-market orientation. Leftist governments will tend to pursue agendas of redistribution through government intervention in the economy. As party system institutionalization decreases, statist policies are likely to become more extreme and comprehensive, including expropriations, land reform, and barriers to trade. Conversely, right-of-center governments will tend to give the market a central role in their government agendas.[22] As party system institutionalization decreases, pro-market policies are likely to radicalize as well, with policies such as privatizations, trade liberalization, and the elimination of subsidies becoming the norm. Figure 3.1 illustrates how the interaction between ideology and party system institutionalization explains economic policy outcomes. The continuum for the type of party system is shown along the horizontal axis and the continuum for the type of transformation is represented along the vertical axis. The shaded area illustrates the extent to which economic policies depart from the prevailing order—represented as the dotted line—as party system institutionalization varies.

Given the theoretical considerations advanced above, this argument would predict policy moderation and the general preservation of the orthodox status quo to be more likely in countries with institutionalized party systems. It would expect

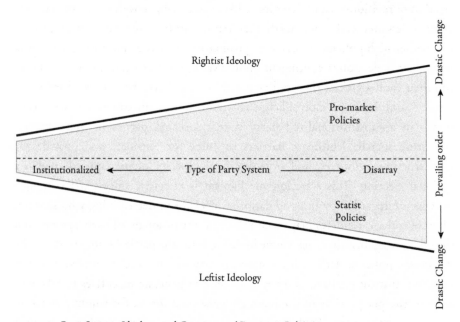

FIGURE 3.1 Party Systems, Ideology, and Governments' Economic Policies

candidates with a history of party politics to be more likely to reach office in such systems, as well as the different political forces represented in Congress to take an active role in shaping the executive's policies. Furthermore, this view would also predict a tendency for less moderate adjustments in countries with party systems in disarray. It would expect outsider candidates—owing their political rise to the explicit rejection of the status quo—to be more likely to reach power, and the disarray of the different political forces to lead to confrontation and impair their ability to influence the president's policies.

The period of dual transitions—economic transitions away from ISI and toward liberalization on the one hand and from authoritarianism to democracy on the other—during the 1980s and 1990s is an instance in which the initial contours of these party system dynamics can be appreciated in comparative perspective. Although the adoption of significant market reforms occurred at a time when several countries were ruled by authoritarian governments—e.g., Chile, Mexico, Peru, and Uruguay—differences in party system institutionalization help explain variation in the depth of market reforms in countries with democratically elected governments. For example, as Chapter 4 will show, during the period in which Venezuela had one of the most institutionalized party systems in the region, presidents in that country found themselves generally unable to carry out significant pro-market economic policy transformations.[23] In contrast, drastic, "shock therapy" style liberalization took place in the context of party system disarray in Bolivia during Paz Estenssoro's (1985–1989) presidency.[24] Without the aura of success that these measures enjoyed at the time, Collor de Mello's market reforms in Brazil were considerably more drastic than those subsequent presidents have been able to implement as the Brazilian party system became more institutionalized.[25] In the case of Argentina, where Menem introduced drastic reforms, the sustained weakening of the Radical Civic Union during the 1990s and the corresponding erosion of the party system has not contributed to the moderation of economic policy.[26] Thus, even though ideology did not play a prominent role as a determinant of the direction of reforms during the region's transition between ISI and market orthodoxy,[27] institutional weakness facilitated drastic economic transformations.

The arrival of leftist candidates to power at the end of the 20th century in Latin America offers a range of cases showing variation between the adherence to a general framework of market orthodoxy and the adoption of extreme policy transformations in the statist direction. In this case, however, all countries can be studied in a context of democracy, at least in the minimal procedural sense, which has allowed different patterns of interparty competition to develop over time.

The evidence regarding the type of economic policies conducted across the region's leftist governments provides empirical support for the theoretical propositions.

Leftist governments that resulted from elections in party systems with low levels of institutionalization—Bolivia, Ecuador, and Venezuela—have carried out policies significantly altering the prevailing model. As the level of institutionalization of the party system increases, so does policy moderation. Those leftist governments that came to power in countries with higher levels of party system institutionalization— Chile and Uruguay—are those exercising policy moderation and departing the least from market orthodoxy.

Based on Pedersen's index of vote volatility as a measure of party system institutionalization,[28] Figure 3.2 reflects the strong correspondence between economic policies and party system institutionalization in comparative perspective. Following convention,[29] I use an index of volatility as a proxy for party system institutionalization since, as Scott Mainwaring and Mariano Torcal have noted, volatility "is the easiest dimension of institutionalization to measure and perhaps the most important because institutionalization is conceptually very close to stability."[30] Since different leftist presidents arrived to power at different points in time, the index reflects vote volatility in the period spanning the three most recent lower/single house elections at the time each leader reached office. This window—spanning between eight and 12 years depending on the country—is large enough to capture the dynamics of interparty competition leading to a leftist leader's election, but small enough to

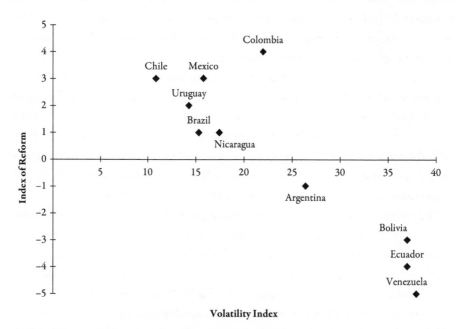

FIGURE 3.2. Economic Reforms and Party System Institutionalization

Source: Author's calculation of Pedersen's vote volatility scores and the index of reform discussed in Chapter 2.

exclude preceding time periods too far removed to accurately reflect the context in which the candidate reached office.[31]

For example, the score for Venezuela is constructed as an average of the volatility scores between 1988 and 1998—the year Hugo Chávez was elected president. The ten-year period captures the dynamics of interparty competition in which Chávez rose to the national stage in politics—i.e., those that made his arrival to power possible. This consideration is particularly important because it shows the degree to which Venezuela's party system had deinstitutionalized *before* Chávez was in a position to further contribute toward this process once in power.[32]

Figure 3.2 illustrates how the empirical evidence conforms to theoretical expectations. Countries are aligned in a < shape, where the lower prong corresponds to leftist governments and the upper prong to rightist administrations. The center of the < shape is in pro-market territory, reflecting the status quo bias that compels policy makers to adhere to the pro-market trend that has prevailed in the region.[33] As party system institutionalization decreases, the extent to which governments carry out significant reforms increases—i.e., countries lie closer to the extremes along the index of reform. The interaction between ideology and party system institutionalization helps anticipate how much governments departed from market orthodoxy. In institutionalized systems, leftist governments' economic reforms tended to slow down the liberalizing impetus prevailing in the region, adopting instead a gradualist approach.[34] As party system institutionalization decreased, leftist governments not only halted the liberalizing trend in many areas but reversed them by introducing statist reforms. Similarly, rightist governments implemented deeper pro-market reforms as institutionalization decreased.

Country-level evidence supports these findings. In the context of governments that have conducted the most radical reversals—Bolivia, Ecuador, and Venezuela—electoral vehicles brought leftist leaders to power. Rather than competing for the presidency through long-established political parties, Evo Morales, Rafael Correa, and Hugo Chávez reached power after running for office with political organizations created explicitly about their persona. The Movimiento Al Socialismo (MAS) in Bolivia, the Movimiento PAÍS in Ecuador, and the Movimiento V República (MVR) in Venezuela were movements transformed into electoral vehicles with the purpose of reaching power by means of antisystem platforms. Lacking the constraints that come with a trajectory within party politics, owing their popularity to the parties' lack of legitimacy, and facing short time horizons, these candidates had few incentives to moderate their extreme policy positions. Furthermore, a product of weak party systems, political forces represented in these countries' legislatures have proved unable to shape the presidents' policies. Instead, their disarray forced them to give in to executive pressure and street mobilizations, even when the opposition commanded legislative majorities.[35] As a result, the legislative bodies in these countries have often been circumvented to conduct statist measures by decree.

In Argentina, the party system has struggled with institutionalization, with some parties appearing and disappearing or shifting alliances, and certain rival factions within parties becoming more salient than political parties proper.[36] Although the Peronist and Radical parties have managed to preserve their traditional identities, new parties—such as the left-of-center *Solidaridad e Igualdad* (Solidarity and Equality) and the right-of-center *Propuesta Republicana* (Republican Proposal)— have gained ground[37] and the coexistence of seasoned politicians with outsiders— the owner of Argentina's soccer team Boca Juniors, for example—has become increasingly common.[38] The parties' lack of a clearly defined programmatic line and their increasingly short time horizons have made the policy making process less predictable and more prone to the adoption of extreme positions. Political issues are often taken to the streets, with *piquetes*—as popular roadblocks are called in Argentina—even encouraged by the government.[39] The result has been little cooperation between the president and congressional forces. Instead, confrontation on economic issues and the executive's reliance on executive decrees have become the norm.[40]

In Nicaragua, economic policy transformations have been moderate in the context of a moderately institutionalized party system. Ortega has managed to pass a mix of statist and pro-market measures, and the parties represented in the legislature have been meaningful actors able to shape the executive's original project. For instance, in the case of a fiscal reform aiming to increase the tax burden, the executive had originally pushed for a 2-percent corporate tax rate, with a provision to increase the rate to 2.5 percent over time.[41] However, Congress moderated the government's fiscal reform to 1 percent.[42] This type of watered down reform has been characteristic of the policy process in spite of Ortega's rhetoric.[43]

In Brazil, the party system has seen progressive institutionalization since the return of civilian rule.[44] Parties like the PSDB and the PT have become increasingly established as fixtures in the political process, and congressional bargaining has taken center stage in the policy making process. As the PT's gradual move toward the center suggests, the Brazilian system's centripetal dynamics have resulted in the moderation of radical positions as a condition to reach power.[45] Although legislative switching and the PMDB's ambiguous ideological stance still undermine the system's predictability, political forces have been able to translate popular support into legislative strength, becoming effective moderators of the speed and scope of Lula's economic reforms.

Although the 1996 electoral reforms undermined voter identification with the three main political forces and eroded the programmatic lines between the Blanco and

Colorado parties,[46] Uruguay's party system institutionalization remains one of the most institutionalized in the region. This country's parties are characterized by discipline and loyalty to the party label.[47] As a result, congressional forces have effectively moderated the president's policies by watering down the executive's policy initiatives, including the proposed Free Trade Agreement with the United States, tax reform, and central bank autonomy.[48] Despite its congressional majority in both chambers—a rare phenomenon in Latin America—the Vázquez government privileged legislative bargaining in order to accommodate the different parties' policy positions.[49]

Departing the least from the pro-market trend, Chile's economic policies have been the consequence of a process of political accommodation and piecemeal reform. A product of one of the most highly institutionalized party systems in Latin America, Ricardo Lagos had to compete in the Concertación's primaries with a government program that would appeal not only to a leftist audience but also to the sectors of the electorate sympathetic to the Christian Democrats. He also had to incorporate sectors of the defeated Christian Democrats and the rest of the parties that formed the Concertación into his government, resulting in the need for consensus building as a condition for governance.[50] Furthermore, intra- and interparty negotiations have characterized the policy process, and parties' strong roots in society have leveraged popular support into legislative strength as well as provided incentives for the executive to seek common ground on important and often contentious issues. Examples include the approval of the Free Trade Agreement with the United States and the government's attempts to pass fiscal reform.

Institutionalization, Fragmentation, and Polarization

How does this explanation based on party system institutionalization relate to other features of party systems to account for economic policy transformations? Most of the work on the effect of party systems for policy making has focused on how increasing levels of fragmentation and polarization are likely to make reforms more difficult. In the case of fragmentation, Haggard and Webb suggest that it "makes coalition rule more likely, increases the difficulty of making compromises and contributes to the instability of governments—all factors that can affect government policy."[51] Lora and Olivera hypothesize that "fragmented party systems are usually considered to be a hurdle for reforms," although they do not find a statistically significant association between the two.[52] Mainwaring argues that party system fragmentation "make[s] it difficult to implement major policy changes."[53] In short, fragmentation is expected to render executives "powerless to pursue their agenda,"[54] although the empirical results have been mixed.

A similar effect is attributed to polarization. Mainwaring suggests that a larger ideological spread among parties in the system hinders the president's capacity to implement significant reforms.[55] Likewise, Haggard and Kaufman expect that "reform will be more difficult in polarized systems [because of] partisan conflict."[56] Focusing on the sustainability of policies across administrations rather than their role for the initiation of reforms, Alesina identifies a "positive relationship between the degree of political and social polarization and the variability of macroeconomic policies [since] populist governments are often followed by right-wing regimes that attempt to reverse these redistributions."[57]

Although an individual effect has been attributed to each of these two factors, their consequences for policy making have often been treated in tandem, both because they are likely to be correlated—as Sartori and others have pointed out[58]—and because polarization is "notoriously difficult to measure."[59] Thus, the theoretical expectations of the effects of fragmentation and polarization can be summarized as follows: "the presence of moderate to high levels of legislative fragmentation [. . .] when combined with moderate to high levels of ideological polarization, should be expected to inhibit effective and efficient policymaking by the president."[60]

However, these considerations have overlooked the fact that fragmentation and polarization become meaningful for policy making when party systems are institutionalized. In order for the number of parties and the ideological distance among them to have a meaningful effect in shaping economic policy, parties must play a consequential role in the policy making process to begin with. This is the case as the level of institutionalization of the party system increases. Otherwise, the proliferation of parties does not translate into multiple relevant veto points, and greater ideological distance does not map onto relevant obstacles to the president's policy agenda.

Without relying on institutionalization as a first dimension to understand the effects of party systems on economic policy transformations, fragmentation and polarization do not provide much explanatory leverage on their own. The empirical evidence from leftist governments in Latin America supports this consideration. First, as Figure 3.3 suggests, drastic economic reforms have taken place in both fragmented and nonfragmented party systems, measured as the effective number of parties in the legislature.[61] According to this perspective, presidents facing highly fragmented legislatures should have a hard time implementing significant reforms. This is the case in Brazil, where parties have become meaningful actors shaping the president's policies, but certainly not in Ecuador or Venezuela, where the proliferation of parties has not prevented executives from carrying out their statist agendas.

Although polarization is much more difficult to measure than fragmentation, there are two ways in which to evaluate its effect on the type of leftist governments'

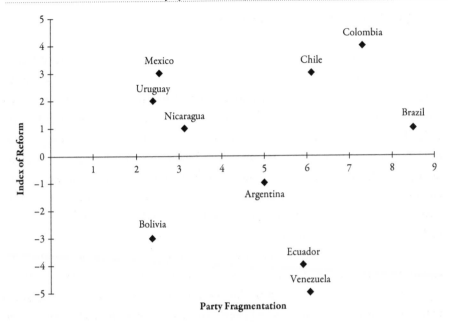

FIGURE 3.3 Economic Reforms and Party System Fragmentation

Source: Author's index of reform discussed in Chapter 2 and calculations of party system fragmentation. Fragmentation was calculated based on the Laagso and Taagapera Index of Seat Fragmentation in the legislature at the time when presidents reached office. The exception is Chile, where Ricardo Lagos became president in 2000 and legislative elections were held the following year. The formula to compute the index is $1/\sum_i^n (P_i^2)$, where n is the number of parties with at least one seat in the lower chamber, and P_i^2 is the square of each party's proportion of all seats.

economic policies. One is to rely on the measure of fragmentation as a general estimate, since polarization and fragmentation tend to be correlated, as was pointed out
earlier.[62] Following this approach, high levels of polarization in Venezuela and Ecuador would be difficult to reconcile with leftist governments' significant statist transformations in these countries.

Alternatively, another approach is to rely on reports of certain events that serve as an
indicator of high levels of polarization in society, such as the occurrence of general strikes,
violent demonstrations, and coups. For example, significant statist reforms have taken
place in Bolivia and Venezuela, where massive demonstrations for and against leftist governments' statist policies have turned violent. In Bolivia, observers have pointed out the
risk of civil war and the military has had to step in upon departmental governments'
threats to secede. In Venezuela, generalized strikes have paralyzed the country and an
attempted coup temporarily removed Chávez from power.[63] As with the first approach
to estimating polarization, significant statist transformations in Bolivia and Venezuela
are also difficult to reconcile with high levels of polarization in these countries. In short,
fragmentation and polarization provide much less explanatory leverage without taking
into account the degree to which the party system is institutionalized.

Assessment of Alternative Explanations

The literature on economic reforms offers several alternative explanatory factors that may account for the left's economic transformations. This body of literature burgeoned during the late 1980s and the 1990s, seeking to account for market reforms across the developing world, in places as diverse as Africa, Eastern Europe, India, Latin America, the Middle East, Russia, and Southeast Asia.[64] Some explanations emphasized institutional determinants of economic reform (regime type, executive powers),[65] others highlighted economic (economic crises, prevailing economic conditions)[66] or more structural factors (state capacity),[67] and still others underscored the role of interest groups (organized labor)[68] and path dependence (embeddedness of the previous model).[69]

The following discussion of alternative explanations relies on these prominent accounts from the reform literature as a point of departure with two exceptions: regime type and state capacity. In the first case, a regime type explanation suggested that democratic governments would tend to increase state intervention vis-à-vis their authoritarian counterparts—in the form of social spending and the creation of state-owned enterprises, for instance—to favor the popular sectors and increase the number of patronage positions for their supporters.[70] However, the arrival of the left to power at the turn of the century does not offer variation in regime type. Since all countries are democracies, at least in the minimal procedural sense, this factor is not plausible in accounting for different economic reforms.[71] In the second case, a view based on state capacity is mainly concerned with policy effectiveness, both at the design level—qualified technocrats conceiving the right policies—and the implementation level—government bureaucracies having the ability to deliver on such policies as planned.[72] However, this factor seeks to explain *performance* rather than why governments took the particular policy direction they did, and is therefore not further explored here.

In addition to these alternative explanations drawn from the economic reforms literature, the following discussion includes a factor advanced more recently to explain variation in leftist policies in Latin America: natural resources. Even though this factor did not play a prominent role in explaining differences in the adoption of market reforms, it has been advanced in scholarly and policy circles;[73] it is therefore worth evaluating whether it can indeed account for differences across leftist governments in the region.

Taken together, these five accounts represent the main existing theoretical challenges to the party system institutionalization explanation advanced in this book. As such, they are a natural place to begin a systematic assessment of why particular countries in the region have adopted statist policies. As with the party system accounts, I first introduce relevant theoretical considerations for each explanatory factor and formulate corresponding hypotheses that apply to the left in government. Next, I rely on established classifications in order to operationalize each factor. Finally, I evaluate whether the empirical evidence supports each hypothesis cross-nationally. Table 3.2 classifies these alternative arguments based on their theoretical grounding.

I. THE ROLE OF NATURAL RESOURCES

One widely held belief about economic policies among leftist governments in the region points to the role of natural resources. Referred to as rentier state theory, this perspective argues that rents from raw materials undermine a country's commitment to economic orthodoxy.[74] Resource rents, according to a cognitive strain of this view, "lead to irrational exuberance, producing a 'get-rich-quick mentality' among businessmen and a 'boom-and-bust' psychology among policymakers, marked by bouts of excessive optimism and frantic retrenchments."[75] Due to the influx of windfall profits into government coffers, the public rejects austerity measures and emphasizes the need for the redistribution of wealth. Following this logic, commodity booms "make the neoliberal quest for wealth creation through productivity, efficiency, and competitiveness look unnecessary."[76]

This perspective has identified a variety of commodities—not just hydrocarbons—as culprits of irrational exuberance in a host of countries. Scholars have studied this "policy myopia" resulting from exports of timber in the Philippines, Malaysia, and Indonesia,[77] to oil in Algeria, Iran, Nigeria, Venezuela,[78] and Russia,[79] to diamonds in Botswana.[80] In the context of the rise of the left in Latin America, this view would anticipate statist policies in countries with undiversified economies and highly dependent governments on commodity revenue—Bolivia, Chile, Ecuador, Venezuela[81]—and economic orthodoxy in countries with more diversified export structures—Argentina, Brazil, Uruguay.

TABLE 3.2

Classification of Alternative Explanations for Economic Reform

Structural	Economic	Path dependence	Interest group or class based	Institutional
- Natural resources	- Economic crises - Prevailing conditions	- Depth of market reforms	- Organized labor	- Executive Powers

Evaluating this perspective with the empirical record in the region, this alternative explanation provides some explanatory leverage. Rentier features could explain statist policies conducted by leftist governments in the most resource-dependent countries since the prices of Latin America's main commodity exports doubled between 2000 and 2009, resulting in a massive flux of resources to government coffers.[82] This view could account for drastic statist policies in, for instance, Venezuela, whose oil exports represented close to 90 percent of the country's total exports and 65 percent of government revenue during this period.

However, this explanation faces two important shortcomings. First, as Ross puts it, there is "little evidence that policymakers collectively fall into wealth-induced stupors."[83] For example, even in Venezuela—a crucial case that should be easily explained by this view[84]—the timing of Chávez's statist policies does not correspond clearly to the psychology of exuberance and restraint cycles. As a candidate, he advocated the government's further control of the Venezuelan oil industry as soon as he got out of prison in 1994 and until his election in 1998, a period in which oil prices reached historical lows.[85] Despite oil prices as low as those prevailing during the "bust years" of the Caldera administration, Chávez took steps to carry out significant statist policies during the first year of his administration, including transferring control of all oil production and distribution from private to state ownership, and an ambitious land reform program.[86] Although additional resources from higher oil prices naturally increased his ability to expand the scope of his program—as is the case with any government in a commodity exporting country experiencing a boom, whether in Botswana, Canada, Chile, Colombia, Norway, or Venezuela—Chávez's statist policies certainly did not begin with price-related exuberance. They both preceded and succeeded the spike in oil prices that began in 2004 and ended in 2008.[87] In short, there is little evidence that these leaders' statist inclinations began or ended with fluctuations in commodity prices.

Second, when evaluated in comparative perspective, this view is unable to account for variation across important cases, such as Chile and Argentina. In the context of Chile, this view cannot explain why this country has preserved a general framework of market orthodoxy in spite of its resource dependence and record high copper prices. Between 2000 and 2006, for example, Chile's commodity exports averaged 85 percent of the country's total; copper represented 49 percent of total exports and accounted for 35 percent of public revenue. To put things in perspective, Chile's share of commodity exports as a percentage of total exports is comparable to those of Ecuador during Correa's presidency (90 percent) and Bolivia during Morales's presidency (85 percent); copper exports in Chile represent as high a share as hydrocarbons do in Ecuador (49 percent) but a higher share than in Bolivia (32 percent); and the Chilean government's dependence on revenue from natural resources is considerably higher than that in Ecuador (24 percent) and Bolivia (22 percent). Figure 3.4 shows countries' average exports of primary goods and main exports as a percentage of total exports. Figure 3.5 illustrates governments' average dependence on natural resource revenue in countries where natural resources play a relevant role in the budget.[88]

According to rentier state theory, statist policies as those in Bolivia, Ecuador, and Venezuela should have been carried out in Chile, whose export structure is similar to those in Ecuador and Bolivia and whose resource dependence is higher. However, in spite of the price of copper tripling to reach record highs during this period,[89] leftist administrations in Chile have furthered pro-market reforms.[90]

Similarly, rentier state theory is unable to account for the adoption of statist policies in countries where rentier features are absent, such as Argentina. Why has this country adopted statist policies if it lacks the factors contributing to a boom and bust mentality? This perspective would predict Argentina to follow orthodox economic policies similar to those in Uruguay, given comparable export structures and low levels of resource dependence. Instead, leftist governments in Argentina and Uruguay adopted very different economic paths.

Figure 3.6 shows the relationship between resource dependence—measured as the average share of the main natural resource export as a percentage of total

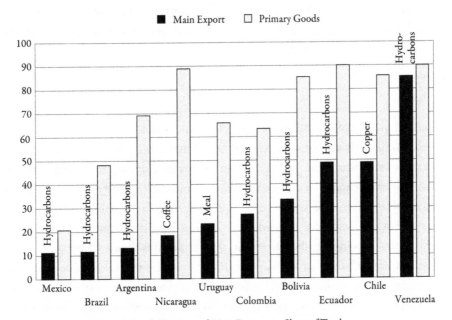

FIGURE 3.4 Average Primary Goods Exports and Main Export as a Share of Total

Source: UN Economic Commission for Latin America and the Caribbean, *Statistical Yearbook 2010* (Santiago de Chile: ECLAC, 2011), Table 2.2.2.1. Each country's average is calculated for the years of the leftist and rightist administration under study.

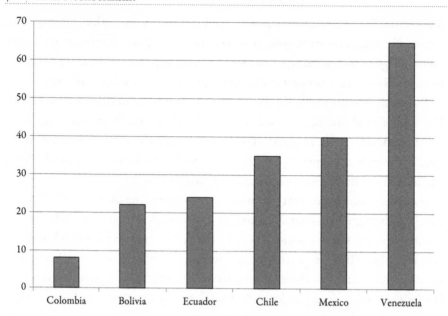

FIGURE 3.5 Average Government Revenue from Natural Resources as a Share of Total
Source: UN Economic Commission for Latin America and the Caribbean, *Statistical Yearbook 2010* (Santiago de Chile: ECLAC, 2011). Each country's average is calculated for the years of the leftist and rightist administration under study.

exports between 2000 and 2009[91]—and the type of economic policies. It illustrates how this explanation fails to account for Chile's pro-market policies in a context of high natural resource dependence, as well as Argentina's statist policies in the absence of resource dependence.

2. PREVAILING ECONOMIC CONDITIONS

A second main explanation in the extant literature submits that the occurrence of an economic crisis has consequences on how drastically a government implements corrective measures.[92] The prevailing economic conditions argument suggests that countries experiencing an economic crisis are more likely to conduct significant reforms since crises make such reforms more palatable to the public, whereas countries without a drastic deterioration of economic conditions tend to have a more difficult time passing significant reforms due to the public's unwillingness to adopt drastic measures.[93] In other words, "economic crises pave the way for a development of a social consensus on the need for policy change and remove potential sources of resistance."[94] They "provide opportunities for the executive to seize the initiative and launch wide-ranging economic reforms."[95] For example, Waterbury suggested that the extent to which Egypt, India, Mexico, and Turkey conducted economic reforms during the 1980s responds to differences in the severity of economic crises

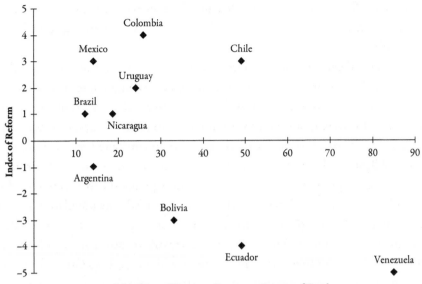

FIGURE 3.6 Economic Reforms and Resource Dependence

Source: Author's index of reform discussed in Chapter 2 and data on resource exports from UN Economic Commission for Latin America and the Caribbean, *Statistical Yearbook 2010*, (Santiago de Chile: ECLAC, 2011).

in these countries.[96] Similarly, the decisive adoption of orthodox measures in Estonia is credited to that country's 1992–1993 crisis.[97]

In Latin America, the adoption of significant market reforms in Argentina, Bolivia, and Peru during the 1980s and 1990s was explained by the public's willingness to switch course after the devastating effects of debt crises and constant bouts with hyperinflation. Dire economic conditions led the public to grant the governments of Alberto Fujimori (1990–2000), Carlos Menem (1989–1999), and Víctor Paz Estenssoro (1985–1989) carte blanche to conduct "bitter reforms."[98] Conversely, governments in Brazil and Venezuela found it more difficult to implement deep neoliberal reforms because economic conditions were not as dismal. In Brazil, Cardoso attempted to pick up some of the reforms his predecessor had left unfinished, but was able to conduct only moderate reforms in some areas.[99] In Venezuela, generalized riots and two attempted coups forced Pérez's second government to back off from more aggressive reforms.[100]

In the context of leftist governments' economic policies, a situation of deteriorating economic conditions may have encouraged governments to reverse the liberalizing trend and dismantle pro-market reforms that may have been perceived as problematic in the postcrisis context. Thus, we would expect to see the most significant statist reactions in countries that experienced serious economic crises, such as Argentina (2001–2002), Brazil (1998), and Uruguay (2001–2002). In contrast, continuity with pro-market reforms would be expected in countries with a vigorous and stable economy, as in Chile, or where economic performance was improving, as in Bolivia and Ecuador.

The empirical evidence in the context of the rise of the left suggests that, while economic crises might account for economic policy changes in some counties, as in Argentina, they are unable to explain the pattern of policy transformations across cases. In Argentina—after the economy contracted by 22 percent as a result of the financial crisis[101]—Néstor Kirchner's government opted for defaulting on its debt obligations, but the country's dramatic economic downturn did not translate into the adoption of statist measures in most policy spheres, as observed in the Andean countries. In Uruguay, where the crisis made the population 20 percent poorer, and in Brazil, where the currency lost 70 percent of its value, leftist governments operated within a general framework of pro-market policies. To put the magnitude of these crises in perspective, the 1994 Peso Crisis, for which the Clinton Administration granted an emergency aid package, contracted the Mexican economy by 8 percent.

Dani Rodrik and Javier Corrales have pointed out with respect to economic crises as an explanatory variable that it is difficult to know *ex-ante* whether a crisis will have any effect. It is only *ex-post* that we can point to them as inflection points without knowing a priori how drastic crises have to be in order to make a difference.[102] Notwithstanding this consideration, it is worth assessing whether less dramatic economic difficulties leading to the election of leftist leaders provide greater explanatory power. In particular, a comparison of financial instability leading up to the election of Lula in Brazil and Chávez in Venezuela is helpful in illustrating how similar crises can have very different effects. In both countries, financial investors panicked about the prospect of a leftist leader reaching the presidency, leading to dramatic selloffs of government bonds, losses in the stock markets, and currency depreciation. One way to assess the magnitude of investors' concerns in each country is by comparing each country's Emerging Markets Bond Index Global (EMBI Global)—a standardized indicator of country risk based on the spread with respect to US treasuries. In both countries the EMBI Global traded at a level higher than 2000 base points for more than 30 days before Chávez's election in 1998 and Lula's election in 2002.[103] Despite these similarities, however, the type of economic policy followed by the two governments diverged considerably: Venezuela, under Chávez, experienced significant statist transformations, while Brazil, under Lula, followed a moderate pro-market reform path. This divergence suggests that investors' panic is not a good determinant in comparative perspective of the two leftist governments' type of economic policies.[104]

Since economic crises do not provide much explanatory leverage for differences in the left's economic policies, it is worth exploring systematically whether economic performance—more generally than crises—can account for the type of governments' economic policies. The logic is similar to that of economic crises: both political elites and masses become disappointed in the failure of a particular economic model—what some authors have called "neoliberal fatigue"[105]—which leads to the adoption of an alternative model in order to fulfill development goals.[106] This view would expect the most drastic departure from pro-market policies to take place in the countries where economic performance was poorest before the left came to power. Table 3.3 reflects changes in GDP per capita between 1995 and 2008. The years when a president was first elected are shaded in gray. Based on these data, we can identify which countries were going through booming, stable, or deteriorating economic conditions before a new government was elected.

The data on prevailing economic conditions does not account for the differences in leftist policies either. Beyond the crises in Argentina and Uruguay that took place right before the left reached power in these countries, Venezuela's and Brazil's GDP per capita remained virtually stagnant in the four years leading to Chávez's and Lula's first elections in 1998 and 2002, respectively; yet their economic policies were very different. In contrast, countries like Bolivia, Chile, and Ecuador experienced sustained growth in the years leading to the election of a leftist president, also with very different outcomes. In Bolivia and Ecuador significant statist policies were adopted during one of their most prosperous periods in decades. Between 1999 and 2006—the year Correa was elected president—the income of the average Ecuadorian grew 26 percent and, for the first time since 1976, Ecuador experienced eight consecutive years of positive GDP per capita growth rates. Although less spectacularly than in Ecuador, Bolivia also experienced an improvement in economic conditions in the years leading to Morales's inauguration in 2006. In the five years prior to Morales's election, real GDP per capita grew almost 2 percent annually, compared to an average performance of 0.3 percent in the preceding five years. The statist economic policies that followed economic booms in these two countries contrast sharply with the general pro-market orientation that prevailed in Chile. Thus, as shown in Figure 3.7, differences in economic performance do not systematically explain the type of economic policies conducted across countries.

3. DEPTH OF MARKET REFORMS

A third alternative explanation for differences in leftist policies is related to the depth of market reforms adopted during the 1980s and 1990s. This view argues that a government's ability to carry out significant economic transformations is contingent on how well-established the previous model was. It implies "policy seriality"—i.e., a country's past policies play an important role in the government's ability to modify

TABLE 3.3

Index of GDP Per Capita, Selected Countries (1995 = 100)

	1995	1996	1997	1998	1999	2000	2001	2002	2003	2004	2005	2006	2007	2008
Argentina	100	104	111	114	109	107	101	90	96	104	113	121	130	137
Bolivia	100	102	105	108	106	107	106	107	108	110	118	121	119	124
Brazil	100	101	103	102	101	103	104	104	104	108	110	113	118	123
Chile	100	106	111	113	111	114	117	118	122	128	134	137	143	146
Colombia	100	100	102	101	95	96	96	97	100	103	107	113	120	121
Ecuador	100	101	103	104	96	97	101	104	106	114	119	123	124	131
Mexico	100	104	109	113	115	121	120	120	120	124	126	131	134	135
Nicaragua	100	104	106	108	114	117	118	118	119	124	128	131	134	137
Uruguay	100	105	109	113	109	107	103	91	92	102	108	121	127	138
Venezuela	100	98	102	100	92	94	96	86	78	90	96	106	113	116
Average	100	103	106	108	105	106	106	105	105	110	116	122	126	131

Source: World Bank, *World Development Indicators Online*, 2011. Relevant presidential election years are shaded in gray.

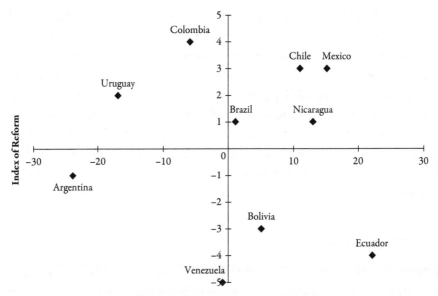

Percent Change GDP Per Capita (5 Years before Election)

FIGURE 3.7 Economic Reforms and Prevailing Economic Conditions

NB: Measures of change in GDP per capita for shorter periods before the election (e.g., one year and three years) are more weakly associated with the type of reforms.

Source: Author's index of reform discussed in Chapter 2 and World Bank, *World Development Indicators*, 2011.

them in the present.[107] This makes sense for several reasons, such as institutions' and bureaucracies' tendency to resist change, society's habituation to neoliberal institutions, and the self-entrenchment of policies throughout time as a result of contracts and international commitments. For example, this perspective explained Chile's and Bolivia's fast and comprehensive adoption of market reforms based on shallow experiences with ISI in these countries. Conversely, it attributed the more gradual and onerous adoption of market reforms in Brazil and Mexico to their generalized and sustained embrace of statist policies between the 1940s and early 1980s.[108]

In the context of the left, this view would expect those countries that most deeply transformed their institutions to accommodate market orthodoxy to find it most difficult to reverse market reforms. For example, Chile's commitment to pro-market policies is often attributed to "its most ambitious agenda of institutional reform" early during the Pinochet years.[109] On the other hand, this view would also expect countries where market reforms were shallow to find it easier to carry out statist policies. Chávez's ability to conduct significant statist policies in Venezuela, for instance, has been attributed to the "cosmetic," rather than substantial, application of market reforms in the early 1990s.[110]

A cross-national comparison provides little support for this explanation, however. As Figure 3.8 shows, differences in the extent to which market reforms were adopted

—measured by Morley, Machado, and Pettinato's index of structural reforms[111]—do not generally correspond to the types of polices carried out across the region. Countries with similar levels of market reforms conducted very different policies. For example, Bolivia, Brazil, and Ecuador had similarly low levels of market reform, but leftist governments adopted divergent economic policies. The same can be said about Argentina and Uruguay with higher levels of market reform, for example. This explanation would have predicted more substantive statist policies in Brazil, less orthodox policies in Chile, and more orthodox policies in Argentina. Thus, although the depth of neoliberalism would seem to explain a couple of cases in isolation, this explanation does not account for differences in the type of policies adopted across the region.

4. INTEREST GROUPS

A fourth compelling explanation focuses on the relative strength of interest groups—predominantly business and labor—to account for the initiation of market-oriented policies during the 1980s and 1990s.[112] It is based on the assumption that interest groups prefer to obtain additional wealth for themselves rather than maximize social welfare or output, and that market liberalization and financial openness favor certain interest groups—capital intensive sectors—through the redistributive effects of

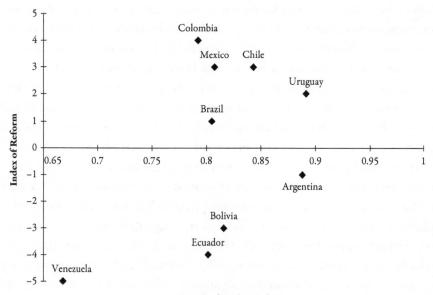

FIGURE 3.8 Economic Reforms and Depth of Market Orthodoxy

Source: Author's index of reform discussed in Chapter 2 and Morley, Machado, and Pettinato, "Indexes of Structural Reforms in Latin America," *Serie Reformas Económicas*, UN ECLAC, January 1999. Nicaragua was not included in the Morley, Machado, and Pettinato's index and is therefore not included here.

reforms.[113] As a consequence of increased liberalization, capital becomes more mobile and can easily adapt—through currency substitution[114] or capital flight, for example—if it finds conditions to be unfavorable. Labor, on the other hand, does not have this luxury.[115] It follows that business sectors—particularly those industries directly benefiting from capital mobility—tend to support liberalizing policies, while labor groups tend to reject them.[116]

In the context of the rise of the left in Latin America, an explanation based on interest groups would seek to account for variation in economic policies based on differences in the strength of interest groups across countries. The strengthening of organized labor could push for the implementation of statist policies, while the strengthening of business groups could push for pro-market measures. Thus, we would expect statist policies in those countries where labor is strongest, and market-oriented policies where labor is weakest.

However, the region's generalized weakening of labor before the arrival of the left to power and the disconnect between the strength of labor and leftist policies in comparative perspective are evidence against this argument. The deterioration of organized labor and the strengthening of business groups as a result of market reforms during the 1980s and 1990s undermine the premise that labor coalitions traditionally associated with the left gained enough leverage to reverse such reforms. Instead, market reforms considerably weakened labor and strengthened business sectors across Latin America in a variety of ways.[117] The reduction in government spending and the privatization of state enterprises translated into the dismissal of bureaucrats and the elimination of special privileges. The exposure of previously protected domestic industries to foreign competition resulted in widespread layoffs particularly affecting highly unionized industries. Stabilization policies that relied on wage restraints to enhance productivity and competitiveness further eroded labor's negotiating power.

Moreover, increased domestic and international competition forced enterprises to reduce costs and improve their production processes and the quality of their products to survive.[118] As a consequence, businesses put pressure on governments to decrease their share of social security contributions and keep wages depressed, effectively transferring the costs of market liberalization to labor. These measures severely undermined labor's political power in Latin America.[119] Thus, organized labor proved to be ill suited to resist the implementation of the Washington Consensus and was severely weakened by trade and financial liberalization,[120] leaving it unable to push for major transformations in the statist direction.

The empirical evidence from the region—regarding both the strength of labor in absolute terms and changes in the strength of labor within countries across time—further undermines the interest group hypothesis. Based on data from the Inter-American

Development Bank on unionization rates as a percentage of the total workforce,[121] a comparison of the levels of strength across countries suggests that significant statist policies were carried out in countries where organized labor was weakest. Two examples are Ecuador and Bolivia, where unionization rates hovered around 13.5 percent and 14.4 percent, respectively. Conversely, pro-market reforms were furthered in countries were labor was strongest, such as Brazil (24.8 percent) and Nicaragua (23.4 percent). As Figure 3.9 illustrates, differences in the strength of labor do not correspond with the types of policies carried out by the left in these countries.

Alternatively, the effect of labor can be assessed based not on labor's absolute strength, but on the relative changes of labor within the same country over time— i.e., whether its strengthening or weakening over time affected labor's ability to push for certain policies. Figure 3.10 shows that, with the exception of Chile, union strength decreased anywhere from three (Uruguay) to 13 (Brazil) percentage points between the mid-1980s and the late 1990s. It suggests that, contrary to the expectation that increases in the relative power of labor would result in statist policies, some of the countries where labor was hit hardest—Bolivia and Venezuela—were also those conducting the most statist measures. In contrast, the most orthodox policies were carried out in countries where labor strengthened, as in Chile, or lost relatively little influence, as in Uruguay. This evidence suggests that the relationship between

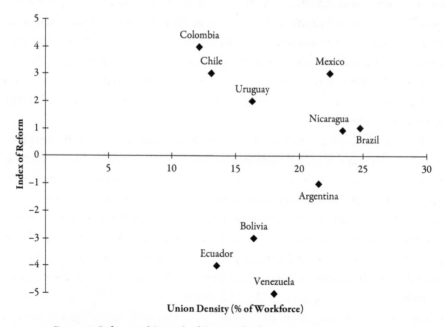

FIGURE 3.9 Economic Reforms and Strength of Organized Labor

Source: Author's index of reform discussed in Chapter 2 and Inter-American Development Bank, *Good Jobs Wanted: Labor Markets in Latin America* (Washington, DC: IADB, 2004). Union density rates ca. 1997.

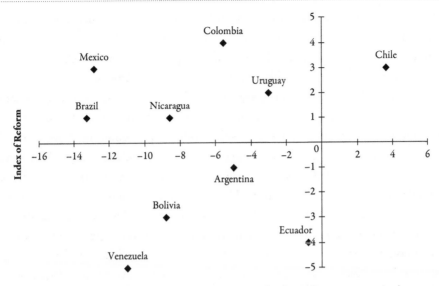

Change in Union Density between 1986 and 1997 (in percentage points)

FIGURE 3.10 Economic Reforms and Changes in the Strength of Organized Labor

Source: Author's index of reform discussed in Chapter 2 and Inter-American Development Bank, *Good Jobs Wanted: Labor Markets in Latin America* (Washington, DC: IADB, 2004).

the strength of interest groups and the type of economic policies carried out by leftist governments in the region is weak.

5. EXECUTIVE POWER

A fifth account suggests that executive strength played a central role in explaining the end of ISI and the adoption of market reforms.[122] When unpopular neoliberal reforms were adopted around the world during the 1980s and 1990s, scholars pointed to the executive's relative strength vis-à-vis the legislature as a useful explanatory factor. According to this view, countries with strong executives were better able to conduct unpopular reforms than those with weak presidents. A president with strong institutional prerogatives over the legislature will have the upper hand in setting the agenda, circumventing opposition legislators, and vetoing opposition initiatives. Conversely, a strong Congress can impair the president's ability to implement his or her government program by consistently blocking presidential initiatives. Nelson, for example, highlighted the role of executive strength to push for "vigorous and wide ranging market oriented reforms" in countries as dissimilar as Ghana, Sri Lanka, and Turkey during the 1980s.[123] Similarly, Holmes found that institutional restrictions on executive powers became an obstacle for the effective implementation of economic reforms in the context of the former communist world.[124] In short, this perspective argues that "the successful initiation of reform depends on rulers who have personal control over economic decision making, [...] and the political authority to override bureaucratic and political opposition to policy change."[125]

During the adoption of neoliberal reforms across Latin America, executive power became a good predictor of the governments' likelihood of carrying out significant economic transformations. Variation regarding executive strength was used to explain why draconian reforms were successfully implemented in Argentina and Chile—with the strongest executives in the region—but only partially in Brazil and very timidly in Venezuela—with considerably weaker presidents. An extreme case of presidential power, Chile's Augusto Pinochet's authoritarian regime was able to drastically reverse Salvador Allende's socialist policies.[126] Also with extraordinary presidential powers but in a democratic regime, Argentina's Carlos Menem carried out ambitious market-oriented transformations as a result of the president's prerogative to issue "Need and Urgency Decrees" (*Decretos de Necesidad y Urgencia*).[127] Conversely, at the other end of the spectrum, Venezuela was the country least able to adopt neoliberal reforms due to extreme executive weakness. Without decree or veto powers, Carlos Andrés Pérez's attempt to implement an ambitious set of orthodox reforms failed.[128] With a stronger executive than that of Venezuela but weaker than those of Argentina and Chile, Brazil's adoption of market reforms was only moderate during the Cardoso administration.

Drawing on the experience of the 1980s and 1990s, we would expect drastic economic transformations to take place in those countries with strong executives at the time leftist candidates reached power. This view would suggest that strong leftist executives—those in Brazil and Chile, for example—would be able to carry out the most drastic transformations, while weak leftist presidents—in Bolivia and Venezuela before new constitutions were drafted, and in Nicaragua—would have a much more difficult time altering the status quo.

The expected relationship between executive powers and the type of economic policies does not hold, however. Relying on the United Nations Development Program's Index of Presidential Powers,[129] Figure 3.11 shows that leftist governments with similar levels of executive strength, such as Brazil and Ecuador, Bolivia and Nicaragua, or Argentina and Uruguay, carried out very different policies. In Bolivia, for example, where presidents are comparatively weak, Morales carried out significant statist policies before the new Constitution was approved in 2009. Conversely, with one of the most powerful executives, Chilean presidents have not relied on their powers to push for drastic reforms.

It is worth noting that the most significant departures from pro-market policies took place in three countries where new constitutions altered executive powers to strengthen the president: Bolivia (2009), Ecuador (2008), and Venezuela (1999). In

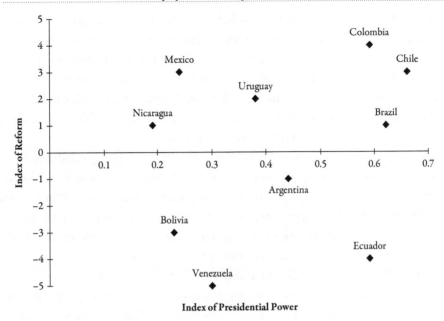

FIGURE 3.11 Economic Reforms and Presidential Power

Source: Programa de Naciones Unidas para el Desarrollo, *La democracia en América Latina* (New York, NY: UNDP, 2004) and author's index of reform discussed in Chapter 2.

all three cases, however, leftist governments were already in office and the transformation of executive powers during their administrations was a *product* of their presidency, not a *cause*. This consideration undermines the causal role of this factor for three reasons.

First, significant statist policies were carried out in these countries before presidential powers were modified as a result of the new constitutions. For example, in Bolivia, Morales carried out a number of statist reforms before the new Constitution was enacted on February 7, 2009. In 2006 he expropriated the energy sector, transferring ownership of all the natural gas produced in the country to the state-owned Yacimientos Petrolíferos Fiscales Bolivianos (YPFB).[130] In 2007 he introduced price controls.[131] In 2008 Morales launched an ambitious land reform effort, expropriated three energy companies—British Petroleum's natural gas producer Chaco, the pipeline company Transredes, and the storage company Compañía Logística de Hidrocarburos Boliviana—and nationalized the telecommunications industry.[132] In January 2009—just days before the enactment of the new Constitution—Morales expropriated Chaco Energy Company, a subsidiary of Pan-American Energy.[133]

Similarly, in Ecuador, Correa carried out several statist policies between his inauguration as president in January of 2007 and when the new Constitution came into force on October 20, 2008. For example, in October 2007 his administration increased taxes on oil companies.[134] In April 2008 he implemented price controls on a variety of goods and services.[135] In September of that year—a month before the enactment of the new Constitution—he expropriated four infrastructure projects including a hydroelectric complex, two irrigation projects, and an airport.[136] Even in Venezuela, where only 11 months passed between Chávez's inauguration in February of 1999 and the approval of the new Constitution in December of that year, Chávez carried out statist policies in the form of tax increases.

Second, it is a logical fallacy to assert that weak presidents strengthened themselves almost overnight based on the same rules on which their weakness was founded. At the time Morales reached power, the Bolivian executive office was one of the weakest in the region, based on the powers conferred in the 1967 Constitution and following the 1995 and 2004 reforms. Similarly, at the time Chávez became president, the 1961 Constitution also made Venezuelan presidents one of the weakest in comparative perspective. In order to change their positions of weakness, presidents had to challenge opposition-dominated legislatures to drastically alter the rules of the game and redesign executive-legislative relations.[137] This was possible due to the disarray of the party system.

Furthermore, changes in executive-legislative relations in Bolivia and Venezuela put these countries in line with the regional average at best, as scholars studying these constitutions have pointed out.[138] Reforms allowed for consecutive reelection, granted presidents the right to call for popular referenda in order to approve legislation or reform the Constitution, and, in Venezuela, extended the presidential term to six years.[139] But even if we assume that the new constitutions put executive powers in Bolivia and in Venezuela in line with countries with the strongest presidents— Brazil, Chile, Colombia, or Ecuador—there would be little variation across the region. This, of course, would render this factor of little value in explaining considerable variation along the dependent variable.

Conclusion

This chapter advanced an explanation based on party system institutionalization to explain governments' economic reforms. It did so by developing a causal logic and revising existing explanations based on fragmentation and polarization in the system. It then argued that the interaction between ideology and the type of party system explains the extent to which governments departed from the prevailing pro-market policy trend. Along these lines, it showed how the number of parties in the system and the ideological distance between them become relevant determinants of economic reforms only when parties are meaningful actors in the policy process.

Where party systems are institutionalized, political actors' time horizons are longer, repeated interactions and participation in local, regional, and national governments give players a stake in the preservation of the status quo, complex rules and procedures favor accommodation over personalistic politics, and parties have the necessary traction in society to shape the executive's policies. These incentives tend to favor piecemeal reform rather than drastic departures from the prevailing order.

The chapter also offered a macro-level test of these theoretical propositions alongside alternative explanations that spanned institutional, economic, interest group-based, structural, and path dependent factors. It found that in countries where parties with a leftist ideology reached power in institutionalized party systems, the pro-market trend was preserved, as in Chile and Uruguay, or moderated, as in Brazil and Nicaragua. As the level of institutionalization decreased, governments with a leftist ideology carried out statist economic policies departing from the pro-market trend, as in Argentina, Bolivia, Ecuador, and Venezuela. In countries where governments had a right-of-center ideology, as in Colombia and Mexico, the degree to which pro-market reforms were adopted increased as party system institutionalization decreased.

Contrary to prevailing institutionalist views based on fragmentation and polarization, significant reforms were carried out in countries with high numbers of effective parties in the system and with considerable ideological distance between parties. In spite of being fragmented, polarized, or both, party systems in Bolivia, Ecuador, and Venezuela did not constrain leftist presidents from implementing significant statist reforms. The disarray of party systems in these countries meant that, regardless of how numerous or ideologically different, parties were not meaningful actors capable of shaping executives' policies, nor were they able to prevent presidents' efforts to alter executive-legislative relations.

The assessment of the alternative explanations showed that other factors are less helpful than party system institutionalization in illuminating policy differences *across cases*. Some alternative explanations are more useful than others in accounting for variation across countries, but their explanatory power is limited to a few cases only. The relative strength of organized labor shows the weakest association, with the empirical evidence entirely contradicting the expected relationship. Contrary to expectations, statist policies were adopted in Venezuela, where the decrease in the relative strength of labor was sharpest, and market orthodox policies were carried out in Chile, the only country where labor gained a better bargaining position.

The rest of the factors are somewhat more clearly associated with policy differences across countries, but not enough to account for variations in the region. Economic crises were expected to encourage leaders to change course, but the 2001–2002 crisis failed to generate drastic statist reactions in Argentina and Uruguay. Similarly, significant statist reforms were conducted in Bolivia and Ecuador in spite of periods of sustained per capita growth preceding the arrival of leftist governments. Additionally, the weakest presidents were expected to struggle in carrying out significant changes, but the most drastic reversal of pro-market policies took place in countries traditionally known for presidents unable to exercise much power over the legislatures (Venezuela) and often incapable of serving their full terms in office (Bolivia and Ecuador) rather than in Chile or Brazil, where presidents have considerably more leverage over their legislative bodies. In countries where weak executives transformed executive-legislative relations to gain the upper hand, the disarray of the party system, rather than existing executive powers, allowed for the adoption of the new rules enabling presidents to carry out important statist transformations.

The depth of market reforms is useful in explaining the extreme cases of Chile and Venezuela, but is of little value in explaining variation in the rest of the countries with leftist governments. Since entrenched policies and institutions were expected to be more difficult to reverse than recent and cosmetic practices, Argentina and Bolivia—countries profoundly transformed by market reforms—should have been more resistant to statist policies than the empirical evidence shows. Likewise, natural resources play a role in understanding statist policies in Venezuela and perhaps Bolivia and Ecuador, but this explanation cannot account for Chile's pro-market policies and Argentina's statist reforms. Although additional income resulting from higher commodity prices will certainly allow any government to do more of what it had originally intended, an explanation based on natural resource rents overlooks the existence of constraints in the political arena.

In sum, upon examination of the extent to which the explanatory factors correspond to the type of economic policies conducted by leftist governments, the degree of institutionalization of the party system remains the explanation with the greatest leverage to systematically account for the type of economic reforms. This does not mean, of course, that other factors do not play any role in explaining leftist governments' economic policies in specific countries in addition to party system institutionalization. Indeed, institutions in general, and political party systems in particular, do not operate in a vacuum; they are shaped by political, economic, and social forces over time.[140] While institutions constitute the rules of the game that shape relevant actors' actions through incentives and disincentives,[141] they are seldom the only explanatory factor leading to the different types of economic policies. Although this chapter presented a general overview of the factors explaining leftist governments' economic policies, country studies in the following chapters identify the relationship between party system institutionalization and other explanatory factors to explain economic reforms in specific cases.

The main objective of the following case studies is to further evaluate the explanations discussed in this chapter. While the analysis conducted in this chapter provided a general picture of the explanatory power for each of the hypotheses at the regional level, case studies allow us to determine whether the causal relationship between party systems and the type of economic reforms indeed holds at the country level, the extent to which other factors play a role, and how these factors interact. Thus, the research in the following chapters shifts the focus from correlations across cases to tracing processes within cases.

4 PARTY SYSTEM IN DISARRAY
Venezuela's Statist Revisionism

"MR. VICE-PRESIDENT!" ORDERED President Hugo Chávez in a martial tone as he turned to his newly appointed cabinet, "I command you to nationalize all of those industries that belonged to the Venezuelan people and were privatized! The electric sector, the oil projects in the Orinoco Belt, the telephone company, return them to the people! [...] I urge the National Assembly," he said, now turning to an auditorium full of sympathizers, "to allow me to continue building the road to socialism by approving the Enabling Law (*Ley Habilitante*) that confers the president the mother of all revolutionary powers."[1] Two weeks later, the legislature gave Chávez broad powers to rule by decree for 18 months. Thanks to this and other Enabling Laws, he carried out statist policies in most areas of the economy. In the president's own words, Enabling Laws were "the main engine of Venezuela's socialist revolution."[2]

The scene captures not just the rhetoric but the ease with which Chávez implemented statist policies in Venezuela. Without much accountability or congressional restrictions, he had free rein to conduct nationalizations and land reform, implement currency and price controls, run deficits, and raise taxes. How did Venezuela, a country once famous for its highly consensual politics, get here?

In this chapter I argue that the sustained deterioration of the party system in Venezuela during the late 1980s and early 1990s, from highly institutionalized to disjointed, favored the rise of outsider, antisystem candidates and steered decision making away from Congress, which undermined the opposition's ability to shape the president's statist transformations.

Once these economic reforms were undertaken, the government's increased leverage from oil revenues allowed the Chávez administration to do more of what it had intended to do and sustain statist policies over time. Although sudden economic crises were absent in the years leading to Chávez's election in 1998, the gradual deterioration of economic conditions played a role in the weakening of the party system in the early 1990s as citizens became disenchanted with politicians' ability to solve the country's problems. Other factors, including organized labor, the depth of neoliberal reforms during the second Carlos Andrés Pérez (1989–1993) and Rafael Caldera (1994–1999) administrations, and the weakness that characterized the Venezuelan executive office at the time Chávez reached power did not play a significant role in explaining his government's ability to roll back market reforms.[3]

The mechanism can be summarized as follows. The sustained decline of economic conditions contributed to the loss of Venezuelans' confidence in the political class as a capable steward of the polity. Generalized disappointment led to the appeal of antisystem alternatives outside the traditional *partyarchy*, undermining the strength of the two-party establishment. The erosion of the party system allowed Chávez to create an ad hoc electoral vehicle—the Movimiento V República—to run for president and rally enough support behind his statist government program. Once in office, the party system's disarray facilitated the president's direct appeal to the people to circumvent existing political parties represented in the legislature, replace existing political institutions, draft a new Constitution, and strengthen the president's powers.

As a result, after the removal of institutional checks on executive power, Chávez conducted the most statist economic transformations among leftist governments in the region. His administration was able to sustain this policy course thanks to the increased leverage provided by record high oil prices. Without a doubt, the influx of money from the oil industry allowed him to maintain high levels of government spending in social programs while preserving macroeconomic stability. The flow of oil resources into government coffers ultimately became one of Chávez's main allies in garnering popular support for his economic policies toward "21st century socialism."

Each of the steps of this process is explained in the following pages. First, I introduce the moderating role that the party system played before its deterioration during the 1990s. Second, I discuss the process of deterioration before Chávez's rise to power along four indicators—(1) parties' legitimacy and roots in society, (2) personalistic politics, (3) electoral volatility, and (4) correspondence between politicians' campaigns and their government policies. Third, I discuss the consequences of the party system's disarray in (1) creating a conducive environment for antisystem candidates to reach the presidency, and (2) replacing congressional bargaining with street politics. Fourth, I provide an account of how these dynamics played out during the Chávez presidency to carry out statist reforms. Lastly, I discuss the role of less prominent explanatory factors and end with a conclusion.

The Legislature as a Moderator of Economic Reforms

Once regarded as a model of stability and institutionalization for the region, Venezuela's party system counted among its most important features the continuity of the main political parties, low electoral volatility, the population's strong party identification, and strong party discipline.[4] Two main political parties, Social Democrat Acción Democrática (AD) and Christian Democrat Comité de Organización Política Independiente (COPEI), alternated in power and governed with generally centrist positions since the establishment of democracy with the Pact of Punto Fijo in 1958.[5] Since then and until the late 1980s, the country became an oasis of consensus building in a region plagued by military coups and institutional breakdown. In the words of Jennifer McCoy, Venezuela was "a model democracy for the hemisphere, withstanding the pressures of a guerrilla war, military rule in its southern neighbors, and the booms and busts of the oil industry."[6]

During this period, the institutionalized party system played an important role in shaping the executive's economic policies. Several instances in which presidents introduced drastic austerity measures following drops in the price of oil, but which were watered down in the legislature, help to illustrate this role. For example, following an important decline in the price of oil in 1986, President Lusinchi introduced a set of stabilization measures including strong cuts in government spending, multitier exchange rate system, debt renegotiation, and fiscal reform.[7] In spite of the mounting fiscal pressures—which at the time led Ramón Espinasa to declare the beginning of Venezuela's post-rentist economy[8]—and Lusinchi's enjoying "the largest ever one party majority in both chambers of Congress," the legislature altered the president's fiscal initiative to give way instead to a modest reform of the *Impuesto Sobre la Renta* (income tax).[9]

Similarly, seeking to address the gap between declining government revenue and spending, President Pérez introduced a set of austerity measures dubbed as *El Gran Viraje* (The Great Turnaround) in 1989. Once again, the political parties represented in Congress, and particularly the president's own Acción Democrática (AD), played a role in moderating the president's initiative.[10] Arguing that it was bringing relief to the middle class, Congress froze the president's proposed reform to ease the burden on the severance payment system and privatize social security,[11] rejected the *Impuesto al Valor Agregado* (value-added tax, or VAT) introduced as part of Pérez's adjustment package, and instead approved "a modest reform of the income tax in 1991 after 2 years of discussion."[12] In the aftermath of Pérez's impeachment and still facing declining oil prices, interim President Ramón Velásquez negotiated with Congress a law that created a national VAT in 1993.[13] In short, regardless of whether the presidents' initiatives or the diluted versions approved by the legislature constituted sound economic policy, institutionalized political parties represented in Congress significantly shaped the executive's economic policies and moderated what otherwise would have been more drastic reforms.

Pre-Chávez Deterioration of the Party System

However, the prolonged deterioration of economic conditions, along with highly visible corruption scandals, deeply eroded support for the political establishment.[14] During the 20 years leading to Chávez's election in 1998, Venezuela's GDP growth rates and per capita income decreased steadily. In sharp contrast with the sustained real average annual economic growth of 4.8 percent during the 1960s and 4.0 during the 1970s, the economy shrank at an annual rate of -0.16 percent during the 1980s and grew at only 2.4 percent during the 1990s.[15] Similarly, real GDP per capita, which peaked at $7,790 in 1977, dropped to $5,654 by 1999.[16] At the time Hugo Chávez took office, Venezuelans' income per capita was 27 percent lower than two decades earlier.

The generalized deterioration of economic conditions resulted in drastic manifestations of popular discontent that evidenced the lack of legitimacy of the existing political order.[17] Such manifestations include the 1989 popular protests, the attempted coups in 1992, and Pérez's impeachment in 1993. In 1989, the first year of Pérez's second presidency, protests against the deterioration of living conditions got out of control and ended in the most generalized and violent riots in Venezuela's modern history. The protests, which came to be known as *El Caracazo* or *El Sacudón*, consisted of "barricades, road closures, the burning of vehicles, the stoning of shops, shooting, and widespread looting."[18] The revolt began in protest for an increase in the official public transportation fares following the government's doubling of gasoline prices, but ended in a general repudiation to the package of orthodox reforms announced by Carlos Andrés Pérez's administration.[19] The riots lasted several days and took a toll of roughly four hundred dead, a couple of thousand wounded, and thousands of businesses destroyed.[20]

Three years later, in 1992, two military coups against President Pérez failed. There was, however, broad popular support for the first coup—organized by Hugo Chávez and Francisco Arias Cárdenas—and as a result the ringleaders were catapulted to the forefront of political stardom.[21] Although the coups failed militarily, public support for the coup leaders was an indication that political parties were failing to represent society's interests.

Before his presidency ended, Pérez was charged for corruption—mismanagement of the secret funds of the state—and impeached. As Edgardo Lander puts it, "the figure of Pérez came to symbolize the turmoil, instability and threats of a coup generated by the deterioration of the living conditions of the population and the increasing loss of legitimacy of democratic institutions."[22] The impeachment, whose real causes were the generalized social discontent and degree of political instability,[23] was dubbed as the "coup of civil society."[24]

Echoing the public's discontent, the Venezuelan party system suffered a dramatic deterioration in the last quarter century before Chávez's election in 1998.[25] With the dramatic disappointment in the traditional parties' ability to solve the nation's problems, AD and COPEI stopped being the main channels through which to voice the people's concerns and articulate their demands. The erosion of the traditional parties' legitimacy and roots in society, an extreme focus on personalistic politics, high electoral volatility, and the lack of correspondence between politicians' campaigns and their government policies provide evidence of the deterioration that took place in the late 1980s and early 1990s.

PARTIES' LEGITIMACY AND ROOTS IN SOCIETY

Venezuelans' support for electoral politics and their identification with political parties—fundamental characteristics of an institutionalized party system[26]—have consistently declined since the beginning of the 1980s.[27] For example, as an indicator of disenchantment or indifference toward party politics,[28] voter turnout decreased steadily during this period, as Table 4.1 shows. Between 1968 and 1983, turnout ranged between 88 and 90 percent of registered voters. However, in 1988, turnout

TABLE 4.1

Voter Turnout in Venezuela's Presidential Elections, 1983–2000

Presidential Election	Abstention Rate (%)
1983	12.25
1988	18.08
1993	39.84
1998	36.55
2000	43.69

Source: Consejo Supremo Electoral, Venezuela

TABLE 4.2

Evolution of Party Loyalty (%) for Venezuela's Three Traditional Parties (AD, COPEI, and MAS), 1973–2000

	1973	1983	1993	1998	2000
Members and sympathizers of AD, COPEI, and MAS	45.9	35.3	27.8	14.0	10.8

Source: Molina, "The Presidential and Parliamentary Elections of the Bolivarian Revolution in Venezuela: Change and Continuity (1998–2000)."

dropped to 82 percent and by 1993 it had reached 60 percent. In the 2000 presidential election, only 54 percent of eligible voters cast their vote. Moreover, for the first time in the party system that emerged from the Punto Fijo Accord, in 1993 there were widespread allegations of electoral fraud. "Popular pressure forced new gubernatorial elections in several states, and the outcome reversed the officially announced results."[29] Claims of electoral fraud reflected a growing mistrust toward electoral authorities.

Parties' roots in society also eroded considerably during the period in question. In the last quarter of the 20th century, an increasingly large proportion of survey respondents were turned off by AD and COPEI—the two main parties that alternated in the presidency—and MAS—the only opposition party that would more or less consistently participate in elections without disappearing.[30] During this period, the proportion of members and sympathizers for these three parties dropped from almost 46 to 11 percent (see Table 4.2). Respondents' identification with these parties in 1973 was more than three times as high as that in 1998, the year Chávez was elected president.

In addition to the decline in party loyalties, confidence in these institutions dropped dramatically. According to survey data from the mid-1990s, political parties were the institutions in which respondents had the least confidence—below trade unions, the police, the business sector, the government, the armed forces, the media, universities, and the Catholic Church.[31] Support for democracy itself had dropped considerably, as evidenced by both the high popularity of the 1992 attempted coup and by the percentage of respondents preferring authoritarian solutions to solve the country's problems (see Table 4.3).

PERSONALISTIC POLITICS

In contrast to the party discipline that characterized the Venezuelan party system between 1958 and 1993, personalistic politics became a prominent feature during the 1990s.[32] One of the main contributors to the erosion of party discipline and

TABLE 4.3

Percentage of Venezuelans Approving of Democracy, 1977–1990

	Venezuela 1977	Venezuela 1983	Caracas 1987	Caracas 1988	Venezuela 1990
Very pleased	29.5	23.4	23.2	23.7	5.2
More or less pleased	55.5	51.4	62.9	58.8	66.2
Should be changed to another political system	15.1	25.2	13.9	17.5	28.6
Sample size	(2,260)	(1,789)	(400)	(400)	(2,500)
Total	100	100	100	100	100

Source: Aníbal Romero, "Rearranging the Deck Chairs on the Titanic: The Agony of Democracy in Venezuela."

the rise of personalistic politics was the 1989 reform allowing for the election of state governors and mayors for the first time.[33] These offices became a showcase through which politicians gained national attention and could circumvent party bureaucracies.

Personalistic politics took the form of *caudillos* starting their own parties, either because they did not get their party's nomination—as in the case of Caldera—or because they completely opposed the Punto Fijo regime—as in the case of Chávez. The new parties constituted electoral vehicles whose only purpose was to win the presidency for their founder. These parties' political life was organized around the caudillo's persona, without much programmatic coherence, organizational complexity, or rank and file.

One of the most visible signs of indiscipline was Rafael Caldera's resignation from COPEI. In an unprecedented act, Caldera, founding member of COPEI since 1946 and COPEI-backed president between 1969 and 1974, broke away from the party and created *Convergencia* six months before the December 1993 elections. Convergencia, which was formed as an ad hoc electoral vehicle with an explicitly antiparty platform,[34] won the presidential election along with a coalition of small parties obtaining 30.46 percent of the vote. This was the first time since 1958 that AD or COPEI did not control the presidency.

By breaking away from the traditional parties, Caldera broke the rules of the game and fractured the stability of the party system. He established a new situation where "the engine now driving pacts is not the array of political parties but the executive power of the presidency itself."[35] Convergencia did not develop a base of supporters or "party identifiers" and its ideological standing was unclear. It often found more coincidence with the rival AD than with the ideologically more proximate COPEI to implement its government program. Toward the end of Caldera's administration, the party was in such disarray that it did not even present a presidential candidate in the 1998 elections. Convergencia was so dependent on Caldera's persona that the party faded away due to the prohibition of another term as president.

PARTY CONTINUITY

Before Caldera's victory with Convergencia in 1993, COPEI and AD had nominated the two main candidates in all of the presidential elections between 1963 and 1988. This pattern of preeminence of two parties would not occur again: at least one of the main contending parties has been different every time since the 1993 election. In 1993 Convergencia's victory left AD and COPEI in second and third place with roughly a fourth of the vote each. However, Convergencia had virtually disappeared by the following election. In 1998 the two main parties—Chávez's MVR and Salas Römer's Proyecto Venezuela, which were founded that same year—left the traditional parties way behind: AD garnered only 9 percent of the vote and COPEI struggled to obtain 2.2 percent. In the 2000 elections Francisco Arias Cárdenas finished second backed by Causa Radical. By then, Proyecto Venezuela had dropped out of the scene. In 2006 the runner-up was Un Nuevo Tiempo, whose candidate, Manuel Rosales, founded the party in 2000 as a trampoline to reach the governorship of the state of Zulia. Instead, the winner of the 1998, 2000, and 2006 elections was the MVR, predominantly organized around the figure of Chávez. Based on Pedersen's index of electoral volatility, a measure of the net change in the vote of all parties from one election to another, Figure 4.1 shows the increase in volatility leading to the election of Hugo Chávez in 1998.

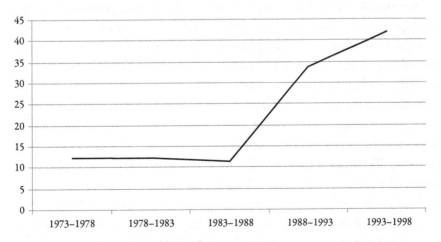

FIGURE 4.1 Vote Volatility in Venezuela's Party System, 1973–1998
Source: Author's calculations based on data for Venezuela's legislative elections from Consejo Supremo Electoral.

LACK OF CORRESPONDENCE BETWEEN CAMPAIGNS AND POLICIES

Another feature of the Venezuelan party system has been the disconnect between the candidates' campaigns and their government policies. The second Pérez administration (1989–1993) broke drastically with both the policies implemented during the first Pérez administration (1974–1979) and those expressed during his second presidential campaign. Although his campaign hinged on an anti-neoliberal platform in line with AD's Social Democrat tradition, the Pérez government opted instead for a "shock therapy" adjustment program. The sudden change of policy took the population by surprise and contributed to recurrent manifestations of violence throughout the second Pérez administration, including *El Caracazo* and the coup attempts.

In the following elections in 1993, Caldera also based his political campaign on an anti-neoliberal platform. He capitalized on the generalized unhappiness generated by Pérez's economic transformations. Although Caldera's economic policies were not as orthodox as those implemented by Pérez, the opening of the oil sector to private investment, the signing of an agreement with the IMF, and a series of privatizations of government assets, marked a continuation of market reforms in Venezuela. The discrepancy between these presidents' campaigns and their government programs became an important source of discontent among the population.[36]

A Fertile Ground for Antisystem Outsiders and the Politics of Antipolitics

A consequence of the Venezuelan party system's disarray was the parties' inability to perform two of its most important functions: mobilizing supporters to further political goals and mediating the demands of competing interests in society.[37] Instead, the legislature's role as a moderating force was diminished and street politics replaced the building of consensus.[38] With political disputes being solved on the streets, the stakes became higher and incentives for compromise decreased.

Throughout the second Caldera administration—well before Chávez's election— there were clear signs that political parties were struggling to perform these functions and that confrontation between the executive and the legislature was increasing. Throughout the 1990s the number of street protests increased steadily along with their level of violence, reflecting both people's discontent with the status quo and the parties' inability to accommodate society's demands.[39] Similarly, the rising confrontation between the president and Congress escalated to the point where even Caldera—a committed Democrat and one of the architects of the Punto Fijo Pact—"expressed a desire to amend the constitution to obtain the power to dissolve Congress."[40] There were even rumors about a possible *Calderazo*—a Fujimori-style presidential coup—and surveys suggested that 35 percent of Venezuelans supported a hypothetical Calderazo.[41] In the eyes of a large sector of the population, Congress had lost its value as the place to reach consensus.

This context provided a fertile ground for, first, the election of an antisystem candidate advocating drastic reforms; second, to the politics of confrontation among the different political actors; and third, to the president's deactivation of Congress to carry out significant statist transformations by decree. After promising to drastically modify the existing political and economic order,[42] Hugo Chávez won the 1998 presidential elections with his ad hoc electoral vehicle, Fifth Republic Movement (MVR). Once in office, the centrifugal dynamics of Venezuela's party system in disarray gave way to increasing confrontation between the MVR and the opposition as well as between the executive and the legislative branches. As a result, Chávez was able to circumvent opposition to his project by convening a Constitutional Assembly that replaced the existing Congress and drafted a new Constitution.[43] These measures enabled him to govern by decree through a series of Enabling Laws—extraordinary powers granted by the legislature—that resulted in drastic statist economic transformations.

THE RISE OF ANTISYSTEM CANDIDATES

The disarray of Venezuela's party system made the election of an insider candidate unlikely. Leading up to the 1998 presidential election, being associated with traditional parties had become extremely damaging for candidates and the incentives to present anti-establishment candidacies were systemic. In line with the emergence of new electoral vehicles that had characterized the 1993 elections, the three main contenders created their own parties shortly before the election.[44]

Former Miss Universe Irene Sáez was the clear front-runner in the first months of the campaign after creating a party named after herself—IRENE—and adopting a stand against the established order. As the traditional parties expressed support for her, however, and her beauty queen status wore off, her popularity plummeted.[45] As COPEI's president revealed in an interview, "the lesson at the time became clear among the candidates: stay away from reformist positions and adopt as radical a campaign as possible."[46] The second alternative was another electoral vehicle formed around yet another personality. Henrique Salas Römer, former governor of the state of Carabobo, founded Proyecto Venezuela months before the 1998 presidential elections.

The third option was Lieutenant Colonel Hugo Chávez, who had jumped to the political stage after attempting a coup to overthrow president Pérez and justified his actions in response to a tyrannical and illegitimate executive, a legislature that did not represent its constituents, and a corrupt judiciary.[47] As former COPEI Congressional leader Gustavo Tarre put it, "the coup was a military failure but quite a political success because many Venezuelans shared Chávez's frustration with the status quo and empathized with his cause."[48] Upon his apprehension, Chávez addressed the nation on TV to call his supporters to surrender. The address catapulted him to national prominence.[49] Following a pardon granted by Caldera and release from prison in 1994, Chávez began his political proselytism by touring the nation and capitalizing on the generalized mistrust toward traditional parties and their organizational disorder.

By the time Chávez founded the MVR—whose statutes explicitly rejected the notion of a political party, strictly speaking, and embraced that of a movement[50]— months before the election, he had solidly earned an antisystem, anti-establishment reputation. His campaign thrived on antisystem rhetoric and the politics of antipolitics, and his promise to radically transform the existing political and economic orders deeply resonated among the population. In particular, Chávez's campaign embodied Venezuelans' discontent with three key factors: the partyarchy system,[51] poor economic performance,[52] and widespread corruption.[53] By denouncing *Punto-fijismo*—the system that emerged from the 1958 Punto Fijo Pact—as too rigid and serving the interests of an entrenched oligarchy; eschewing the failed economic policies of the last two partyarchy administrations—Pérez's orthodox push in his *Gran Viraje* and Caldera's oscillating erratically between heterodoxy and his orthodox *Apertura* (Opening)—and condemning the squandering of oil wealth as a "moral catastrophe"[54]—Chávez's campaign became particularly appealing across social sectors.[55] In sum, the deterioration of the party system set the stage for an outsider to politics to reach the presidency and capitalize on the population's animosity toward the prevailing political and economic order. In the words of Javier Corrales, Chávez's "anti-party platform was unquestionably the preeminent rallying cry for almost every Venezuelan in the late 1990s."[56]

In this context, as the dominance of three new parties in the 1998 election suggests, the rise of an electoral vehicle without the need for consensus building and intraparty accommodation faced little opposition. Having become a prominent national figure and with the MVR in place, Chávez's election was not guaranteed,[57] but the conditions were ripe for Chávez to become president. At the end of the day, political parties had so little traction among the electorate that Venezuelans opted for supporting a candidate who attempted to breach the constitutional order through a violent coup rather than continue supporting the traditional "partyarchy" order. As a result of the convergence of these factors, Hugo Chávez would begin pushing for major statist transformations soon after taking office on February 2, 1999.

THE POLITICS OF CONFRONTATION, THE CONSTITUTIONAL
CONVENTION, AND CHÁVEZ'S ENABLING LAWS

In line with the trend of decreasing relevance of the legislature as a check to the executive that prevailed throughout the 1990s, Chávez's first years in office were characterized by increasing confrontation among parties and interbranch conflict. Shortly after his inauguration in February 1999 he clashed with the opposition-controlled Congress over a request for an Enabling Law—extraordinary decree powers—to renegotiate or incur additional debt and decree legislation related to Venezuela's oil industry. Upon Chávez's request for "power to dictate extraordinary measures regarding economic and financial issues required by the public interest,"[58] Congress refused to grant him the authority to renegotiate or incur additional debt and to decree legislation related to Venezuela's oil industry, which the president had originally requested.

Following the legislature's refusal, Chávez vowed to declare a state of emergency unless his requests were granted.[59] The opposition-led majority in Congress openly called the president authoritarian, while the president's MVR denounced the opposition as an entrenched oligarchy. The conflict escalated until, in a press conference aired during prime time, Chávez denounced Congress's shortsightedness and threatened to declare a state of emergency and dissolve the legislature.[60]

By appealing directly to *el pueblo* and taking the conflict to the streets, Chávez bullied the opposition into stepping aside—in spite of the opposition-dominated Congress he inherited—and into granting him the authority to conduct the first wave of significant policy changes. With a diminished ability to organize resistance,[61] legislative opposition gave in within a week.[62] In an interview granted after security forces had to protect him from street demonstrators as he arrived at the Senate, former President and then Senator Carlos Andrés Pérez warned that Congress was "self-dissolving" given that popular protests frequently impaired its ability to function.[63]

After sending a desperate letter to the Organization of American States,[64] the opposition conceded defeat a few days later and began drafting the Enabling Law granting extraordinary powers.[65] On April 21, 1999, among what the President of the Chamber of Deputies, Henrique Capriles Radonski,[66] described as "an atmosphere of commotion and disconcertment that prevailed in Congress,"[67] the legislature passed the first of several Enabling Laws. The 1999 Enabling Law would empower Chávez to conduct a series of statist policy changes by decree, regarding land reform, the ownership of hydrocarbons, and the tax structure, among others.[68]

In the ensuing months, the attacks between the president and the legislature escalated to the point where Chávez deactivated Congress. On April 23, 1999, a referendum was held to convene a Constituent Assembly, which superseded the National

Congress. Although the opposition took the resistance to the streets, it lacked the necessary traction among the population, resources, and organizational capacity to make a difference, as suggested by the 62.2 percent abstention rate.[69] In the aftermath, pro-Chávez candidates gained control over the Constitutional Assembly in charge of drafting the new Constitution, which resulted in a severe institutional transformation in Venezuela.[70]

The deterioration of the party politics transformed the Venezuelan political system from one where political parties were an effective mechanism to solve disagreements to one where they became secondary and dispensable in channeling society's demands. As a result, with people taking to the streets instead of relying on parties as mediating institutions, the legislature's ability to act as a moderating force was severely undermined. In the end, the political parties represented in Congress were so weak they could not even guarantee the legislature's own survival.

Marking the beginning of Venezuela's "Fifth Republic," the new Constitution was approved in a referendum held on December 15, 1999. It transformed the bicameral Congress into a single-chamber National Assembly and granted the president the ability to dissolve the legislative body. The new text also increased the length of the presidential term from five to six years, and allowed one consecutive reelection.[71] Most importantly, it extended the powers granted by Enabling Laws from strictly financial to general.[72] By expanding the decree powers of the president, it provided Chávez the necessary leverage to conduct drastic economic reforms including nationalizations in the banking, cement, electric power, oil, and telecommunications industries; price and foreign exchange controls; and the expropriation of more than 1.5 million hectares.

On July 30, 2000, the first presidential and legislative elections of the Fifth Republic were held concurrently under the new Constitution. Chávez won the presidency comfortably with 59.7 percent of the total vote, followed by Causa R's candidate and Chávez's former comrade-in-arms Francisco Arias (37.5). In the parliamentary election, the MVR won with 44.4 percent of the vote to obtain 92 of the 165 total seats at stake in the National Assembly. AD finished in a distant second place with 16.1 percent and 33 seats. COPEI, one of the pillars of Venezuela's partyarchy, was reduced to six seats in the legislature. With friendly parties controlling 60 percent of the seats in the National Assembly,[73] Chávez emerged from these elections with a comfortable control of the legislative body.

Having changed the terms of Enabling Laws, and in the context of a Chavista legislature, the National Assembly granted Chávez a second Enabling Law in November 2000.[74] The new unicameral legislature approved a 12-month prerogative enabling the president to issue decrees along six main spheres: financial, economic and social, infrastructure and transportation, public safety, science and technology, and the organization of the state. These reforms considerably expanded the degree of state intervention in the economy. Among the 49 decrees that resulted from this prerogative were changes regarding land reform, hydrocarbons law, and income taxes to oil companies.[75]

Chávez's first reforms increasing state intervention in the economy contributed toward a series of protests and confrontations outside the realm of institutional politics, which in turn resulted in the radicalization of economic policies. With political parties unable to represent their interests or shape economic policy, and in the context of deteriorating economic conditions, several sectors of society took their demands to the streets.[76] The Venezuelan Federation of Chambers and Associations of Commerce and Production (*Federación Venezolana de Cámaras y Asociaciones de Comercio y Producción*—FEDECAMARAS), with the support of the Venezuelan Workers Confederation (*Confederación de Trabajadores de Venezuela*—CTV), called for a one-day general strike on December 10, 2001, to pressure the Chávez administration. Another work stoppage organized by the same actors on April 9, 2002, set in motion a series of violent clashes that led to the April 11, 2002 coup. The general strike/lockout of 2002–2003 paralyzed the oil industry and contributed to a drastic economic contraction of -8.9 and -7.8 percent in 2002 and 2003, respectively.[77] A recall referendum called for by opposition sectors in April 2004 also threatened to interrupt Chavez's project.

Against this backdrop of intense confrontation between Chavistas and anti-Chavistas that extremely raised the stakes—to the point of Chávez's brief ouster during the April 2002 coup—the politics of antipolitics emboldened Chávez to accelerate the pace and increase the magnitude of statist reforms. As Chavez's Vice President Adina Bastidas put it, "these serious challenges to the survival of Hugo Chávez's government became a wake up call for us and served as a catalyst for the president's economic program."[78] In the words of Ambassador Bernardo Álvarez, "those very powerful interests attacking the government accelerated the pace of President Chávez's Bolivarian Revolution; their attacks forced the president to compress his government's time horizon for reforms into months rather than years."[79] This translated into more ambitious and frequent statist policies. Although the steady increase in oil prices after 2003 undoubtedly gave the Chávez administration considerable room for maneuver, these events crystallized Chávez's economic program toward further state intervention. The creation of thousands of worker cooperatives, the expropriation of companies occupied by workers, the implementation of price controls, the further expropriation of land, and the provision of health and educational services and subsidized groceries through Misiones ensued.

The opposition's strategic mistakes in the 2005 legislative election and Chávez's sound victory in the 2006 presidential election further contributed to the deepening of statist policies. The opposition's decision to boycott the 2005 congressional elections increased Chávez's control over the legislature. Five opposition parties, namely AD, COPEI, Proyecto Venezuela, Primero Justicia, and Un Nuevo Tiempo, decided not to participate in the elections to renew the National Assembly. They complained that the electronic voting mechanism, which included finger print scanners, did not guarantee the anonymity of the vote. Beyond the technical complaint, the boycott was meant to be a broader political statement. "Its political objective was to protest Chávez's dismantling of the legislature and to denounce his authoritarianism to the eyes of the world."[80] Only the MVR and its satellite parties, including Patria Para Todos, Por la Democracia Social, and Partido Comunista de Venezuela, participated in the election. The MVR won 116 of the 167 seats in the National Assembly, and the remaining 51 went to Chávez's satellite parties. This result gave the president the two-third majority required to change the Constitution without having to negotiate support with other political parties.

In December 2006 Chávez handily won the presidential election with 62.8 percent of the vote.[81] In his inauguration speech, he unveiled a plan to set in motion five strategic processes—the Five Engines of the Revolution—in order to take the country down the path toward 21st century socialism. The five engines corresponded to economic transformations, constitutional reform, socialist education, territorial reorganization of political units, and the formation of communal councils.

Responding to the first engine's call for "a direct way to socialism" through statist reforms by decree, a third Enabling Law was published in the official gazette on February 1, 2007. It included eleven spheres, and the scope of the decree powers went well beyond economic and financial issues to include the military and national defense, public safety, energy, and infrastructure. Regarding the economy, it enabled the president to implement measures toward "a new economic and social model that introduces the collective into the country's development to accomplish equality and the equitable distribution of wealth."[82] This time, extraordinary powers were granted for an unprecedented period of 18 months.

As a result of the 2007 Enabling Law, Chávez issued the Law of Nationalization of the Electric Sector (*Ley de Nacionalización del Sector Eléctrico*), which effectively nationalized the power company Electricidad de Caracas and all of its subsidiaries. He also issued decrees mandating the currency conversion at the end of 2007 from Venezuela's traditional bolivar to the "Bolivar Fuerte";[83] the nationalization of the Orinoco Belt (*Faja Petrolera del Orinoco*)—transferring at least 60 percent of ownership to the state[84]—and sanctions for speculators and violators of price controls.[85]

On December 17, 2010, the National Assembly granted Chávez a fourth Ley Habilitante. After legislative elections were held in September 2010 in which the main opposition parties returned to the National Assembly with 40 percent of total seats, the outgoing legislature approved the president's extraordinary powers for a period of 18 months.[86] This concession was controversial because it mortgaged the work of the incoming legislature, but the Supreme Court (*Tribunal Supremo de Justicia*) validated the constitutionality of the Ley Habilitante.[87] Although no decrees had been issued in the economic domain at the time of writing, the continuation of Chávez's statist reforms through this enabling law remains a distinct possibility.

In short, Chávez intimidated the National Congress into granting him extraordinary powers through an ambitious Enabling Law that sidelined the opposition and contributed to set the stage for his economic transformations. Appealing directly to the public, and with the opposition parties unable to present significant resistance, Chávez was able to refound the political system by deactivating Congress and convening a Constituent Assembly to draft the new Constitution. Following these profound institutional changes to the now Bolivarian Republic of Venezuela, Chávez encountered little resistance to conduct drastic economic transformations by decree.

Before discussing other factors, it is important to address a consideration regarding the timing of the deterioration of the party system. The concern is that the deterioration of the Venezuelan party system did not precede the rise of Hugo Chávez, but that these events occurred at the same time and reinforced each other.[88] Although the rise of Hugo Chávez to power contributed to the further deterioration of Venezuela's party system—indeed, institutions do not exist in a vacuum—the party system's decline preceded, and allowed for, Chávez's election. Scholars started documenting this steady deterioration process throughout the late 1980s and early 1990s. For example, Gómez Calcaño and López Maya were writing about the decline of the Venezuelan party system throughout the 1980s.[89] McCoy and Smith described the signs of the system's deterioration by 1989 as "inequivocal."[90] Coppedge wrote about Venezuela's party system's "pathological tendencies" of the 1980s and described the state of Venezuelan politics during the Caldera administration as "especially plagued by confrontation."[91] Domínguez declared the Venezuelan party system as having "collapsed in the early 1990s."[92]

As discussed in the previous section, there were several indications of severe deterioration during the second Pérez and Caldera administrations. General trends beginning in the 1980s—rising abstentionism, declining party identification, fuzzy programmatic positions, and decrease in people's support for democracy—as well as specific events—street protests and riots, attempted coups, impeachments, and party splits—were among the telltale signs. Even though it is difficult for one person to single-handedly deteriorate an entire party system to the extreme of the Venezuelan case, presidents Pérez and Caldera significantly contributed to this phenomenon before Chávez was in a position to do so. Pérez's—and the political establishment's—tolerance for naked corruption undermined parties' roots in society and people's trust in the political class. Moreover, by publicly expressing support for the coup, founding his own electoral vehicle to reach the presidency, and appealing to the public to close Congress, Caldera dealt significant blows to the party system. Weak parties led to confrontational dynamics between the executive and the legislative branches, which contributed to Caldera's administration's erratic economic policies—swinging back and forth between orthodoxy and heterodoxy. Thus, the deterioration of the party system and parties' ability to perform their basic functions had been an ongoing process for years before Chávez's electoral campaign.

Natural Resources and the Expansion of Chávez's Statist Program

Venezuela's resource dependence has indeed played a role in Chávez's disregard for market orthodoxy. The steady increase of oil prices between 2003 and 2008 undoubtedly helped augment his room for maneuver and improve the sustainability of his statist policies over time. Revenues from oil have done this in two ways. First, they created government liquidity that supported state intervention in a number of policy areas.[93] Oil windfalls provided resources to pay for nationalizations in the energy, minerals, telecommunications, banking, cement, steel, and tourism industries; helped create new state-owned companies in the aviation and telecommunications industries; supported a currency peg and foreign exchange controls; and contributed to establishing price controls and subsidies of basic food items, utilities, and medicines, to name a few examples.[94] Without the oil revenues resulting from the commodity boom, the scope of many of these policies would have been considerably more limited.

Second, oil revenues helped co-opt public support for the continuation of his economic policies toward "21st century socialism." They have done so by funding high levels of government spending on popular social programs. In 2004, for example, the state-owned oil company Petróleos de Venezuela (PDVSA) transferred the equivalent of 4.5 percent of the country's gross domestic product (GDP) to a special fund managed by the presidency for discretionary spending.[95] This fund financed 70 percent of the social spending exercised through Chávez's Misiones, constituting one of the largest social spending funds in Latin America. Although the opacity of Chávez's discretionary spending makes it hard to estimate the total amount and the destination of the funds, by mid-2007 the president's discretionary fund was believed to have more than US$15 billion—or close to 8 percent of Venezuela's GDP in 2007.[96] Discretionary spending ballooned along with Chávez's popularity, ability to remain in power, and capacity to undertake additional statist policies.

Notwithstanding the importance of oil revenue for the sustainability of Chávez's policies, however, a resource-based explanation often fails to account for the empirical record of Chávez's proclivity for state intervention—both as a candidate and as president—regardless of significant fluctuations in international oil prices. As a candidate—when the price of oil was severely depressed—Chávez openly advocated state intervention in the economy through campaign speeches, party manifestos, and government programs. In a document entitled "Alternative Bolivarian Agenda: A Patriotic Proposal to Exit the Labyrinth" ("Agenda Alternativa Bolivariana: Una propuesta patriótica para salir del laberinto"), which was crafted as a rejoinder to President Rafael Caldera's (1994–1999) orthodox stabilization measures,[97] Chávez mocked the policies as "the end of intelligence" and considered them "an extension of the fundamentalism and rampant capitalism imposed by Washington and Caracas elites."[98] The manifesto advocated an end to privatizations; the moratorium, renegotiation, or forgiveness of the foreign debt; foreign exchange controls; and the subordination of monetary policy under the president's control. Similarly, in his 1998 government platform Chávez blamed the country's economic problems on the process of globalization and proposed instead import substitution and inward-looking development.[99] As Teodoro Petkoff, Caldera's minister of planning at the time of the election, former Movement toward Socialism (MAS) presidential candidate, and former *guerrillero*, put it, "Chávez clearly campaigned as an outspoken critic of neoliberalism during his presidential bid in 1998."[100]

Chávez's election in 1998 came just as the price of oil reached its lowest point in history (US$16/barrel).[101] According to rentier state theory, Chávez's statist campaign at a time when oil prices were at historical lows—the "bust" part of the cycle—should have been extremely unpopular and his election unlikely. Instead, he conducted statist policies before, during, and after the spike in oil prices.

In the first few years of his presidency, with the price of oil averaging US$27/barrel—Chávez took important steps toward increasing the role of the state in the economy. In April 1999 he requested extraordinary powers from Congress to increase the state's control over the oil industry.[102] In that same year he oversaw the drafting of a new Constitution with an underlying statist tone, including a section explicitly outlining the role of state intervention in the economy.[103] In 2001 a Hydrocarbons Law was passed in which oil production and distribution were transferred to the state.[104] That same year a Land Law was passed, aimed at establishing limits on land ownership[105] and redistributing 1.5 million hectares—an area slightly larger than the state of Connecticut in the United States.[106] Similarly, the approval of the Social Security Law guaranteed state control of the pensions system.[107]

Initially, these measures were not systematic or comprehensive. During the first two years of the administration there was continuity in some economic policy areas in the early months[108]—Caldera's Finance Minister Maritza Izaguirre was ratified to appease international markets and fiscal stringency remained a priority.[109] As José Alejandro Rojas, Chávez's second finance minister, put it, "this was a consequence of both the relative inexperience within Chavismo to manage the economy and the president's undivided attention to the drafting and approval of the new Constitution and the strengthening of the executive office."[110] However, the statist measures implemented during a period of depressed oil prices were highly consequential and consistent with Chávez's campaign documents.

The series of statist measures continued into the period of oil-induced bonanza as the price of oil steadily climbed to US$126/barrel in June 2008, including the establishment of foreign exchange controls in 2003[111] and further nationalizations—extra heavy oil fields in 2004, the telephone company CANTV and electricity company Electricidad de Caracas in 2006, and the steel company Ternium Sidor as well as the cement company CEMEX in 2008.[112]

However, despite the precipitous decrease in oil prices following the global financial crisis, Chávez continued with his statist plans. In November of 2008, after the price of oil fell by 62 percent from its peak to US$49, he nationalized Santander's Banco de Venezuela,[113] and in January 2009—as the price of oil reached an intrayear low of US$33 and in the midst of a global recession, his government continued with the wave of nationalizations by taking over the mining complex Las Cristinas.[114] The government's expropriations continued throughout the year, including the nationalization of the coffee producers Fama de Américas and Café Madrid,[115] the sardine processing plant La Gaviota,[116] a rice mill owned by US company Cargill,[117] and the Hilton Hotel in Isla Margarita.[118] As Figure 4.2 shows, Chávez's statist policies in the face of the volatility of oil prices makes it difficult to attribute statist measures exclusively to oil-induced bonanza.

In other words, the increased revenue made possible by oil windfalls has given the Chávez administration ample room to maneuver. As former Vice President José Vicente Rangel put it, "President Chávez skillfully contributed to the increase in oil prices early in his presidency. He made a point to work with OPEC countries toward this end. And oil has certainly helped the government in its revolution, although the importance of oil for the Venezuelan economy has been grossly exaggerated by the opposition and the United States. The Bolivarian project has been much greater than oil."[119]

Although not directly responsible for Chávez's ability to carry out important statist policies during the first years of his presidency, the unprecedented price of oil pushed the boundary of the policy choices at hand farther out, allowing his government in subsequent years to maintain high levels of social spending while compensating for

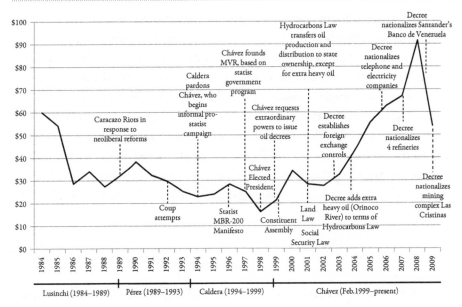

FIGURE 4.2 Annual Average Crude Prices and Selected Events in Venezuela, (1984–2009)
NB: Prices are in Constant 2009 US Dollars.
Source: Oil prices from the US Energy Information Administration.

capital flight and the lack of private investment.[120] As Teodoro Petkoff confided, "The extra revenue resulting from historically high oil prices allowed Chávez to first ease and then eliminate altogether the austerity measures articulated in the so-called Washington Consensus."[121]

Organized Labor

Although organized labor has historically shown a preference for statist policies,[122] it did not play a prominent role in Venezuela for two main reasons. First, in line with the declining strength of organized labor across Latin America, the power of labor groups in the Andean country suffered a sustained erosion during the last three decades. This was due in part to the deterioration of economic conditions, which affected salaried workers and the underemployed most significantly, and in part to the loss of prestige of the once powerful workers' umbrella organization—the Confederation of Venezuelan Workers (CTV)—because of its close association with AD and COPEI.[123] Due to the close ties that labor had with the traditional parties, the decline of AD and COPEI severely damaged the CTV's and labor's organizational capacity and resources.

Second, since the CTV was controlled by the traditional parties—particularly AD—organized labor became an important critic of the leftist president's project and even sided with the business sectors in opposing Chávez's economic transformations. In an unusual alliance between labor and business, the CTV promoted a series of strikes in 2001 among workers of the steel, oil, teachers, and public employees unions, and the Venezuelan Federation of Chambers of Commerce (FEDECAMARAS)—the main umbrella business organization—endorsed the general strike upon the CTV's request.[124] The strikes constituted a concerted attempt to repudiate the president's economic policies and bring down the Chávez government. Throughout his presidency, rather than governing with organized labor, Chávez has relied on the informal sector to create structures of political mobilization in support for his policies, including the Círculos Bolivarianos, Consejos Comunales, and Comités de Tierra Urbana y Rural.[125]

Executive Powers

At the time Chávez reached power, the Venezuelan executive was relatively weak compared to other Latin American countries.[126] This weakness contributed to Venezuelan presidents' inability to carry out market reforms during the 1990s, compared to countries like Argentina or Chile where powerful executives implemented neoliberal reforms in spite of popular opposition. When Chávez became president, the executive branch enjoyed the same powers as his predecessors who were unable to implement market reforms. Chávez was able to carry out significant transformations in spite of this initial weakness, including the approval of a new, explicitly statist Constitution. Thus, the existing rules of the game at the time he was elected cannot be held responsible for his ability to carry out drastic economic reforms.

This does not mean that Chávez has been a weak president—quite the contrary. As discussed in this chapter, the 1999 Constitution transformed executive-legislative relations to give the president the upper hand. In addition to extending the length of his term and allowing for reelection, he turned the legislature into a single-chamber body and gained the ability to dissolve it. These provisions gave the Venezuelan executive unprecedented formal powers, transforming one of the weakest executives in the region to one in line with the regional average.[127]

However, these transformations in executive-legislative relations were a consequence of his presidency. It is therefore difficult to attribute any causal role to them regarding the arrival of Chávez to the presidency. They cannot account for the predominance of antisystem candidates during the 1990s, for instance. Additionally, these transformations are not helpful in accounting for the events that allowed Chávez to strengthen the executive office in the first place. For example, they cannot explain Chávez's ability to replace the National Congress by convening a Constitutional Assembly that was widely contested by the opposition.[128]

Instead, Chávez's ability to significantly alter executive-legislative relations is a consequence of the country's party system disarray. In spite of having a majority in the legislature at the time Chávez was elected, the country's traditional parties failed to preserve the existing power balance. Unable to translate popular support into legislative strength, opposition forces became spectators of the president's redesigning of the rules of the game via a new Constitution. These events would have been considerably less likely in the presence of organized parties with solid ties to the population and organizational capacity.

Depth of Market Orthodoxy

With the lowest levels of neoliberal reforms in Latin America,[129] Venezuela's market reforms were too superficial to become an obstacle for Chávez's statist policies. In the words of Eleazar Díaz Rangel, director of the Venezuelan newspaper *Últimas Noticias*, "In contrast to the rest of the region, throughout the 1990s Venezuelans continued to be used to ISI-style policies."[130] Reform efforts attempted during the second presidencies of Pérez and Caldera were shallow, erratic, and brief. In the case of Pérez, the reform effort undertaken during his second presidency was ephemeral due to the severe public opposition and the interruption of his tenure after his impeachment on corruption charges.[131] Neoliberal reforms stalled during the caretaker government that finished Pérez's term and were carried out irregularly by Caldera, who experimented with a mix of orthodox and heterodox policies. Thus, political instability, the interruption of Pérez's term, and Caldera's economic "ad hocery" became important factors contributing to the superficiality of neoliberalism in Venezuela. As a result, Chávez faced little neoliberal inertia against his statist transformations.

Conclusion

The Venezuelan case shows the central role that the disarray of the party system played in allowing a candidate with an antisystem agenda of radical transformation to reach the presidency, encouraging the politics of street confrontation instead of legislative consensus, and weakening the legislature's ability to serve as a moderator of the president's policies. The precarious state of the party system generated conditions conducive to the electoral victory of an antisystem candidate such as Hugo Chávez and his sidelining of political parties in order to circumvent the legislature. Unable to prevent their own demise through the dissolution of the National Congress, the traditional political parties could do even less to influence the economic transformations following the 1999 Constitutional Convention. In a context of an institutionalized party system, Chávez's election and his ability to conduct drastic economic policies without the moderating force of political parties represented in the legislature would have been extremely unlikely.

The case study also suggests that Chávez's statist policies did not directly correspond to fluctuations in the price of oil as some scholars have suggested. Significant statist measures, including nationalizations, land reform, and tax increases took place before and after the spike in oil prices between 2003 and 2008. Additionally, an explanation based on oil cannot account for key factors behind Venezuela's statist reforms, from the rise of outsider candidates during the 1990s, to the transformation of executive-legislative relations during his presidency or the opposition's void in the National Assembly following their decision to boycott the 2005 legislative election. A product of the disarray of the party system, these factors made significant statist transformations possible without the moderating role that the legislature had played until the early 1990s.

However, although this chapter highlighted important shortcomings of oil-based explanations, it would be wrong to dismiss altogether the importance of oil for Chávez's economic transformations. Oil windfalls provided significant resources to support Chávez's popularity following the 1998 election through social assistance programs. Oil revenue also gave Chávez significant room for maneuver in order to overcome some of the constraints that the globalized financial system imposes—including capital flight and access to foreign debt—on governments seeking to depart from economic orthodoxy. In short, even though commodity windfalls did not cause Chávez's unchecked statism, they certainly expanded their scope and contributed to their sustainability over time.

Several factors contributed to the process of deinstitutionalization of Venezuela's party system, of which the gradual deterioration of Venezuela's economic conditions played a significant role. Unlike Argentina, Brazil, and Uruguay's sudden economic crisis, Venezuela's economic woes were slow moving and protracted. The economic troubles that began early in the 1980s after Pérez's first presidency eroded the people's trust in the competence of the political class. To make matters worse, unpunished corruption scandals along the way convinced Venezuelans that the traditional partyarchy was not only inept but also corrupt. The 1989 decentralization reforms—introducing the direct election of state governors and mayors for the first time—further contributed to the erosion of the parties' strength. Taken together, these factors became the silent malaise that would poison Venezuela's once exemplary party system.

5 PROGRESSIVELY INSTITUTIONALIZED PARTY SYSTEM

Brazil's Moderate Reforms

"*O BRASIL QUER mudar*," or "Brazil wants to change," were the first words in Lula da Silva's 2002 letter to the Brazilian people, in which he denounced President Cardoso's economic policies and expressed the need to change course. However, the letter reassured Brazilians that "the PT and its partners are fully aware that the change of the current model, emphatically called for by the people, will not take place with a magic wand, overnight. [...] What was undone or neglected in eight years cannot be accomplished in eight days. The new model cannot be a product of unilateral government decisions, nor can it be implemented by decree."[1]

The message had little in common with Lula's rhetoric during his first presidential bid in 1989. Long gone were the days in which the PT candidate claimed that "land reform is for the PT what oxygen is for mankind."[2] No longer did he advocate defaulting on Brazil's foreign debt or sustain that, "in order to carry out the redistribution of wealth the PT stands for, the people who benefited from the prevailing economic order necessarily have to lose."[3]

The letter highlights not only the significant moderation of Lula and the PT's agenda between 1989 and 2002, but also Lula's understanding of the need to govern by seeking consensus among broad sectors of society. By the time Lula launched his fourth bid for the presidency, the party system that emerged from military rule had become increasingly institutionalized, which gave political parties represented in Congress a prominent place in shaping the president's policies.

In this chapter, I argue that Brazil's gradual institutionalization of the party system over time played a central role in accounting for the leftist government's moderate economic policies. Undergoing progressive institutionalization since the return of civilian rule, the Brazilian party system lies between the Venezuelan and the Chilean extremes. More institutionalized than its Venezuelan counterpart, Brazil's party system is able to shape the executive's economic policies and is less prone to the emergence of outsider, antisystem presidents with little stake in preserving the status quo. On the other hand, less institutionalized than that of Chile—discussed in detail in Chapter 6—Brazil's party system does not generate legislatures with stable, predictable policy positions where broad consensus-seeking becomes the norm.

In the following pages, I first discuss the progressive institutionalization of Brazil's party system over time. I suggest that, contrary to early characterizations as a party system in disarray, the Brazilian case became increasingly institutionalized during the 1990s and 2000s, although some personalistic features remain. Second, I show how progressive institutionalization played a role in the moderation of Lula's economic policies. I show how the institutionalization of the PT contributed to the arrival of a candidate with a moderate agenda to the presidency. I also show how intra- and interparty negotiations moderated Lula's policies, underscoring the cases of pensions reform, fiscal reform, and central bank autonomy. Third, I discuss the role of alternative explanations, with an emphasis on two factors that played a secondary, albeit important role in accounting for the leftist government's economic policies in Brazil: the economic instability facing the country in the months leading to Lula's election in 2002 and the use of executive powers. Lastly, I present a conclusion in the fourth section.

Progressive Institutionalization of the Party System

As this section outlines, early studies characterized the Brazilian party system following the end of military rule as inchoate.[4] However, it underwent progressive institutionalization for a quarter of a century following the return of civilian rule.[5] In this process of increased institutionalization, the initial, highly unpredictable system—with very unstable congressional alliances, constant renewal of parties, and renegade legislators—became more predictable, allowing presidents to garner more stable working majorities. Although short of the predictability of the Chilean party system, the net effect of increased institutionalization has been a relative moderation of extreme positions in order to appeal to a variety of constituencies and the formation of ad hoc, issue-by-issue legislative majorities.[6]

The Brazilian party system was first described as one with short-lived political parties, extreme ideological positions, low party discipline, weak roots in society, and low ideological congruence.[7] In their influential classification of Latin American party systems, Mainwaring and Scully initially placed Brazil in the inchoate category.[8] They blamed Brazil's electoral rules—open list proportional representation, a variety of district magnitudes ranging from a minimum of eight to a maximum of 70, and low thresholds for congressional representation—for the party system's main ailments: extreme fragmentation, low discipline, pork-barrel politics and, consequently, difficult governance.

Whereas the post-Pinochet political parties could be traced back to the pre-coup period in Chile, Brazil's military dictatorship (1964–1985) was successful in disrupting traditional party affiliations. Following the artificial creation of two main parties—the pro-government National Renovating Alliance (*Aliança Renovadora Nacional*—ARENA) and the Brazilian Democratic Movement (*Movimento Democrático Brasileiro*—MDB)—the introduction of new electoral rules in 1981 fragmented the party system taking shape toward the end of the authoritarian regime and the beginning of civilian rule in 1985.[9]

In addition to the loss of programmatic continuity with respect to the pre-coup political parties, the new party system was especially prone to patronage politics.[10] In contrast to other Latin American military regimes, congressional activity was allowed during the dictatorship but legislators lacked any meaningful role. As a result, legislators had little incentive to try to affect policy. Instead, they developed clientelistic networks among local constituencies.

Moreover, in an attempt to compensate for the restrictions on political liberties during the military regime, a series of electoral reforms introduced after 1985 further contributed to the fragmentation of the party system and legislative indiscipline. Such reforms allowed the formation of legislative coalitions, permitted legislators to switch parties, and did away with the threshold to obtain representation in Congress.[11] These changes, along with the presidential runoff format introduced for the 1989 presidential election encouraged the proliferation of political parties. Consequently, it is common to find parties represented in Congress after receiving as little as 1 percent of the vote. Not surprisingly, the *Congreso Nacional* is highly fragmented to the point where the effective number of parties commonly reaches eight.[12] The combination of these features earned the Brazilian party system the labels of "pragmatic, personalistic, and non-ideological."[13]

The Brazilian party system experienced an important process of institutionalization during the 1990s and 2000s, however. The old conception of Brazil's party system has been replaced by stronger party labels, higher levels of discipline, more predictable policy positions, and a decreasing volatility than those observed during the first years of civilian rule. Although Brazil's party system has not overcome indiscipline and unpredictability, it has certainly ameliorated them.[14] In the next paragraphs, as with the cases of Venezuela in the previous chapter and Chile in the following one, the level of institutionalization of the party system is illustrated along four dimensions: party continuity, roots in society, congruence between campaigns and policy, and personalistic politics.

PARTY CONTINUITY

Brazil's political parties have become increasingly stable across time. Compared with the final years of military rule and the first years of civilian government during the 1980s—when the appearance and disappearance of parties prevailed—parties are increasingly resilient to changes in the political tide from one election to another. This resilience is reflected in Brazil's decreasing electoral volatility across time. As Figure 5.1 shows, Brazil's Pedersen's index of electoral volatility, which measures the net change in the vote of all parties from one election to another, dropped from 42.5 percent between 1982 and 1986 to 15.6 between 1998 and 2002, when Lula was elected. Following Lula's presidential election, volatility has stabilized around 13 percent. This steady decrease of volatility across almost three decades is an indication that political parties are becoming stable political referents in society.

Additional evidence of the increased continuity and decreased volatility is seen in the preeminence of two parties, the PSDB and the PT, in the last five presidential elections (1994, 1998, 2002, 2006, and 2010). Although in two of them incumbent

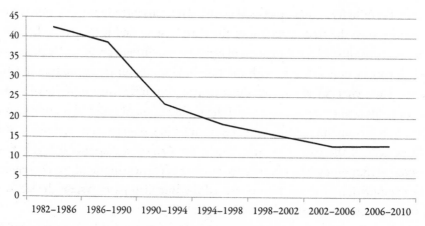

FIGURE 5.1 Vote Volatility in Brazil's Party System, 1982–2010
Source: Author's calculations based on electoral data from Brazil's Tribunal Supremo Eleitoral.

presidents have been reelected—Cardoso in 1998 and Lula in 2006—the dominance of these parties for almost two decades bodes well for party continuity in this country.[15]

PERSONALISTIC POLITICS

Brazil's party system has become less personalistic over time, although party switching is still common and some candidates maintain a "supra-party" image that allows them to supersede party politics. As party labels became more established, presidential candidates with a record of party politics became increasingly prominent players. Since 1994 the main presidential contenders have been candidates with a history of accommodation in party politics. For example, Fernando Henrique Cardoso's political career began with the MDB—which was succeeded by the PMDB at the end of the military regime—party with which he became a senator in 1982. Explicitly rejecting the personalistic style of the PMDB, Cardoso broke with the party and founded the Party of Brazilian Social Democracy (*Partido da Social Democracia Brasileira*—PSDB) in 1987.[16] Following his participation in President Itamar Franco's cabinet as finance minister, he became president in 1995 and was reelected in 1998.

Lula's trajectory also reflects a move toward institutionalization and away from personalistic politics. Although a very charismatic figure with a strong personal following, Lula was far from an outsider candidate. He was involved in party politics since he contributed to the foundation of the PT in 1980[17] and was the president of the party until 1994. He ran twice for elected office with the PT, unsuccessfully for governor in São Paulo in 1982 and successfully for Congress in 1986. He relinquished his right to run as an incumbent at the end of his term and ran for president with the PT in 1989, 1994, and 1998. After three national campaigns for the presidency, Lula was elected president in 2002 and reelected for a second term in 2006.

Cardoso's and Lula's main contenders have also been political insiders. José Serra had a long history in politics by the time he ran for president with the PSDB in 2002 and 2010. He was elected federal deputy in 1986 and 1990 and senator in 1994 for São Paulo state. In 2004 he won the mayoral race in the city of São Paulo and in 2007 became the governor of São Paulo state. One of the founders of the PSDB along with Cardoso, Serra served as his minister of planning and health. Likewise, Geraldo Alckmin, the PSDB candidate in 2006, has had a similar trajectory in politics. He was elected local deputy in São Paulo state in 1982 and federal deputy in 1986 and 1990. Also one of the founding members of the party, he was elected first vice governor in 1994 and then governor in 2002 of São Paulo state. Both Serra and Alckmin lost to PT candidates in presidential runoff elections, known in Brazil as *segundo turno*.

Although the main contenders in presidential elections since 1994 have been political insiders, some personalistic features remain in Brazil's increasingly institutionalized party system. For instance, politicians can switch parties without significant electoral consequences, as long as they are able to maintain high levels of personal popularity.[18] In the 1995–1998 legislature, for example, 26.5 percent of the chamber switched parties. In the 1999–2002 period, 30 percent changed labels, and in the 2003–2006 period, it was 31 percent.[19] Although some of these switches are due to disciplinary expulsions,[20] voluntary party switching takes place in most cases.

One of the most visible examples of personalistic politics is former president Collor de Mello's ability to successfully run for office on five occasions, each time with a different party label. He first became mayor of Maceió, the capital of Alagoas state, with ARENA in 1979. Next, he successfully ran for Congress in 1982 with the Democratic Social Party (*Partido Democrático Social*—PDS).[21] Afterward, he became the governor of Alagoas running with the Brazilian Democratic Movement Party (*Partido do Movimento Democrático Brasileiro*—PMDB) in 1986. He then won the presidency with the Party of National Renewal (*Partido da Reconstrução Nacional*—PRN) in 1989. In 2006 he was elected senator with the Brazilian Renewal Workers' Party (*Partido Renovador Trabalhista Brasileiro*—PRTB) and once in office he joined the Brazilian Labor Party (*Partido Trabalhista Brasileiro*—PTB) in 2007.

Another prominent example is Anthony Garotinho, who gained a disproportionate share of the vote in the 2002 presidential election (17.9 percent) compared to his party's base (5.3 percent). A former sports commentator and declared Marxist, Garotinho became a messianic evangelical preacher after surviving a car accident in 1994.[22] Even resorting to hunger strikes as part of his political strategies, he switched ideological positions several times. In 1998 he became the governor of Rio de Janeiro state with the PDT. However, in the 2002 race, he ran with the Brazilian Socialist Party (PSB) and finished third, only 5 percent of the vote behind runner-up José Serra (PSDB). In 2009 he switched to the PMDB, and in 2010 he was elected federal deputy with the Republic Party (*Partido da República*—PR), which was created in 2006 as a merger of the Liberal Party and the Party of the Reconstruction of the National Order (*Partido da Reedifição da Ordem Nacional*—PRONA). In spite of the frequent party switching, Garotinho was among the federal deputies receiving the most votes in 2010. He was second only to Tiririca the Clown (Francisco Everardo Oliveira Silva), another Partido da República candidate elected federal deputy in 2010.[23] The embodiment of personalistic politics, Tiririca's first political stint in São Paulo state was characterized by campaign slogans such as "Worse than it is, it can't be, so vote for me" and "If elected I promise to help all Brazilian families, especially mine."[24] In these cases, personal following proved to be more important than whichever party label a candidate was running with at the time. In short, the two dominant parties alternating in the presidency since 1994, the PT and the PSDB have fielded highly insider candidates for the presidency, but personalistic politicians still coexist in the Brazilian party system.

PARTIES' ROOTS IN SOCIETY

Following the return of civilian rule, Brazilian parties have progressively strength-ened their roots in society, as evidenced by higher levels of party identification and electoral turnout. Slight increases in party identification suggest that the extreme fluidity that characterized the party system in the first years of civilian government gave way to moderate levels of allegiance in society. During the Sarney administra-tion (1985–1990), roughly 30 percent of the population identified with a political party, whereas in the period between 1989 and 2002, the level of party identification oscillated between 41 and 53 percent.[25]

Some parties have been able to develop a label that society clearly recognizes and associates with a particular ideological position, although others still remain foreign to a sizable share of the population. Regarding party recognition, for example, parties such as the PT and the PMDB show high levels of recognition (80 and 59 percent, respectively). Other parties, such as the PSDB (40 percent), the (former) PFL (36 percent), and the PTB (21 percent) had moderate recognition. Several other parties had less than 21 percent.[26]

Moreover, as Table 5.1 shows, the abstention rate has gradually decreased over time. As parties develop stronger ties with the population and voters are able to recognize parties' ideological positions and candidates, turnout has also increased.

CORRESPONDENCE BETWEEN CAMPAIGNS AND POLICIES

The correspondence between political campaigns and government policies remains mixed in Brazil, where ideologically consistent parties coexist with opportunistic parties lacking a clear ideological position. Although undergoing slight shifts over time, several of the main parties have been generally consistent in ideological terms. On the right of center, Democratas (former PFL) has traditionally occupied

TABLE 5.1

Voter Turnout in Brazil's Presidential Elections, 1994–2010

Presidential Election	Abstention Rate (%)
1994	29.3
1998	21.5
2002	18.0
2006	16.8
2010	18.1

NB: Turnout results correspond to the first round of presidential elections.

Source: Tribunal Superior Eleitoral do Brasil.

conservative positions. The PSDB has maintained a centrist orientation with a social democratic slant. On the left, the PT has adopted positions to the left of the previous two parties.[27] Many of the smaller parties have also shown consistent ideological orientations. The Partido Comunista do Brasil (PC do B), Partido Socialista Brasileiro (PSB), Partido Popular Socialista (PPS), and Partido Democrático Trabalhista (PDT) have traditionally been associated with the left-of-center of the ideological spectrum, while the Partido Liberal (PL) and Partido da Reedificação da Ordem Nacional (PRONA)—which merged to form the Partido da República (PR) in 2006—and the Partido Progressista (PP), have adopted conservative positions.

In the second category is the PMDB, which tends to control a sizable proportion of Congress and lacks programmatic conviction. Siding sometimes with the government and sometimes with the opposition, it has no ideological identity and is prone to switch positions to gain political favors. For example, the PMDB has switched alliances repeatedly across administrations. After fielding its own candidate in 1989, it formed a coalition with the PSDB to support Cardoso's presidential bids in 1994 and 1998. In 2002, 2006, and 2010, however, it supported the PT's presidential candidates.

Even within administrations, it is unclear whether the PMDB will vote with its nominal coalition of parties. In 2003, for example, the PMDB voted with Lula to pass the social security reform, but then voted with the opposition against Lula's attempt to levy a tax on financial transactions to pay for social programs in 2007. By most accounts, the promise of patronage—known as *fisiologismo* in Brazil— not ideological congruence, is what drives the PMDB's policy positions. As PT Senator Tião Viana put it, "The PMDB is the essence of patronage. It has good cadres, but it lives off the exchange of favors. Programmatic conception and doctrinary vision are sacrificed to satisfy its legislators, who are only interested in reassuring reelection."[28] In the words of former President Fernando Henrique Cardoso, "the PMDB is a confederation of local interests whose ideological views span the political spectrum."[29]

Brazil's Party System and Economic Policy Moderation

The progressive institutionalization of the Brazilian party system has important consequences for the leftist government's moderate economic policies. Consequences can be divided into two groups: (1) those contributing to the type of candidate who reaches the presidency, and (2) those playing a role in the parties' ability to shape economic policy. The implications of each are discussed next.

1. ACCOMMODATION AND MODERATION IN THE PT'S
PROGRESSIVE INSTITUTIONALIZATION

The party system's progressive institutionalization has played a key role in the PT's policy moderation over time. Institutionalization in the form of routinization of party rules and procedures, continuous participation in electoral politics, participation in local governments, and increasingly stable legislative contingents greatly contributed to the moderation of the PT's program in general and its economic agenda in particular. As this section shows, progressive institutionalization contributed to the development of cadres with experience in accommodation and negotiation. It provided the PT with powerful incentives to appeal to broader sectors of the electorate by abandoning extremist positions based on antisystem and anticapitalist views and forging alliances with other parties. As a result, by the time Lula launched his fourth bid for the presidency in 2002, the PT occupied the broad center-left and its economic agenda was significantly more moderate than it had been in 1989.

During the early 1980s, the main groups in the party were characterized by adhering to a movement mentality and positions rejecting the state, capitalism, and its institutions.[30] The different groups that gave birth to the party in 1990—unions, ecclesial base communities, Marxist intellectuals, and former guerrillas—"formed a mosaic of social forces resembling a range of parties within the party."[31] Their radicalism verged on antisystemic behavior—and had "a clearly anti-capitalist program."[32] For instance, the PT, refused to support the electoral college election of Tancredo Neves to head the transition to democracy in 1985, and refused to approve the new Constitution of 1988.[33] It presented itself as for socialism and land reform and against social democracy, which it understood "as a bureaucratic socialism that does not serve workers but only a governing cast of technocrats." [34] It explicitly advocated the "socialization of the means of production."[35] For example, referring to the number of words in its slogan "Work, Land, and Liberty," one of the party's battle cries was "*um, dois, três, o resto é burguês!*" or "one, two, three, the rest is bourgeoisie!"[36] In the words of José Genoino, former guerrilla, congressman, and president of the PT, the party was "extremely radical during the early 1980s."[37]

A first moderating impetus took place in the party's 1987 Fifth National Encounter (*5º Encontro Nacional*), when rules were formulated to put an end to the multiple "parties within the party," each of which had its own headquarters, finances, press, leadership, and procedures. The new rules (*Regulamento das Tendencias*) formalized or institutionalized the different forces into factions or *tendencias*, forced them to abide by the resolutions of the party's decision making bodies, and restricted their ability to issue communications to the party membership only, as opposed to the general public.[38] The enforcement of these rules in the following years played an important role in the PT's transformation from a party-front to a political party proper.[39]

A slight change in the PT's views on the economy can also be appreciated by the 5° Encontro Nacional in that the party's resolution made for the first time an explicit commitment to the struggle for socialism within democratic institutions and underscored the willingness to form electoral alliances with likeminded, leftist parties, although defining itself strictly as a class-based party.[40] The main economic message remained radical, however. In an open letter to the Brazilian people announcing Lula's candidacy for the 1989 election, the PT emphasized the struggle for land reform and debt moratorium as central economic concerns, and called for the "preeminence of workers' interests over those of bankers, landowners, industrialists, and the military."[41] In the 5° Encontro Nacional's resolution, the party stated that "in order to extinguish capitalism and begin with the construction of a socialist society, it is necessary, in the first place, to carry out a radical political transformation; workers have to become a hegemonic and dominant class within the state, ending the political domination exerted by the burgeoisie."[42] The resolution also called for the statization of the banking and financial system and the public transportation systems.

Lula's electoral defeat in the 1989 presidential election against Collor also contributed to the party's slow but consistent moderation. The party maintained among its goals the "triumph of socialism over the bourgeoisie and its apparatus for ideological domination" and the "generation of political conditions and accumulation of forces for a socialist revolution,"[43] but it also began to define itself as a party "committed to the struggle for democracy."[44] By the 1991 First National Congress (*I Congresso Nacional do PT*),[45] although socialism remained the long-term goal of the party, the PT moderated its rhetoric by explicitly rejecting the dictatorship of the proletariat and the idea of abolishing the free market system by decree.[46] In addition to emboldening the party's membership, Lula's close second place also generated a real sense that participation through institutions provided a feasible avenue to transform Brazil.

The moderating push resulting from the institutionalization of the party's *tendencias* and Lula's 1989 defeat generated frictions with the most radical sectors of the party. In 1992 *Convergencia Socialista*, a radical Trotskyist group on the extreme left of the party, was expelled.[47] This exit responded to the party's gradual rejection of extremist positions on the left and further contributed to the strengthening of moderate sectors and the party's continuous movement toward the center.

Throughout the second half of the 1980s, *Articulação*, a faction occupying the party's ideological center, dominated the National Directorate or *Diretório Nacional*—the leadership body of the party. This faction had strong labor union representation and incorporated a wide array of sectors, although with a diminished presence of the Marxist end of the spectrum. During this period, Articulação's main challenge over positions in the National Directorate came from more leftist sectors of the party—which adopted different names depending on the Encontro (e.g., *O PT se Constrói na Luta* (1984); *Alternativa Operária e Popular* (1986); *O PT pela Base, Em Defesa da Democracia, Luta Socialista* (1987); *PT de Luta e de Massas, Alternativa Socialista e Revolucionária* (1990).[48]

Between 1990 and 1993, however, a further moderating factor began to take shape: the emergence of a relevant tendencia to the right of Articulação. The merger of the tendencias *Nova Esquerda* and *Vertente Socialista* softened their original Marxist principles and gave way to a common program under the tendencia *Projeto Para O Brasil* at the PT's First National Congress in 1991. This group presented a document by the same name, "Um Projeto para o Brasil," whose goal was to generate proposals to "break with the tradition of intolerance and authoritarianism that have character-ized the left; renew ideas, positions, and practices; and review conventional paths."[49] By the 1993 Encontro, this group had evolved into *Democracia Radical*, adopting social democratic positions. Led by José Genoíno, Eduardo Jorge, Marina Silva, and Tarso Genro among others, one of *Democracia Radical's* distinctive features was its advocating the party's electoral alliances with non-leftist parties.[50]

As the PT label became more established, electoral victories in the early 1990s gradu-ally generated additional incentives for moderation (see Table 5.2). Being in govern-ment—as opposed to criticizing the government from the opposition—gradually transformed the PT from a radical leftist party to a center-left party much closer to the median voter.[51] In the words of Glauco Arbix, former PT member, head of the Office of the President's Strategic Planning Unit, and head of IPEA between 2003 and 2005, "once the PT candidates began to reach office they realized they faced laws, budgets, human resources, an opposition, the press, and many other constraints. Reaching power at the local level made them understand the limits to demands based on ideolog-ical considerations as well as the need to govern beyond the narrow PT constituency."[52]

TABLE 5.2

PT Electoral Victories, 1982–2010

Election Year	1982	1986	1990	1994	1998	2002	2006	2010
Governors	0	0	0	2	3	3	4	5
Federal Deputies	8	16	35	49	58	91	83	88
% of Chamber	1.7	3.3	7.0	10.0	11.0	18.0	16.2	17.2
Election Year	1982	1985	1988	1992	1996	2000	2004	2008
Mayors	1	2	38	54	110	186	410	558
Mayors in Capital Cities	0	1	3	4	2	5	6	6

Source: Tribunal Superior Eleitoral do Brasil.

The PT's moderation resulting from electoral victories in prominent mayoralties—including São Paulo, Porto Alegre, and Vitória[53]—help to illustrate this point. For instance, the PT government in São Paulo between 1989 and 1992 has been described as one of the first experiences in government that fundamentally transformed the party, contributing toward "a shift from a contestatory position of the state's institutional-representative order to one of acceptance of institutionality and one to which it would adapt."[54] Identified with the leftist base of the party at the time of her election, São Paulo Mayor Luiza Erundina confronted those radical sectors upon their urging her to govern from the opposition. Instead, she urged them to "take into account public opinion, that of the PT supporters that made their election possible, and even that of those who oppose the PT administration."[55] Similarly, there were important tensions between the mayors of Diadema and Fortaleza[56]—two of the PT's first mayoral victories—and the party leadership due to the challenge involved in governing for an entire city and not just a narrow faction of the electorate. As the PT's President Olívio Dutra recognized at the time, "the PT needs to learn that, in heading municipal governments in a capitalist society, it cannot govern for itself without taking into account the interests of society as a whole."[57]

Additionally, the arrival of the PT to power at the local level contributed not only to a change of mentality but also to the financial strengthening of those pragmatic cadres within the PT with government experience. Since the moderate sectors of the party were those advocating participation in the electoral arena rather than mass mobilizations, resources available to the party from the party's elected officials tended to favor the moderate factions within the party.[58] Significantly, the electoral growth of the party in the executive and legislative branches at different levels of government led to the steady increase of participants in the PT's Encontros and Congressos nominated by senators, federal representatives, state representatives, mayors, and councilmembers, which further contributed to the consolidation of pragmatic, pro-system positions and the replacement of the party's antisystem and strictly ideological views. As shown in Figure 5.2, the share of delegates linked to the state in the party's Encontros and Congressos more than doubled between 1997 and 2001, from 33 to 74 percent of the total.[59] The increase in the proportion of delegates with some form of government experience, reaching three-fourths of total delegates in 2001, contributed to the moderation of the party's positions over time.

The effects of having to govern for broader sectors of society than those strictly represented by the PT combined with the availability of resources from elected offices to more moderate sectors contributed to the relative strength of the party's moderate tendencias throughout the rest of the 1990s. This resulted in two centers of gravity pulling the Articulação away from the center—the existing left-wing and

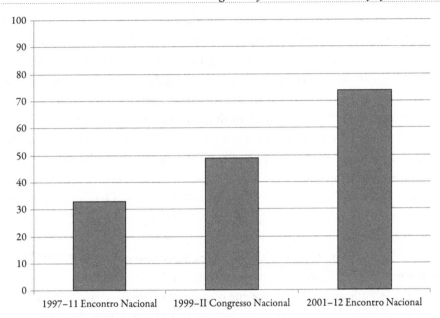

FIGURE 5.2 Share of PT Delegates Linked to the State, 1997–2001

Source: Pedro Ribeiro, *Um partido em mutação: A transformação do PT e seus reflexos sobre as campanhas presidenciais* (1989, 2002) (PhD diss., Universidad Federal de São Carlos, 2004), 127.

the emerging right-wing. As a result, the leftist sectors of the Articulação broke with the rightist groups within this tendencia in the 1993 8° Encontro. Denouncing *"eleitoralismo,"* or the willingness to form electoral alliances at the expense of socialist principles,[60] the leftist wing formed the group *Hora da Verdade*, which would become known as *Articulação de Esquerda*.[61]

The remaining group of the former Articulação became *Articulação Unidade na Luta*, which would occupy the center-right of the PT's spectrum. Led by some of the most visible PT politicians—including Lula da Silva, José Dirceu, Aloízio Mercadante, Vicente Paulo da Silva, Marco Aurélio Garcia, Eduardo Suplicy, and Benedita da Silva—Articulação Unidade na Luta consistently joined forces with Democracia Radical throughout the 1990s to form a social democratic majority controlling the leadership of the PT.[62]

In the 1994 9° Encontro, an anti-extreme left movement began to take shape under the leadership of Lula. In the face of the 1994 presidential election, the center-right sectors pushed to make the party's positions less radical and more appealing to broader sectors of voters. Rhetoric including phrases such as "anti-imperialist struggle" would be softened, and proposals such as defaulting on the country's foreign debt would be eliminated.[63] However, Articulação de Esquerda was able to gain control of the Diretório Nacional in the 9° Encontro— with Rui Falcão occupying the presidency in an interim fashion and managing

Lula's campaign—which would shape both the decision to assemble a coalition formed exclusively by traditional leftist parties and a more radical message in the 1994 campaign than was palatable to the growing center-right-wing of the PT.[64] Although mentions to socializing the means of production had disappeared, the PT's government program still promised to *"mudar radicalmente o Brasil"* or "radically change Brazil."[65] It presented wealth redistribution as a sine qua non for the country's development, underscored the importance of land reform as a fundamental step in this direction, and proposed a "de-privatized state" as the engine of the country's development. However, there was special recognition that keeping inflation down was one of the PT's top priorities, and land reform efforts were presented in the context of the legal framework granted by the 1988 Constitution and phased out over a 15-year period.

The defeat in the first round of the 1994 presidential election further contributed to the party's moderation. For the moderate tendencias Unidade na Luta and Democracia Radical, the defeat was due to the party's adherence to proposals that only appealed to a narrow sector in society, its lack of touch with the population's demands, and an underestimation of the benefits of the Plano Real.[66] In spite of strong opposition from Articulação de Esquerda and the rest of the left-wing of the party, the PT allowed alliances with centrist parties in the second round for the first time and devolved alliance decisions to state leaderships.[67]

Moreover, in 1994 the PT won gubernatorial races for the first time, in the Federal District and Espírito Santo, and expanded its legislative presence in the Congresso Nacional, from 35 to 49 seats in the lower house and from 1 to 4 in the Senate. These electoral victories put further pressure on the party to adopt an institutional perspective to accommodate the interests of broad sectors of the population over which the PT governed.

The gradual shift of the PT's center of gravity toward the moderate wing of the party also became manifest as other groups appeared in the ideological space between Articulação de Esquerda and Unidade na Luta, and the rightist tendencias garnered a growing majority in the Encontros between 1993 and 2001.[68] Groups such as *Socialismo e Liberdade* and *Nova Democracia* occupied the space between Articulação de Esquerda and Articulação Unidade na Luta and often sided with the latter.[69] As a result, their joining of forces came to be known as *Campo Majoritário*, or Majority Camp.

In 1995 the moderate sectors regained control of the party—under the presidency of José Dirceu—and continued isolating the leftist sectors. They prevented Articulação de Esquerda from occupying the position of secretary general, restructured the party's finances, and maintained control over the campaigns for the 1996 municipal elections. In the 11° Encontro in 1997, Nova Democracia broke away from Articulação de Esquerda and joined forces with Articulação Unidade na Luta and Democracia Radical, further strengthening the moderate sectors of the PT and isolating the extreme left of the party. During this period, the moderation resulting from being in government continued to play out: the PT doubled its mayoralties in 1996 from 54 to 110, and in 1998 it added a third governorship and expanded its congressional contingent from 49 to 58 seats.

As a result, by the PT's Second National Congress (*II Congresso Nacional*) in 1999, the moderate wing of the party controlled approximately 67 percent of total delegates and Lula's Articulação Unidade na Luta dominated the election with 43 percent of delegates alone.[70] Moreover, a change in the rules to elect the party's leadership at all levels took place. In spite of strong resistance from the leftist sectors, the Campo Majoritário introduced direct elections in order to appeal to the growing electoral strength of moderate PT members. Banking on the shift of the median PT voter from the left to the center-left toward the end of the decade, the Campo Majoritário successfully consolidated its control over the reins of the party.[71] Empowered by its control over the PT's government body, the moderate wing began a strong push for alliances beyond the left in an attempt to "loosen the party's restrictive alliance policy in order to have a chance of capturing an electoral majority."[72]

By the 12th National Encounter (*12° Encontro Nacional*) of December 2001, Lula's moderate group controlled 69 of 108 seats in the Diretório Nacional and was able to elect José Dirceu to the PT's presidency for a third time.[73] Consequently, the center-right-wing realized its quest to reach broad sectors of the population through alliances beyond the traditional left. The 12° Encontro's resolution announced Lula's campaign to the presidency with the objective of forming a "democratic and popular government."[74] In the document *Um outro Brasil é possível* (Another Brazil is Possible), the party formally declared its intention to establish a broad coalition across social sectors to win the 2002 election. In March 2002 the National Directory issued a document—*Resolução do Diretório Nacional sobre a Política de Alianças*—outlining its coalitions policy and its decision to "pursue a framework of alliances incorporating political forces in opposition to Fernando Henrique Cardoso, being this decision competence of the Diretório Nacional along with the final decisions on the government program, the selection of the vice presidential candidate, and coalitions. In this sense, the Diretório Nacional, informed of ongoing conversations, authorizes the maintenance of the dialogue with the PL and sectors of the PMDB who oppose the Cardoso government."[75]

By early 2002 the moderate wing's strategy of reaching out across the spectrum to form electoral alliances had clearly solidified. Several months before the election, the PT was actively reaching out to forge alliances with the PMDB and the PL. During the last days of May of that year, for example, the PT offered the vice presidency to PMDB senator Pedro Simon—who declined the offer—and maintained informal communications with other prominent PMDB leaders including former President Itamar Franco and former governor of São Paulo state Orestes Quércia.[76] On June 20th, José Alencar, tycoon and then-PL senator for Minas Gerais state, accepted the offer to join Lula's campaign as the vice presidential candidate.

The progressive moderation of the PT discussed above can be perceived by observing the party's ideological movement with respect to the other main parties in the system. While the party system was weakly institutionalized in the late 1980s, parties with extreme positions had a distinct chance of reaching power. New parties were emerging and existing ones were searching for their place in the political spectrum. With the fluid positions of the PMDB and PSDB—shifting positions between the center-left and the center-right—the PT had the incentive to differentiate itself as a party on the extreme left. In this context of extreme volatility and ideological positions constantly in flux, the PT maintained an "everything is possible outlook."[77]

However, as parties' ideological placement became more stable and volatility decreased, the chances of "maverick parties" reaching power also decreased, and the PT had incentives to occupy a broader spectrum on the center-left as the PSDB moved toward the center-right. Figure 5.3 shows the ideological movement of Brazil's main political parties over time and how the PT moved to occupy the ideological space that the PSDB used to occupy in the early 1990s. Based on legislators' ideological placement of the parties in Congress, Figure 5.3 highlights how the PSDB and PMDB crossed positions between 1993 and 1997, with the PSDB moving to the right of the PMDB during the time that the PSDB headed the national government during Cardoso's presidency. The results also suggest that the PT's sharpest movement rightward took place between 2001 and 2005, during the same time that it became the governing party at the federal level.

Not surprisingly, a 1987 survey asking all 17 PT legislators which economic system they preferred revealed that 10 of them supported radical socialism and six favored moderate socialism, but not a single petista supported social democracy or a market economy.[78] In contrast, the same question asked in 2005 revealed that 14 percent of petistas supported a market economy, with the least possible participation by the state, 33 percent favored social democracy, 52 percent preferred moderate socialism, and no legislator expressed sympathy for radical socialism.[79]

In short, the PT that reached power in 2002 was very different from the party of Lula's first presidential bid in 1989. Moderation of the PT's economic views over time, as this section has shown, was largely the result of the formalization of internal rules; the routinization of democratic procedures; the gradual occupying positions

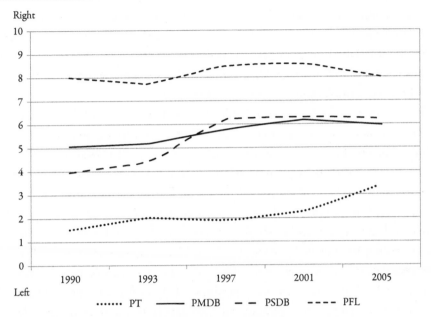

FIGURE 5.3 Ideological Placement of Parties by Congressional Elites, 1990–2005

NB: Respondents were asked to locate all parties on a scale where 1 equals Left and 10 equals Right. PFL became Democratas. The respondents' placement of their own parties were disregarded in the calculation of these means in order to neutralize the tendency of Brazilian politicians to situate their party to the left of where everyone else locates it. On the need to eliminate self-placement scores see Scott Mainwaring, Rachel Meneguello, and Timothy Power, "Conservative Parties, Democracy, and Economic Reform in Contemporary Brazil," in *Conservative Parties, the Right, and Democracy in Latin America*, ed. Kevin Middlebrook (Baltimore: Johns Hopkins University Press, 2000).

Source: Timothy Power, "Centering Democracy? Ideological Cleavages and the Convergence of Brazil's Political Class," in *Democratic Brazil Revisited*, ed., Peter Kingstone and Timothy Power (Pittsburgh, PA: University of Pittsburgh Press, 2008), Table 5.3.

in government—first at the local, then state, then national level—leading to the formation of cadres with experience in the process of accommodation with broader sectors of society; and the formation of legislative alliances forcing politicians to seek common ground among varying positions. Having discussed the features of intraparty competition that led to the moderation of the PT and Lula's platform over time, the following section explains how the patterns of interparty competition effectively shaped the Lula government's economic reforms.

2. PARTIES' ABILITY TO SHAPE ECONOMIC POLICY AND LULA'S PIECEMEAL REFORMS

The mix of institutional and personalistic features of the party system has a moderating effect on economic policy transformations. The low levels of identification and the fragmentation of the party system result in the president's need to form legislative majorities with several other parties in addition to his or her own. For example, despite winning the presidency in 2002, 2006, and in 2010, the PT was able to garner only between 15 and 18 percent of the vote for Congress. Cardoso's PSDB faced a similar situation in 1994 (14 percent) and 1998 (17.5 percent). Thus, it is virtually impossible for presidents to get legislation passed in Congress without reaching out to other parties and forming government alliances.

In contrast to the Chilean experience (discussed in Chapter 6), however, these alliances are not consistent across time and do not necessarily respond to ideological affinity. Sometimes cutting across the political spectrum, alliances are often formed on an issue-by-issue basis and on postelectoral convenience.[80] For instance, in addition to the PC do B, the PSB, and other natural allies on the left, Lula's PT government enjoyed the congressional support of the conservative Liberal Party (PL),[81] the vice president's party.[82] Conversely, the more like-minded PSDB is the PT's political adversary in spite of being ideologically closer. Moreover, the formation of alliances also responds to the distribution of cabinet positions and material benefits. For example, the PMDB—one of the main parties since the end of the military regime—has chosen not to present a presidential candidate in recent elections in order to have the freedom to form coalitions at the local level and to support any resulting government depending on the issue at hand.

Notwithstanding the party system's progressive institutionalization, however, the formation of alliances in this fashion generates a degree of uncertainty since the government is unsure whether it can count on congressional allies' support for difficult votes. Consequently, as former President Fernando Henrique Cardoso observed, "presidents have trouble predicting the policy positions of the different parties represented in Congress. A party that voted with the president on the last initiative may fiercely oppose the next one. Moreover, even if the party leadership supports the president on a given initiative, a sizable proportion of the congressional delegation may challenge the party line and vote differently."[83]

In contrast to the Venezuelan case (discussed in Chapter 4)—where the party system is fragmented but in disarray—the comparatively institutionalized party system in Brazil makes fragmentation more important in policy making: policy compromises result because they must be compatible with the preferences of all the parties in the legislative alliance, since parties are relevant actors to articulate society's preferences. The formation of legislative alliances in this fashion—a combination of loosely associated parties, some sharing ideological affinity with the government and others unabashedly selling their legislative support—results in moderate, diluted policies. The reason is that, in order to get legislation approved, executives need to appeal to the lowest common denominator among the allied parties—with different positions in the ideological spectrum—and ensure that the appropriate price is paid in the form of spoils to opportunistic parties. Otherwise, the government may find itself without enough congressional support to pass legislation.[84]

The legislative fate of several issues during the Lula administration—pensions reform, central bank autonomy, comprehensive tax reform, and the tax on financial transactions to pay for social assistance, to name a few—illustrates how the Brazilian party system contributed to moderate economic reforms and sometimes gridlock. They show how Lula's attempts to conduct economic policy changes have been considerably diluted or even blocked when common ground is not found. Three examples show this dynamic. First, Lula's reform of the pensions system is an example of an initiative that was significantly toned down from its original conception before it was passed. Second, the attempt to grant autonomy to the central bank is a case in which the initiative failed to reach a minimum consensus in spite of substantial watering down. Finally, comprehensive tax reform illustrates the government's failure to secure the vote of the PMDB in exchange for political prerogatives. These issues are discussed next.

PENSIONS REFORM, CENTRAL BANK AUTONOMY, AND THE FINANCIAL TAX

Shortly after his inauguration in 2003, Lula submitted a pensions reform bill to Congress. The initial government proposal included a series of changes aimed at improving the financial health of the pensions system for public sector employees. Among the main changes envisioned were a new calculation for pensions based on the person's average historical salary; the end of pension increases based on wage increases; the equalization of civil servant pensions with those of the private sector; and an eight-year increase in the retirement age. Although the changes were unpopular, they were deemed by the government to be extremely necessary. Lula decided to make this issue the first relevant change of his presidency and take advantage of the political capital resulting from his honeymoon period with voters.[85]

On paper, the president had the three-fifths majority needed in both houses to make the necessary constitutional changes. In practice, however, a consensus appealing to the lowest common denominator had to be reached and political loyalties secured. The support of the PMDB was obtained in exchange for the post of government leader in Congress. But, as with any vote in the Brazilian congress, negotiated support at the top did not guarantee the three-fifths majority since it was uncertain how many pledged legislators would indeed vote along party lines.[86] The PMDB, for instance, had problems compelling all of its legislators to vote together because of the broad range of ideologies that form the party. In doing the math days before the vote was introduced in the Chamber of Deputies, Eunício Oliveira—the PMDB leader in the lower house—had trouble guaranteeing 20 votes out of his party's 68 legislators.[87] Due to the high stakes of the vote, even the PT had difficulty reining in all of its legislators.[88]

The government tried to negotiate a set of measures acceptable to all congressional allies—*a base* or "the base" as the government coalition is called in Brazil—shortly after Lula's inauguration in January 2003. By July 2003 the president was publicly willing to make important concessions to guarantee the support of pro-government parties.[89] Rather than giving retirees a pension based on the average of their historical salary, the government accepted giving them 100 percent of their last salary. Pensions would be increased in line with wage increases, in contrast to the government's proposal to dissociate the two. The government also removed the original cap proposed on civil servants' pensions to equalize them with private sector pension recipients. Two important points left untouched were the eight-year increase in the retirement age for full pension eligibility, and the payroll tax of 11 percent for retirees—the same as active civil servants. The PMDB, whose votes were crucial for the reform's approval, refused to endorse the bill until these concessions were made.[90]

The diluted version differed considerably from the original proposal envisioned by the Lula administration. As Brazil's Social Security Minister Ricardo Berzoini—in charge of shepherding the reforms through Congress—put it, the government had to make these concessions in order to maintain "congressional harmony."[91] The moderated version was passed on August 7, 2003, in the lower house and on December 19, 2003, in the Senate. In the words of PSDB Congressman Ronaldo Dimas, "the reform was extremely limited."[92] Given the difficulty to pass pension reform the way the government wanted, it decided to postpone the introduction of the tax reform.

The Lula administration's inability to renew a tax on financial transactions (*Contribuição Provisoria de Movimentação Financeira*, CPMF) through Congress in December 2007 constitutes another example of the government's dependence on fragmented, loose, and undisciplined alliances to pursue its agenda.[93] Considered one of Lula's biggest setbacks, the tax on financial transactions intended to raise 40 billion reais (US$22 billion) to pay for Bolsa Família, the government's social assistance program.[94] In 2007 87 percent of program's expenditures—about $3.75 billion of the program's $4.3 billion total budget—were funded through this tax. Thus, as Patrus Ananias, Brazil's minister of social development, put it when Congress rejected the renewal of the financial tax in December 2007, "the survival of Bolsa Família was jeopardized."[95]

In contrast to the experience with pensions reform, this time the government was unable to garner the PMDB's support. The PMDB refused to side with the government to renew taxes earmarked for a variety of social programs. Instead, the PMDB organized a strong campaign against Lula's initiative, likening it to a 21st century Robin Hood that, as Senator Gérson Camata characterized it, "stole from the rich to give to the poor."[96] The bill reached the floor in the hope that some legislators would unexpectedly support the initiative, but it fell short of reaching the required majority.[97] In the final vote, legislators from the government's allied parties—including the PMDB, PTB, and PR—sided with the opposition and the bill was defeated in the Senate.

Lastly, Lula's attempt to modify the law governing the central bank ran a similar course, but no minimum agreement was reached in the end. In this case, Lula's original intent was to grant the central bank full autonomy from the government to control monetary policy and introduce fixed terms for the board of directors.[98] After several months of negotiations, in a watered-down version designed to appeal to a working majority, the federal government would continue to establish inflation targets that the central bank board would have to meet through monetary policy.[99] In the face of lack of consensus among pro-government allies, the initiative was never approved. Lula's government, in particular Finance Minister Antônio Palocci, believed that Brazilians had come to value the importance of price stability. The government understood this reform in pragmatic terms, following the trend in the rest of the world. When the Senate began debating the issue in 2005, they were encouraged that autonomy would move forward, but in the end it became clear there was no consensus within the government's base, not even within the PT. Instead, the Lula administration was forced to freeze indefinitely efforts to push the reform through Congress.[100]

Other reforms, such as comprehensive tax reform attempting to unify different states' VAT rates into a federal one,[101] a bill seeking to reorganize the power industry,[102] and an initiative to carry out labor market reform followed a similar fate. Instead, Lula opted to pursue initiatives where garnering allied support was more likely.[103] A prominent example is Lula's Growth Acceleration Program (*Programa de Aceleração do Crescimento*—PAC), a series of measures aimed at promoting growth. With the improvement of the country's infrastructure as one of its main objectives, "Lula used the PAC as means to bolster consensus among allies and keep a pro-government coalition together."[104]

In brief, Lula's reforms have been subjected to the same pattern: diluting the president's initiatives in order to reach a minimum agreement, or oblivion in the legislative process if an agreement is not reached. The resulting moderation and gradualism of economic changes are direct consequences of the need to appeal to loose and diverse coalitions in a fragmented system where parties matter.

Alternative Explanations

The path to moderation has not been monocausal, of course. Other factors have had some moderating effect on Lula's economic policies. In the following paragraphs, I discuss the extent to which these factors—prevailing economic conditions, executive powers, depth of neoliberalism, organized labor, and natural resources—played a role in explaining Brazil's piecemeal economic policy transformations.

PREVAILING ECONOMIC CONDITIONS

Leading up to the 2002 presidential election, Brazil experienced a period of financial instability. Naturally, this instability cannot be held responsible for Lula and the PT's moderation during the 1990s, but it played a role in consolidating the leftist government's moderate economic project. As this section will discuss, the deterioration of market indicators and the depreciation of the real during Cardoso's last year in office was a far cry from major economic downturns in Mexico (1994), Argentina (2001–2002), or Uruguay (2001–2002),[105] but instability was significant enough to prompt Lula to emphasize a moderate economic agenda during the campaign and even give priority to policies aimed at restoring investors' confidence once in office.

Although President Cardoso succeeded in controlling Brazil's chronic hyperinflation and bringing macroeconomic stability to the country during his first term (1995–1998), signs of deterioration of macroeconomic conditions began to appear throughout his second term in office (1999–2002). During the last four years of his presidency, the economy grew at an annual average rate of 2.1 percent, a lower figure than the 2.6 percent observed during his first term. These growth rates placed Brazil on par with the Latin American average for the period but were considerably lower than those of the group of developing countries labeled as BRICs.[106] Furthermore, after bringing inflation down from more than 2,000 percent when he took office in 1994, to 3 and 4 percent in 1998 and 1999, the government missed its inflation targets by a couple of points in 2001 and 2002.[107] Unemployment increased from 6 percent when Cardoso took office in 1995, to 8 percent by the time he left in 2002,[108] and the real, Brazil's currency, depreciated from a one-to-one parity with the dollar in 1995 to 3.8 reais to one dollar toward the end of 2002.[109] Although Cardoso was successful in stabilizing the economy in his first term, the last four years of his presidency were characterized by such slow growth and slipping economic conditions that "even PSDB candidate Serra took pains to distance himself from Cardoso's low-growth, tight-money policies."[110]

Notwithstanding these difficulties, the Brazilian economy's performance toward the end of the Cardoso administration was highly regarded among the international financial community. In the words of Juan Martínez and Javier Santiso, "At the beginning of 2002, the country's sound economic track record was being praised by almost everybody from New York to London and from Washington to São Paulo."[111] In March of that year, not only was the decoupling between the Argentine and Brazilian economies celebrated among investors, but Brazil's Central Bank Governor Arminio Fraga was elected Man of the Year by *Latin Finance* and heralded as "The Man Who Saved Brazil" at the Inter-American Development Bank's Annual Meeting in Fortaleza, Brazil.[112]

The optimism about Brazil's economy eroded during the second half of 2002, however. When early polls in April of 2002 began to give the first indication that Lula was ahead in the public's electoral preferences, fear that a leftist government would be unwilling or unable to meet its debt commitments began to spread among the international financial community. This concern was fueled by Argentina's default in 2001, Brazil's low levels of foreign reserves, and the PT's previous presidential campaigns' proposals for the renegotiation of the country's US$260 billion in domestic and international debt—approximately 46 percent of GDP.[113] By June— five months before the election—a slew of brokerage firms downgraded Brazil from overweight to neutral.[114]

The source of the instability is a matter of debate,[115] but the implications were severe enough to prompt Lula to signal heavily throughout the campaign his willingness to maintain fiscal prudence in order to appease financial markets. The signaling took place in several ways. First, the invitation to PL's Senator and tycoon José Alencar to become Lula's vice presidential candidate sent a strong message that notable leaders of the business community did not fear Lula's economic policies. Second, Lula published the *Letter to the Brazilian People* on June 22, 2002. In the open letter, Lula made a case for his moderate economic agenda: "We will preserve the primary budget surplus as long as necessary to prevent a growing debt from destroying the trust in the government's ability to meet its commitments." He also reassured Brazilians that his government would be a careful steward of the economy: "Nobody needs to teach me the importance of controlling inflation. From my very first years as a union leader I was outraged by the process of erosion of workers' purchasing power."[116] Third, Lula, along with all presidential candidates, signed a commitment to honor an agreement with the IMF in which the Cardoso administration had secured a US$30 billion loan as long as the government maintained a primary budget surplus (i.e., pre-debt) of 3.75 percent.[117]

Evidence of the credibility of these efforts was the strong backing of Lula's campaign among prominent business sectors, mostly domestic industry. In contrast to Wall Street's reaction, Brazil's "Main Street" was more attuned to Lula and the PT's progressive moderation over time. In the 2002 campaign, the reaction of Brazilian business sectors—the real or industrial sector rather than the financial sector—to Lula's electoral prospects was considerably different from that in 1989 when the party's ability to govern was an unknown quantity. In 1989 Mario Amato, the head of the country's most powerful business organization—Federation of Industries of São Paulo State (*Federacão das Industrias do Estado de São Paulo—FIESP*)—publicly declared that Brazil's largest 800,000 businesses would leave the country following a Lula victory in that year's presidential elections. In contrast, Lula's 2002 campaign enjoyed the outspoken support of some of Brazil's most prominent businesspeople and tycoons, including Eugenio Staub—owner of the country's electronics giant, Gradiente—Sergio Haberfeld—head of packaging giant and plastics manufacturer, Dixie Toga—and Paulo Feldmann—director of the international accounting and consulting firm, Ernst & Young. For example, as early as June 2002, Staub would express support for Lula in a public communication to Alencar declaring that he "could not understand the absurd reservations toward Lula, which generate incomprehensible criticism of an alleged radicalism."[118] Similarly, in the words of Haberfeld leading up to the 2002 election, "Lula has grown up a lot. He became less of a revolutionary and more of a statesman. I wouldn't have supported him before."[119]

This rhetoric was backed by a surge in campaign donations where business groups played a crucial role.[120] In contrast to Lula's previous campaigns, where the PT's coffers trailed those of the winning candidate by far, in 2002 his campaign raised R$39.5 million, much more money than his main competitor's R$28.5 million.[121] Even though many business leaders probably donated to both the Lula and the Serra campaigns, their willingness to overwhelmingly back the PT candidate financially in 2002 signaled support toward—or at least much less concern about—Lula's economic policies. This support would likely not have taken place without a credible record of moderation preceding the 2002 campaign.[122]

Once Lula was in government, there is evidence that financial instability played a role as a catalyst for his economic policy moderation. One of the Lula administration's first tasks upon taking office was to stabilize deteriorating economic indicators and generate confidence among investors. "Otherwise, there would be no room to implement the president's economic agenda, or any agenda really," in the words of Bernard Appy, deputy minister of finance.[123] One of Lula's main policies to address instability was the decision to go beyond the IMF target of 3.75 percent primary budget surplus and set it at 4.25 percent. As Deputy Finance Minister Nelson Barbosa and BNDES Economist José Antônio Pereira have noted, "One of the main objectives of this measure was to signal to the markets the government's commitment to fiscal discipline and therefore assuage any concerns about government debt."[124]

However, other aspects of the economy required less intervention because instability was merely speculative.[125] For example, in spite of the severe currency depreciation during the second half of 2002, "the exchange rate was left alone because the real had risen to historically high levels in real terms, so it was clear that Brazilian assets were extremely cheap for foreign investors and that the nominal exchange rate would go down in 2003. The government was confident that the increase in exports would bring the economy back to growth, and this is what happened in the second half of 2003."[126] Once the economy recovered in 2004, "the government was able to focus on public investment in infrastructure and income transfers through conditional cash transfer programs and adjustments to the minimum wage."[127] Thus, as another one of Lula's vice ministers of finance put it, "deteriorating financial conditions contributed to solidify or crystallize Lula's long-forged economic pragmatism. But fiscal and social security reforms, for example, have been among the country's most pressing since Fernando Henrique [Cardoso]. And given limited progress in the Lula administration, they will continue to be pressing for the next administration."[128]

In short, Brazil's financial instability in 2002 contributed both to Lula's moderation of his economic program as a candidate and to his government's adoption of a tight fiscal policy in order to appease investors early in his administration. Although instability did not account for the gradual moderation of Lula and the PT over the course of the 1990s or for the process of interparty accommodation that diluted Lula's reforms in the legislature, it made the government go out of its way to appease the markets. As a result, the government's fiscal policy was tighter than it originally envisioned.

EXECUTIVE POWERS

Comparatively high by regional standards, the powers of Brazilian executives could be expected to be instrumental in pushing for significant transformations. They cannot, however, account for the rise to power of an insider president with a moderate agenda, nor can they account for the president's inability to carry out such transformations due to intra- and interparty accommodation. Nonetheless, they have played a supporting role in furthering some aspects of the president's agenda.

Brazilian presidents enjoy important prerogatives, including the exclusive authority to introduce bills in some policy areas and the capacity to implement reforms through provisional decrees, known as *Medidas Provisórias*.[129] Introduced in the 1988 Constitution, these prerogatives have assisted Brazilian presidents in passing legislation whenever they are unable to garner congressional support for a particular initiative.[130] Even though these decree powers have a temporary character—they expire in 60 days unless Congress votes on the measure—the executive's reissuing of the provisional decree is not unusual.[131]

However, there are important limitations associated with provisional decrees. They often end in constitutional review courts, tend to alienate Congress, and do not apply to all policy areas.[132] As one of Lula's vice ministers of finance noted, "Policy changes regarding fiscal reform, pensions reform, or central bank autonomy necessarily require congressional approval."[133] Or in the words of DEM's congressional leader Deputado José Carlos Aleluia, even though Lula's government has "often abused his prerogative to issue Medidas Provisórias in some cases, Lula's main economic transformations have not been a product of provisional decrees."[134]

Even if Lula's main economic reforms have not been a product of executive decrees, there are examples in which this measure helped the president to carry out his agenda. One of the most prominent cases is the president's decree granting ministerial status to the chairman of the Central Bank of Brazil (*Banco Central do Brasil*). In August 2004 Lula responded to the inability to build consensus among the president's congressional base on a bill granting formal autonomy by issuing an executive decree: *Medida Provisória 207, 2004*. The decree formally incorporated the head of the central bank as a member of the President's Council of Social and Economic Development and granted the same immunity from prosecution by all but the Supreme Court that legislators and cabinet members enjoy.[135] According to Finance Minister Guido Mantega, this measure, which allowed the chairman of the central bank to report directly to the president without the minister of finance as intermediary, was meant to give the central bank "an additional layer of autonomy."[136] Even though the PSDB and the PFL (now DEM) introduced unconstitutionality complaints—*Ações Diretas de Inconstitucionalidade 3289 e 3290,* respectively—before the country's Supreme Federal Tribunal (*Tribunal Federal Supremo*—TFS), the ruling favored the Lula administration.[137] This arrangement far from grants formal central bank autonomy—the central bank's budget is still subordinated to the ministry of finance and its chairman reports to the president—but it does offer an example of the president's use of executive powers to further his agenda.

Another prominent instance is Lula's expansion of Bolsa Família by lowering the previous age limit of 18 for teenagers ages 16 and 17 to be eligible to receive a direct allowance through the *Programa Nacional de Inclusão de Jovens*—Projovem. Given Congress's refusal to vote on this issue because the measure was perceived as an electoral strategy,[138] the president issued a provisional decree in December 2007 (*Medida Provisória 411, 2007*). Upon the expiration of the temporary measure, Congress voted on a modified version in April 2008.[139] Other examples include modifications to the structure of the federal bureaucracy (*Medida Provisória 103, 2003* and *Medida Provisória 437, 2008*), restrictions on land use in the Amazon (*Medida Provisória 458, 2009*); additional resources for Brazil's National Bank for Social and Economic Development (BNDES) (*Medida Provisória 431, 2008*); and changes to the minimum wage (*Medida Provisória 248, 2005*). These examples notwithstanding, the highly visible initiatives discussed in the previous section, including tax reform, central bank autonomy, and the expansion of social programs "were beyond the scope of the president's Medidas Provisórias."[140] In short, Lula certainly relied on executive decrees to advance his government agenda, but his administration's main economic transformations were not advanced through Medidas Provisórias.

DEPTH OF MARKET ORTHODOXY

Brazil is a late and somewhat shallow adopter of neoliberal reforms.[141] Compared to the early adoption in Chile during the 1970s or Bolivia during the mid-1980s, Brazil was among the last Latin American countries to pursue market reforms. Their adoption did not take place until the early 1990s. Once adopted, they were not implemented as deeply as in Argentina, Bolivia, or Chile, but they were not as shallow as those attempted in Ecuador and Venezuela.[142] Thus, as this section will argue, Lula's economic policies are not a product of a path dependence set in motion by deep reforms in place by the time the PT reached the presidency.

The adoption of neoliberal reforms in Brazil began during Collor de Mello's short presidency (1990–1992) and gained momentum during Cardoso's first term in office (1995–1998). In what became known as the Plan Collor,[143] Collor de Mello's reforms included the elimination of the majority of nontariff barriers and cutting average tariff levels by half.[144] He also began with the process of privatizations in Brazil, mostly in the steel, petrochemical, and fertilizer industries.[145] This effort was interrupted by Collor's impeachment in October 1992 due to a corruption scandal.

Brazil's adoption of market reform accelerated when Cardoso took office in 1995. He expanded privatizations to utilities, transportation, and infrastructure, and pushed through with financial liberalization.[146] He modified the Constitution to grant domestic and foreign firms the same legal status and allowed foreign capital to invest in previously reserved industries such as oil exploration and utilities. Other reforms, such as tax reform and the autonomy of the central bank, remained pending.

However, reforms during the Lula administration—or lack thereof—cannot be attributed to neoliberal inertia from the Cardoso administration. Instead, the Lula administration faced considerable resistance to pass major reforms, and many of his intended reforms—fiscal reform, central bank autonomy, and pensions reform, to name a few—were attempted by Cardoso and remained pending for President Dilma Rousseff's administration to resolve. There is no indication that Lula's economic moderation has been a product of the degree to which neoliberal reforms were implemented, or that neoliberal policies conducted in previous administrations have impaired the leftist government's ability to conduct statist or pro-market reforms.

Changes in the two policy areas where Lula's reforms have materialized—furthering of fiscal discipline and reorganization and expansion of social programs—have not been determined by policies set by the president's predecessors. On the contrary, Lula interrupted his predecessor's privatizing effort. Similarly, the government's targets for fiscal surplus are set every year, and Lula's tightening from the 3 percent observed during Cardoso's last year in office to the 4.5 percent adopted by the leftist government responded more to sending a signal of responsibility to investors than to path dependency or policy seriality.[147] Further, regarding Lula's reorganization of social programs, Bolsa Família was not impaired in any way by neoliberal policies or institutions established in previous administrations. Instead, Bolsa Família built upon existing programs put in place by Cardoso.[148] The only obstacles facing Bolsa Família were budgetary constraints determined by the legislature and the lack of infrastructure.[149] In short, Lula's piecemeal reforms were not constrained by the depth of predecessor's neoliberal reforms but by the different political forces represented in the legislature.

ORGANIZED LABOR

Although organized labor benefited from policies adopted by the Lula administration, it did not play a prominent role in shaping the government's economic reforms in a statist direction since statist policies were largely absent. Instead, some of Lula's main initiatives found important opposition among sectors of organized labor. Two prominent examples are the government's fiscal stringency and public pensions reform. In the first case, some sectors of organized labor viewed the government's decision to exceed the IMF's target primary surplus as responsible for maintaining interest rates unnecessarily high, hindering investment, and sacrificing the generation of employment.[150]

In the second, Lula's social security reform directly affected civil servants by eliminating a series of prerogatives for government bureaucrats. Expressing extreme discontent toward this effort, public sector unions characterized the reform as "anti-democratic, anti-republican, and promoting an upside-down redistribution of income to benefit business groups."[151] This disagreement led to a schism within Brazil's largest federation of workers' unions, the *Central Única dos Trabalhadores* (CUT), and the formation of a rival federation, the *Coordenação Nacional de Lutas* (CONLUTAS).[152] As stated by CONLUTAS's founding documents, its creation responded to the explicit objective of "opposing the continuation of Cardoso's and Lula's neoliberal policies" and "opposing further reforms to the social security system."[153] In subsequent years, other federations broke with the CUT, leading to the formation of rival federations or *centrais*, including the *Instrumento de Luta e Organização da Classe Trabalhadora (Intersindical)* in 2005 and the *Central dos Trabalhadores e Trabalhadoras do Brasil (CTB)* in 2007.[154] Even though the dissident sectors did not represent the majority of the unions forming the CUT, these divisions undermined organized labor's ability to shape Lula's main economic reforms.

Another source of discontent among sectors of organized labor was the secondary role assigned to representatives of labor in the president's cabinet.[155] The appointment of conservative cadres from the PT—and even from the opposition—to the main economic posts in Lula's first cabinet disappointed labor representatives from both the CUT and the PT. Lula appointed Antônio Palocci as his finance minister, one of the most orthodox leaders of the party and a former mayor of Ribeirão Preto in São Paulo state known for stringent expenditure cuts and privatizations.[156] Henrique Meirelles, a conservative banker and member of the PSDB who had been elected deputy in 2002, became the chairman of the central bank.[157] Luiz Fernando Furlan, the chairman of the board of Sadia, Brazil's largest producer of processed meat, was offered the Ministry of Development, Industry and Foreign Trade.

In contrast, leaders of the most leftist sectors of the party occupied less relevant positions in government. José Fritsch, one of the leaders of the Articulacão de Esquerda, occupied the Fisheries Ministry (*Secretaria Especial de Aquicultura e Pesca*) and former union leader Miguel Rossetto became the head of the Ministry of Agrarian Development. The exception was Jaques Wagner's appointment as minister of labor, which was a natural position for organized labor. As Deputy Minister of Finance Bernard Appy put it, "Although important in their own right, this distribution of cabinet positions did not grant organized labor the weight to influence the government's main economic policy decisions."[158]

This does not mean, however, that the Lula administration failed to benefit unionized workers. For example, real minimum wages rose significantly during Lula's presidency. Between 2003 and 2010, real minimum wages increased by 56 percent.[159] Additionally, Lula strived to strengthen unions. As promised during his campaign, he formed a consultation mechanism, the National Labor Forum (*Fórum Nacional do Trabalho*—FNT) among labor and business groups to generate consensus for a labor reform. Although the consensus that emerged was precarious and unions were divided over issues such as the right to strike, job guarantees for union officials, and the union tax, the government's objective was to strengthen organized labor.[160] In March 2005 the government sent to Congress its labor reform, with the strengthening of the *centrais* and the guarantee of a union presence in the workplace as pillars.[161] Despite the reform's failure to pass in Congress, the government's efforts suggest that the Lula administration sought to benefit organized labor.

Thus, rather than playing a prominent role in influencing Lula's economic policies, labor organizations faced divisions among their ranks and were unable to generate enough political support to pass a labor reform. Sectors disappointed in the government's policies regarding fiscal surpluses and public sector pension reform were unable to prevent their implementation and perceived such policies as Lula's betrayal to his roots as a union leader.[162]

THE ROLE OF RESOURCES

Although the importance of oil in Brazil has increased steadily during the 1990s and 2000s, Lula's economic reforms did not follow the statist orientation predicted by natural resource-based explanations. Rentier state theory argues that Lula's moderate economic policies are explained by the absence of significant rentier pressures in Brazil's diversified economy. It suggests that, since natural resources carry little weight as a share of Brazil's GDP, total exports, and government revenue,[163] presidents are not tempted by fluctuations in the price of commodities to pursue significant statist policies.

This argument is plausible from a static perspective. Indeed, the Lula administration increased the government's share in Petrobras from 57.5 to 64.25 percent of the company's common stock as part of a capitalization effort.[164] The capitalization of Petrobras responded to the government's interest in exploiting the country's pre-salt fields and the need to raise funds to maintain the company's investment-grade credit raiting.[165] The public share offering of more than 4 million shares raised R$120.2 billion reais (approximately US$69.9 billion) in state and private capital.[166] As part of the transaction, the government exchanged 5 billion barrels in pre-salt reserves— to be exploited in 2015—for its newly acquired stock.[167] Thus, the increase of the government's stake in Petrobras could be attributed to rentist pressures.

However, this view is unable to account for the PT's and Lula's progressive moderation over time. Instead, the PT's gradual moderation discussed above coincides with Brazil's growing oil production.[168] As Figure 5.4 illustrates, the country's oil production has experienced an increasing trend since 1980, with an inflection point in the first years of Cardoso's presidency. During the second half of the 1990s as well as the 2000s production increased at higher rates than in the 1980s and early 1990s. The capitalization of Petrobras through private investors following the 1997 Oil Law (*Lei do Petróleo*)[169] and the discovery of new oil fields[170] have contributed to the dramatic increase in production. In 1996, the year before the law was passed, the oil sector represented 2.8 percent of GDP. By 2004 this sector's participation in the economy had reached 8.1 percent.[171] In 2009 oil represented 10 percent of Brazil's GDP.[172]

During this period, Brazil has become an important oil player globally. The increase in production has turned Brazil into a net exporter of oil and the ninth producer in the world. In 2009 the country produced more barrels per day (2.57 billion) than Venezuela (2.47 billion) and exported more barrels (505,000) than Ecuador (325,000) and Colombia (348,000). In that same year, Brazil's proven reserves totaled 12.6 billion barrels, which surpassed those of Mexico (10.5 billion) and made Brazil the country with the second largest reserves in Latin America after Venezuela and the fiftinth largest in the world.[173]

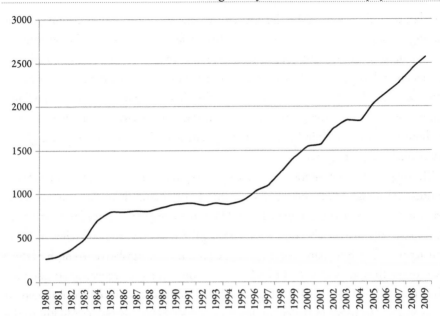

FIGURE 5.4 Evolution of Brazil's Oil Production (Thousands of Barrels/Day), 1980–2009
Source: Dados Estatísticos Mensais, Agência Nacional do Petróleo—ANP

In short, the growing importance of oil in Brazil since 1980 runs counter to the progressive moderation of the PT during this period. Rather than adopting increasingly statist positions as resource wealth became more salient and relevant for the country's economy, the PT moved from the left to the center-left of the political spectrum. The two opposite trajectories suggest that the explanation behind the PT's moderation over time must lie elsewhere.

Conclusion

The analysis of the case of Brazil shows the importance of the country's progressive institutionalization of the party system for the moderation of economic policy transformations. Before the party reached the presidency, the PT's routinization of rules and procedures, continuous participation in electoral politics, growing experience in government, and accommodation within the party and among political allies, played a significant role in the moderation of the party's government program and economic agenda. These dynamics contributed to the development of cadres with experience in accommodation and negotiation, and provided incentives to abandon extremist positions in order to appeal to broader sectors of the electorate.

Once the PT reached power, it had to bargain both with political allies and the opposition in order to pursue its government agenda. Instead of circumventing the legislature, Lula had to take the legislature seriously and find common ground among a working majority. In some cases, his initiatives were diluted but eventually materialized, as in the public sector's pensions reform. In others, Lula was unable to garner enough support in the legislature, sometimes among allied parties—as in the renewal of the CPMF—and other times within his own party—as in central bank autonomy. To be sure, the scope of Lula's economic reforms would have been greater without the moderating influence of the legislature in the country's increasingly institutionalized party system.

The degree of fragmentation in Brazil's party system must be taken in appropriate context. Although fragmented party systems do not naturally result in policy moderation, as the experiences of Ecuador and Venezuela suggest, the need to form broad multiparty alliances can become a moderating force when parties are relevant political actors. Since Brazilian executives cannot rely on the legislative strength of their own party, they are compelled to take into account the preferences of ad hoc pro-government alliances often cutting across the political spectrum. For fragmented party systems to result in policy moderation, party labels must be meaningful to the population and parties must show continuity across time so that strong roots in society and long time horizons provide incentives to seek consensus in the legislature.

In contrast to the Venezuelan case, where the sustained decline of economic conditions is identified as the main cause for party system deterioration, there are several reasons why Brazil's party system has achieved progressive institutionalization. Despite its institutional design—rules allowing for legislators' party switching and incumbents' right to appear on the ballot—several factors have contributed toward this outcome. Uninterrupted democracy since the return of civilian rule in 1985 has allowed parties to gradually stake out positions in the ideological spectrum and society to become more familiar with party labels. The economic stability achieved since the mid-1990s has provided the political class with a floor of legitimacy among the population. The leadership of the main parties—particularly Cardoso for the PSDB and Lula for the PT—has worked to improve their parties' organizational life.[174] Although accounting for the evolution of Brazil's party system is not the objective of this study, there are signs that the factors encouraging further institutionalization have steadily gained ground, trumping the country's electoral rules pushing in the opposite direction.

Other factors play a secondary role in explaining Brazil's moderate reaction. Financial instability leading up to the presidential election in 2002 contributed to crystallize Lula's economic moderation in the first years of his presidency. Executive powers were useful in carrying out the administration's agenda, as in the case of ministerial status to the central bank's chairman, but they did not assist the president in conducting the main reforms it intended, as was the case of fiscal reform, pensions reform, and the central bank's formal autonomy. Regarding the depth of neoliberal reforms, Lula's piecemeal transformations were not constrained by previous administrations' pro-market reforms; instead, Lula's reforms slowed down his predecessors' liberalizing impetus. Moreover, organized labor was divided and largely unsuccessful in pushing for significant statist reforms during Lula's presidency. From a resource wealth perspective, the increasing role that oil has played in Brazil's economy cannot account for Lula's and the PT's progressive moderation across time.

The analysis of the Brazilian case constitutes another piece of evidence to support the claim that as the level of institutionalization of the party system increases, so does parties' ability to shape and moderate governments' economic policies. In the following chapter, I discuss how Chile's highly institutionalized party system contributed to Lagos's general adherence to market orthodoxy.

6 HIGHLY INSTITUTIONALIZED PARTY SYSTEM
Chile's Pro-Market Continuity

"WE HAD TO be very realistic about the limits imposed by the institutional legacy of the dictatorship and the need to maintain cohesion among the different parties in government. Without a doubt, the pace of the Concertación's economic reforms has been slowed down by the need to find consensus among the country's political forces, both from the left and the right."[1] This is how Senator Carlos Ominami, former minister of the economy, chairman of the Senate Public Finance Committee, and vice president of the Socialist Party, characterized the role of the party system in shaping the Concertación's economic policies.

His words are a reminder that, even though Chile has become a poster child for successful economic orthodoxy in Latin America, the Concertación's economic policies were a product of accommodation and reconciliation of competing views across the political spectrum. In the Chilean system, competing views have been reconciled not just between the government and the opposition, but also among the "many souls" of the government coalition.[2] Although none of these souls advocated dramatic statist transformations—for reasons discussed in this chapter—the centripetal forces characteristic of Chile's institutionalized party system have functioned as a moderator for economic policy changes.

In this chapter I argue that Chile's highly institutionalized party system played a central role in explaining the pro-market orientation of the leftist government's economic policies. The party system's role hinges upon two main factors: the arrival of moderate candidates—those who climb through the ranks of party politics, build a reputation, and develop a stake in the system—to power, and the different parties' ability to shape the executive's economic policy through deliberation and accommodation in the legislature. Furthermore, Chile's solid economic performance and deep market-oriented reforms discouraged any drastic changes to the model inherited from the military dictatorship. As this chapter shows, other factors—executive strength, natural resources, and organized labor—do not play a significant role in explaining Chile's general adherence to pro-market policies.

The mechanism at work in the Chilean case can be summarized as follows. First, the highly institutionalized party system provided incentives for the arrival of moderate candidates to the presidency. Among the main factors contributing to this phenomenon are the complexity of the process of accommodation required to maintain stable electoral coalitions, the control that coalition and party leaders have over political nominations and resources, the strong ties between the parties and society, and the importance given to programmatic coherence and political trajectory. As a result, radical, antisystem candidates have been "weeded out" in the process of party politics. This would not be possible without the broad legitimacy conferred to political parties by the population. The trajectories of the Concertación's presidents and the opposition's presidential candidates show such leaders rose to the top after being tested in party politics, holding party leadership roles, and running for lesser offices. In contrast, candidates who have attempted to circumvent the party system have failed. Thus, Chilean presidents have been a consequence of a process of political accommodation, consensus reaching, and popular legitimacy.

Second, the highly institutionalized party system in Chile provided incentives for the political forces to reach agreements through deliberation and consensus-building, giving parties represented in Congress the opportunity to shape policy outcomes. Policy making in Chile has been the result of a system of incentives and disincentives for intraparty, interparty, and intercoalition negotiation that obviate the president's need to rely on executive powers. Rather than exercising their executive powers—among the strongest in Latin America[3]—Chilean presidents tend to navigate the congressional waters to form broad majorities in order to get legislation passed. The party system's stable coalitions and predictability of the parties' policy positions made the *Congreso Nacional* the heart of political negotiations par excellence, resulting in a process of policy making by consensus that minimizes room for extremism. Consequently, the left-of-center governments' general adherence to pro-market policies stemmed from an environment where presidential candidates are the result of a moderating trajectory within party politics on the one hand, and congressional bargaining is favored over street politics and compromise prevails over executive discretion, on the other.

In the following pages I first present evidence of the high level of institutionalization of the Chilean party system, and discuss how some of the legacies of the military dictatorship contributed toward the system's centripetal dynamics. Second, I present an account of how these factors played an important role in the Lagos government's adherence to economic orthodoxy. Third, I discuss alternative hypotheses, and conclude that, in addition to the party system's institutionalization, booming economic conditions and the depth of market reforms have played a fundamental role in encouraging the left's general adherence to market orthodoxy.

Chile's Highly Institutionalized Party System

Following the transition to democracy, Chile's party politics has been highly institutionalized.[4] With the return of competitive politics after 17 years of Pinochet's military rule, parties resumed their role as the backbone of the Chilean political system.[5] The opposition's victory in the October 1988 plebiscite rejecting Pinochet's attempt to remain in power until 1997 helped political parties reclaim the prominence interrupted by the military dictatorship. After regaining legal status in March 1987, parties were able to tap into the organizational capacity set up for the plebiscite campaign and connect with civil society organizations belonging to the different ideological subcultures that survived the interruption of democracy.[6] Thus, the three main ideological subdivisions—left, center, right—that prevailed before the military regime's proscription of political parties reemerged to claim the center stage of Chilean politics.

Four features have made the Chilean party system the most highly institutionalized in the region.[7] First, there has been a remarkable continuity among the main political parties. Although the parties' institutional life was interrupted during the Pinochet years (1973–1991), party loyalty and identification were able to remain largely unchanged during the proscription of some political organizations. Second, the party leadership has been characterized by politicians with a long trajectory of party accommodation and negotiation. There tends to be little room for personalistic politics and antisystem candidates. Third, there has been a strong connection between political parties and society. Although showing some signs of decline in recent years, parties maintain close ties with the population and party identities permeate everyday life. Lastly, there has been a clear correspondence between the candidates' platforms and the policies implemented once they reach government. Once elected, candidates do not turn their back on their campaign promises. Each of these four features is briefly explained next.

PARTY CONTINUITY

In spite of the Pinochet regime's efforts to alter the traditional cleavages represented in the party system, the main ideological divisions around the right, the center, and the left of the ideological spectrum remained largely unchanged from their pre-coup versions.[8] Although the party labels have slightly evolved throughout time, party platforms and cadres can be traced back to their pre-coup versions. Since the restoration of democracy in 1990, party continuity has been remarkable: parties rarely appear and disappear from one election to another and the main coalitions tend to be consistent across time.

Due to the roughly equal support for the left, center, and right, the Chilean party system is often referred to as a three-thirds system (*sistema de tres tercios*). In terms of the right, Chile's two main right-wing parties, National Renewal (*Renovación Nacional*—RN) and Independent Democratic Union (*Unión Democrática Independiente*—UDI), drew supporters from the pre-coup National Party (*Partido Nacional*—PN) and the *Gremialista* movement.[9] Representing the conservative vote before the breakdown of democracy, the PN was born in 1967 when Liberals and Conservatives merged to contain the Christian Democrats' increasing popularity. Supportive of the Pinochet regime, the PN embraced the "recess" on political parties mandated by the dictatorship and gradually dissolved as a formal organization.[10] Following the economic and political difficulties in the early 1980s, however, the right began to reassemble party cadres to prepare for a civilian government. In 1987, leading to the plebiscite, three conservative organizations, National Unity Movement (*Movimiento de Unidad Nacional*—MUN), National Labor Front (*Frente Nacional del Trabajo*—FNT), and UDI, joined forces to create National Renewal as the rightist political party that would carry on the National Party's project.[11] The UDI—formed mainly by Gremialistas from the Universidad Católica[12] and former officials of the military government that advocated Pinochet's remaining in power—broke away shortly thereafter. The two parties remained as the main rightist alternatives since the restoration of democracy. They have formed an electoral coalition presenting common congressional lists—and often a common presidential candidate—since democracy was restored.

The Christian Democrats (*Partido Demócrata Cristiano*—PDC), who displaced the Radical Party as the main centrist option during the 1960s, continued to hold the center of the electoral spectrum after the end of the dictatorship. The Catholic

Church's progressive social doctrines shaped the party's thought and—in parallel with the Vatican's shift toward a reformist position on social issues—the party underwent a gradual transformation from the right-of-center to a more progressive stance.[13] A year after its foundation in 1957, the PDC obtained 20 percent of the presidential vote in the 1958 presidential elections. Six years later, Eduardo Frei Montalva (1964–1970) became the first PDC president. Although part of the PDC supported the military coup, the party was heading the opposition to the regime by 1980.[14] PDC presidents Patricio Aylwin (1990–1994) and Eduardo Frei Ruiz-Tagle (1994–2000) headed the first and second democratically elected governments after Chile's transition to democracy. The PDC is one of the main parties comprising the Concertación.

The main parties on the left of the spectrum, the Party for Democracy (*Partido Por la Democracia*—PPD), the Socialist Party (*Partido Socialista*—PS), and the Communist Party (*Partido Comunista*—PC) can be traced back to the precoup socialists and communists.[15] The PC was founded in 1922 and traces its origins to the *Partido Obrero Socialista* created in 1912. Officially founded in 1933, the PS benefited from a multiclass appeal that included blue-collar workers, members of the middle class, and even intellectuals, until the military coup. Both parties participated in Allende's Popular Unity government (1970–1973) and remained proscribed throughout the military dictatorship. Notwithstanding the severe repression they suffered during the military dictatorship, their cadres were able to survive the authoritarian period, either in exile or clandestinely. Due to the ban that prevented these parties from participating in the 1988 referendum, the PPD was created in 1987 as an instrumental party in order to circumvent the ban. Through the PPD, many left-of-center sympathizers were able to participate in the electoral opposition to Pinochet's extended rule. The PS and the PPD joined the Christian Democrats and the Radicals in the Concertación coalition. Remaining outside the Concertación, the PC constitutes the extra-parliamentary left.[16] Although two main coalitions—the center-left Concertación and the right-wing Alianza—emerged after the end of authoritarian rule, each of the main parties forming the two coalitions maintained its membership, internal procedures, and identity.[17]

In the post-Pinochet period, these parties have also experienced remarkable continuity. Based on Pedersen's index of electoral volatility, Figure 6.1 shows how the net change in the vote of all parties from one legislative election to another has remained low, hovering between 8 and 12 percent.[18] In sharp contrast to the case of Venezuela, where parties win the presidency only to disappear by the next election, Chilean parties have become examples of stability.

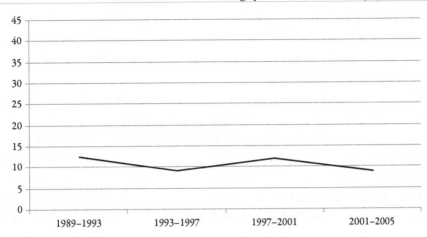

FIGURE 6.1 Vote Volatility in Chile's Party System, 1989–2005

Source: Tribunal Calificador de Elecciones de Chile.

PERSONALISTIC POLITICS

In contrast to the experiences in other countries, personalistic politics have not been successful in the Chilean party system since democracy was restored.[19] Situations in which a *caudillo* jumps to the national stage by starting a new party are rare, and support for antisystem or protest parties has been extremely low.[20] The fate of the Progressive Union of the Centrist Center (*Unión Centro Centro Progresista—* UCCP) party is a case in point. The party was created around the leadership of Francisco Javier Errázuriz, a businessman-cum-populist who participated in the 1989 elections. A supermarket tycoon, Errázuriz attempted to situate the UCCP as the true centrist alternative—hence the emphasis in the name. In spite of these efforts to become the main centrist party, most of the UCCP support came from the right.[21] The UCCP had no party organization and lacked a clear government program. Consequently, Errázuriz's electoral vehicle disappeared as he faced legal trouble and retired from politics.[22]

Instead, party leaders are selected among cadres with a long trajectory within the party.[23] In the case of the left, leaders of the PPD, Socialist, and Communist parties—such as Ricardo Lagos and Gladys Marín—were drawn from the pre-coup Socialist and Communist parties. In the case of the right, leaders of the UDI, such as Hernan Buchi—UDI's 1989 presidential candidate—and Joaquín Lavín—UDI's candidate in 1999 and 2005—can be traced back to Pinochet's economic team of technocrats, the Chicago Boys. Arturo Alessandri Besa—UDI and RN's 1993 presidential candidate[24]—was a member of Congress with Partido Nacional at the time of the coup. RN's 2005 presidential candidate, Sebastián Piñera, served as senator and the president of the party. Similarly, there is cadre continuity among the Christian Democrats, whose presidents Aylwin and Frei were prominent members of the party long before the military coup.

A recent example of the importance of party trajectory for candidate selection is the Concertación's nomination of former president Eduardo Frei as its candidate for Chile's 2009 presidential election. When his candidacy was challenged after the primaries by Marco Enríquez-Ominami—a former filmmaker and first time representative *(diputado)* from the Socialist Party—the Concertacion's leadership closed ranks to support Frei's nomination.[25] Marco Enríquez-Ominami resigned from the party and ran instead as an independent, which severely jeopardized his chances of reaching the presidency. Frei's nomination shows the weight of an established trajectory within party politics, the leadership's esprit de corps to protect the established candidate selection mechanism, and tight grip over the candidate selection process.[26]

PARTY ROOTS IN SOCIETY

Political parties in Chile have been well-established national organizations that reach the most remote villages in the country and effectively shape political life.[27] They have constituted the main channels to voice concerns and reach office. Party membership has worked as an important organizing principle in private institutions and associations, including university life, labor unions, and professional associations. Political preferences are passed from one generation to another, and constitute an important part of Chileans' identity.[28] Party roots in society are particularly relevant to understanding the high levels of institutionalization of the party system in Chile. Political tendencies in this country are the result of collective memories of past political divisions that shaped and reshaped the party system. They also embody political identities, values, sentiments, and traditions that are passed to the new generations mainly through families, including the way parents structure the sociability of their children through, for instance, schools, neighborhoods, and churches.[29]

Two indicators of the degree to which political parties are considered legitimate actors representing society's interests are voter turnout and party identification. As Table 6.1 shows, the abstention rate in Chile remains at remarkably low levels. Similarly, party identification oscillated between 70 and 80 percent in the years following the transition to democracy.[30] There are some signs, however, of decreasing trends over time as elections become less plebiscitary and the rigidity of the binomial system turns off voters, particularly young ones.

TABLE 6.1

Voter Turnout in Chile's Presidential Elections, 1989–2005

Presidential Election	Abstention Rate (%)
1989	5.3
1993	8.7
1999	10.1
2005	12.3

Source: Tribunal Calificador de Elecciones de Chile.

CORRESPONDENCE BETWEEN CAMPAIGNS AND POLICIES

Since the return of democratic life in Chile, Concertación presidents maintained a general continuity with the policies expressed during their political campaigns. There were no surprises regarding candidates promising to follow a particular economic model during the campaign and changing their minds once in office. In contrast to the Venezuelan experience—when Pérez and Caldera neglected their campaign promises during their second presidencies—the correspondence between party platforms, campaigns, and policies has been the norm in Chile.

Post-Pinochet Features

Changes to the electoral rules during the military dictatorship considerably structured the party system to reach high levels of institutionalization.[31] Although Pinochet attempted through different means to interfere in party life and alter Chile's historical ideological cleavages through the 1980 Constitution, the 1987 Law of Political Parties, and the 1988 Electoral Law,[32] the unintended consequence was the increase in predictability and cooperation among parties. Four fundamental changes contributing to the consolidation of the Chilean party system in its current form were (1) the establishment of the binomial electoral system with high thresholds to register political parties; (2) the introduction of legacy senators; (3) the need for congressional supermajorities to pass important legislation; and (4) the democratization of the selection of the party leadership.[33]

First, the bipolar logic of the Chilean binomial electoral system—*sistema binominal*, as it is called in Chile—virtually forces parties to create broad alliances or lists before the elections.[34] Intended to eliminate small parties and create a two-party system, the Chilean electoral system provided for congressional districts with a magnitude of two. A party list is required to double the total vote of the closest list to win both seats in each district—i.e., a list needs at least 66 percent of the vote to carry both seats. Otherwise, the first and second lists get one seat each. This formula tends to systematically overrepresent the minority list, which, at the time of the transition, corresponded to the rightist parties sympathizing with Pinochet. Moreover, the 1987 Law of Political Parties made it considerably more difficult to register a political party by requiring signatures equivalent to 5 percent of the electorate in at least eight regions or in at least three neighboring regions to register a party. This provision increased the minimum threshold from 20,000 signatures before the coup to roughly 200,000 at the time of the 1988 plebiscite.[35]

Second, after losing the 1988 plebiscite, Pinochet's appointment of nine "institutional" or "legacy" senators—one fifth of the senate—distorted the relationship between parties' share of the vote and congressional representation.[36] Article 45 of the 1980 Constitution established that, of the nine institutional senators, four would be chosen by the National Security Council—controlled by Pinochet during the 1990s—among retired commanders in chief of the army, navy, air force, and national police. Three would be chosen by the Supreme Court—two among former justices and one among former attorney generals. The president would appoint one from ex-rectors of academic institutions, and another from a former cabinet member. The Concertación governments were not able to appoint like-minded senators until 1998. On August 16, 2005, Congress abolished the provision for institutional senators, beginning on March 11, 2006.[37]

Third, the 1980 Constitution made it particularly difficult to form working majorities to approve legislation, forcing the Concertación to reach out to opposition parties in order to govern. Previously, the 1925 Constitution facilitated the approval of legislation without broad congressional support—often introduced by presidents who won by a slim plurality—making the system particularly volatile.[38] Passing legislation required a simple majority in either house of Congress and only one third plus one in the other. In order to preserve changes introduced by the military regime, the 1980 Constitution raised the bar to pass legislation, requiring a majority in both houses, or a supermajority, depending on the issue.

Lastly, the 1987 Law of Political Parties mandated the selection of party leaders by the membership through democratic means. This provision turned the elite-driven, behind-the-scenes, decision making process that characterized the parties before the military coup into a more transparent one. The change contributed to strengthen the legitimacy of the party leadership and engage the rank-and-file in the parties' internal life. A developed form of this democratic principle is the selection of candidates through primaries. Although party primaries have not been the norm in every political party, their introduction as the Concertación's preferred mechanism to select presidential candidates has played an important role in strengthening the connection between the parties and society.[39] The Concertación has considerably democratized their candidate selection process, moving from a smoky room model to an openly democratic one. It replaced the elite conclave mechanism employed in 1989 with an indirect primary in 1993, which was in turn replaced by an open primary system in 1999.[40] In contrast, the right-wing coalition Alianza has maintained a leadership-centered selection process.

Together, these four features of the post-Pinochet regime acted as powerful incentives for political parties to form stable coalitions and favor accommodation in order to maximize chances of reaching power.[41] As a result, the two main coalitions—the left-of-center Concertación and the right-of-center Alianza—have routinely engaged in a series of multilevel negotiations at the party and coalition level. A prominent example is the intense pre-electoral negotiations that take place in order to select the lists of candidates for each district in congressional elections. The parties forming each coalition—mainly the centrist PDC and PRSD and the leftist PS and PPD comprising the Concertación and the UDI and RN comprising Alianza por Chile—have to negotiate 60 two-seat electoral slates for the chamber of deputies and nine or 10 similar slates for the senate, depending on the electoral cycle.[42] Since the binomial formula favors the election of one candidate from each coalition, coalitions need to present two particularly strong candidates in a district to double the vote of the opponent's list and win both seats at stake. If a coalition fails to win both seats, however, a strong candidate is "wasted" in that district. Therefore, in order to entice strong candidates to take the risk and pair up with another strong candidate in the same district, the coalition needs to compensate them politically in the event of a defeat.

In the case of the governing coalition, prominent positions in the executive's cabinet are awarded as compensation.[43] Additionally, "formal transversal coordination across the government's parties is conducted by the General Secretariat of the President (*Ministerio de la Secretaría General de la Presidencia*)."[44] In the case of the opposition, negotiations are somewhat more complicated because it is more difficult to offer some form of political compensation without controlling the executive branch. However, the process itself is meaningful because it involves true sacrifice and generates enduring loyalties to the party and the coalition. This practice of accommodation has contributed greatly to generating a sense of allegiance—both to the party and the coalition—maintaining discipline among the coalitions' legislators.

Furthermore, not only has party discipline become a sine qua non to reach the supermajorities required to pass legislation, but it has also generated the strong sense of predictability required to work with all the parties represented in Congress. The system of accommodation within coalitions results in the congressional loyalty, party discipline, and predictability that have helped to institutionalize the system of congressional deliberation and bargaining.[45] In the words of Pamela Figueroa, director of the Office of Governability at the Ministry of the Interior and member of the PPD's National Directorate, thanks to this predictability, "the government has a pretty good idea of how many votes it can count on from legislators and what it will have to give up in exchange in order to negotiate with the opposition."[46]

These qualities proved to be essential to seek broad consensus beyond the political forces forming an electoral coalition. The institutional constraints inherited from the military dictatorship forced Concertación presidents to negotiate most of their government program with the conservative opposition.[47] Since the restoration of democracy in 1990, the Concertación was forced to negotiate with at least one of the parties of the right in order to approve legislation. Consequently, the Concertación governments adopted a piecemeal reform strategy that incorporated a broad consensus across the ideological spectrum. This approach excluded the implementation of any major reforms advocated by the Concertación—such as modifying the binomial system—but proved to be effective in passing a compromise version of the original proposals—as was the case with labor and health care reforms.[48] As Senator Carlos Ominami pointed out, "the need to negotiate these reforms with all the political forces represented in congress certainly slowed down the pace and scope of the policy transformations advocated by the Concertación in general and the Socialist Party in particular."[49] Although the Concertación presidents never advocated radical economic policies, the party system put the breaks on the left-of-center governments' reform agenda—an opinion shared by several of Lagos's cabinet ministers and close advisers.[50]

In sum, the combination of the binomial system, the designated senators, the supermajorities required to legislate on important matters,[51] and the democratization of party life transformed the Chilean party system into one with stable, disciplined coalitions with predictable policy positions, deep roots in society, and the habit of negotiating virtually every initiative with the entire political spectrum. These characteristics would result in a system encouraging a high level of moderation among the different political forces.[52]

Party System Institutionalization and Economic Policy Moderation

The high degree of institutionalization of Chile's party system has been a key factor in conducting moderate economic transformations. This is due to two main reasons. First, Chile's system tends to generate moderate candidates with a history of negotiation and a stake in the system, so gradual reformers are likely to be elected rather than radical transformers. Second, Chile's party system fosters accommodation and consensus seeking in the legislature, generating an essential "framework of predict-ability for economic decision-making."[53] Disciplined political parties with strong social roots and predictable positions in Chile force executives to interact with them to negotiate policy courses of action. In other words, in Chile, seasoned, moderate executives opt for deliberation and negotiation rather than rule by decree or plebi-scitary appeals in order to conduct policy.

MODERATE CANDIDATES LIKELY TO REACH OFFICE

The process of negotiation characteristic of the Chilean party system has resulted in the selection of presidential candidates with a history of political accommodation, consensus building, and party loyalty. A product of party politics, presidential can-didates develop a stake in the system after climbing through parties' ranks. Candi-dates then strive to preserve this same system. This has been the case for every candidate reaching the presidency since the return of civilian rule.

The political careers of leftist candidates and their opponents are cases in point. By the time Ricardo Lagos ran for president in December 1999, he was well known for being a moderate socialist. He had participated in two primary elections for pres-ident and one election for senator.[54] He acquired a reputation as an orthodox, pro-market economist while serving as the minister for public works during the Frei Ruiz-Tagle administration (1994–2000). One of the main factors contributing to this reputation was his proactive partnership with the business sectors in activities that were previously controlled by the government. Lagos was appointed minister of public works after losing the primary to select the Concertación's candidate between Frei Ruiz-Tagle (Christian Democrat) and Lagos (PS/PPD) in 1993.[55]

A product of the same party system, Lagos's successor shared the same features. Michelle Bachelet was also a political insider with a stake in the system. She served as minister of health (2000–2002) and minister of defense (2002–2004) during the Lagos administration. Before serving in these capacities, she unsuccessfully ran for mayor of Las Condes (a *comuna* in eastern Santiago) in 1996 and participated in Ricardo Lagos's 1999 campaign. Before becoming the Concertación candidate for president, she had to beat Christian Democrat Soledad Alvear in a primary elec-tion.[56] By the time that Bachelet became the Concertación's presidential candidate in 2005, she had navigated a system of party accommodation and consensus seeking in order to achieve the nomination of the Socialist Party first, the Concertación second, and—most importantly—the presidency itself.

Opposition candidates have had similar records of party work. Joaquín Lavín, UDI's presidential candidate in the 1999 and 2005 presidential elections, had a long history of accommodation within the party. He first ran unsuccessfully for Congress in 1989 and was later elected mayor of Las Condes in 1992. Following his defeat by a narrow margin in the 1999 presidential election, he became the mayor of Santiago until he ran again for the presidency in 2005. Likewise, Sebastián Piñera, the RN candidate in 2005—when the right did not present a unified candidacy for the presidential election—and 2010—when he won the presidency—had served as a senator between 1990 and 1998 and president of RN between 2001 and 2004. In brief, all of the presidential candidates put forth by the parties forming the main coalitions share similar trajectories in party politics.

PARTIES' ABILITY TO AFFECT ECONOMIC POLICY

Institutional constraints forced the Concertación administrations to govern by trying to obtain the consent of a predictable and stable opposition.[57] This practice in turn generates a culture of compromise that reinforces the government's ability to "reach consensus among a wide array of political forces."[58] Consequently, the opposition has had the ability to substantially shape the content of policy in Chile. As a result of the predictability of the rules of the game, the opposition has responded with a responsible position. It has engaged in intense parliamentary negotiations and supported the government in passing important economic reforms. "Coalitional discipline helped the Concertación to enlist rightist support for a hike in the value-added tax that paid for expanding social programs in the early 1990s, as well as to pass anticorruption legislation during Lagos's term."[59] Perhaps the best example is the opposition's overwhelming support for the 2005 constitutional reform eliminating several of the "protected democracy" provisions—legacy senators, the president's inability to remove and appoint the top commanders of the military, and the military's mandate as the sole warrantor of the constitutional order. Only four representatives—all retired military personnel and only one of them elected—voted against the reforms.[60] After all, the left's responsible management of the economy and the political parties' responsiveness to society's demands obviated the need for such provisions.

The approval of the FTA between Chile and the United States—a very controversial issue that generated heated debate across the political spectrum—constitutes another example of the politics of accommodation and the consequent responsible reaction of the opposition. After President Lagos's three-year negotiation with the United States, the agreement that was signed in June 2003 was approved 87 to 8 in the Chilean Chamber of Deputies and 34 to 5 in the Chilean Senate.[61] Among the votes against the FTA in the lower house, one was a socialist member of the Concertación, five were from UDI, and two from RN. In the Senate, votes against came from two Christian Democrats, two members of RN, and one from Chileve (a short-lived spin-off from the PPD).[62] The vote tally is a reflection of the successful accommodation of the different party preferences even in the context of highly contentious issues.

The unanimous approval of Lagos's poverty alleviation program, Chile Solidario, is another case in point. Originally, the opposition rejected the president's initial bill, particularly those provisions related to the centralization of resources in the hands of the Ministry of Planning and away from local governments.[63] The bill was watered down by eliminating contentious issues and approved by consensus in both houses of Congress.[64]

Consensus is not reached on every policy initiative, of course, and the government's attempts to substantially alter the status quo without fully reconciling policy positions have been unsuccessful. The tax and labor reforms—pursued at different times by Presidents Aylwin, Frei, and Lagos—are illustrative. In these cases, the versions approved by Congress were only a shadow of the changes pursued by the executive,[65] particularly regarding the labor reform attempts in which the government fell considerably short of its goals (Aylwin), was shut down by Congress (Frei), and even struggled to get on board its own coalition members (Lagos).[66] These governments' failures to loosen restrictions on unionization and collective bargaining— explicitly one of their main government goals[67]—constitute one of the most visible examples of the moderating role of the process of legislative accommodation.

Thus, the incentives for negotiation in the Chilean party system have scaled down the Concertación's policy initiatives in order to gradually move forward its agenda. As Francisco Díaz, Office of the President's director of public policy confided, "the Concertación's economic agenda has been slowed down by the need for compromise that congressional dynamics impose."[68]

Alternative Explanations

In addition to party system institutionalization, two other factors have played an important role in accounting for the left's economic policy moderation in Chile: the country's solid economic performance and the depth of market reforms. Conversely, other factors including executive powers, natural resources, and the strength of organized labor are much less useful in explaining that country's piecemeal economic transformations.

ECONOMIC CONDITIONS

Growing steadily since the mid-1980s, and with declines in poverty rates and improvements in wealth distribution, the Chilean economy has provided little incentive to conduct substantial economic policy transformations. After the economic recovery following the crisis in 1983 through 1984,[69] the opposition coalition Alianza Democrática (AD)—formed by Christian Democrats and some Socialists—was compelled to moderate its economic program. As the economic situation improved and the social unrest was overcome, AD lost important negotiating leverage to lure business into forcing a transition to democracy before 1989.[70] Clear economic improvement drove AD to commit to pro-market policies—dropping its demands for a mixed participation of state and private enterprise—and focus on political openness rather than economic revisionism. The AD even stopped referring to state intervention as such, and thereafter attempted to shape economic policy within the boundaries of market orthodoxy.[71] In other words, economic success generated a risk aversion among the main economic actors—why change the model if this one is working so well?—which boxed in the opposition into committing to the prevailing model. In contrast to experiences in Venezuela—where market reforms were unable to survive popular opposition and thus failed to detonate economic recovery—and in Brazil—where economic growth was modest after partial reforms—economic success became a compelling reason for the opposition to embrace market orthodoxy in Chile. In the words of Jorge Frei, deputy minister of justice and one of Lagos's former policy advisors, "it was the Concertación's embrace of market orthodoxy that made the transition to democracy even possible."[72]

The economic model's sustained success during the Christian Democrat governments of the 1990s made it even more difficult for the Socialists to reverse market orthodoxy once they reached the presidency in 2000. In fact, although Pinochet is credited for laying the foundations for sustained economic growth, the economic performance during the Concertación governments surpassed that of the dictatorship.[73] Although far from the double-digit growth rates experienced in China and India during the 1990s, the country experienced the fastest economic expansion in Latin America since 1980. The continuation of economic success during the first two Concertación governments, along with the Socialists' participation in important cabinet posts, became compelling reasons for not making any significant changes to the general economic orthodoxy followed in Chile.

A relevant counterfactual question is, then, had Chile experienced deteriorating economic conditions, would Lagos's response have departed from economic orthodoxy? Chile's generally vigorous economic performance under Concertación governments provide us with few hints to answer this question. However, there is evidence that a brief economic crisis was not enough to prompt a departure. The only time in which declining economic conditions could have prompted a change in economic policy was Chile's 1999 economic recession—the country's worst economic performance since 1983. In 1999, the last year of the Eduardo Frei Ruiz-Tagle administration and the year of the presidential election, Ricardo Lagos's commitment to economic orthodoxy was put to the test. For the first time in the post-Pinochet period, Chile's economy experienced an economic recession, recording a negative growth rate of -0.8 percent. After experiencing double-digit growth (10.6 percent) in 1995, the recession marked the country's fourth year of decreasing economic performance.[74] Unemployment, which had averaged 5 percent in the 1990s, doubled in 1999 and remained at 10 percent until 2006.[75] The situation during the electoral year deteriorated to the point where presidential approval levels reached 28 percent, the lowest level for any Concertación president between the return of democracy in 1990—when Aylwin's approval surpassed 70 percent—and 2006—when Lagos's approval during his last year in office hovered around 68 percent.[76]

Despite the economic recession, Lagos's commitment to maintaining the pro-market policy trend remained firm. Although the 1999 recession turned out to be temporary, economic performance in Chile had clearly been deteriorating—along with the president's approval—since 1995.[77] At the time of the election in December 1999—the height of economic uncertainty—the Lagos campaign maintained its pledge to continue with economic orthodoxy. This continued to be the case even during the first three years of the Lagos presidency, which were characterized by sluggish growth. Although Chile's recession leading up to the change in government was not as drastic as other economic crises such as, for example, the 1994–1995 peso crisis in Mexico or the 2001–2002 financial crisis in Argentina and Uruguay, the sudden drop in GDP growth was unusual enough—the worst performance since 1983—to raise the issue of whether the prevailing economic model was reaching exhaustion. Instead, rather than taking the opportunity to advocate more drastic economic transformations, the Lagos administration adhered strictly to a piecemeal reform program focusing mostly on labor issues and leaving untouched the pro-market model adopted by Pinochet.

Notwithstanding this instance in which a brief crisis failed to prompt a change in the economic model, however, it would be difficult to argue that a sustained erosion of economic conditions—such as the one experienced in Venezuela over more than two decades—would have no effect on the party system. As seen in the Andean country, a prolonged state of sharp economic deterioration would probably result in citizens' discontent and the mistrust of political parties as capable representatives of society's preferences, even in the most institutionalized party systems.

DEEPLY ROOTED MARKET REFORMS

The depth of neoliberal reform can be measured in terms of longevity of market-oriented policies and their scope. In other words, how long has neoliberalism been around and to what extent has it permeated relevant sectors of Chilean society?

Chileans have become habituated to neoliberal economic policies as the dominant paradigm in that country since 1973—the longest period in Latin America. Even though initially neoliberalism was reserved for Pinochet's government elites, in the aftermath of the 1982 debt crisis the model reached wide sectors of society and became the common currency of business sectors, academics, and even the opposition.

Pioneers of neoliberal economic policies in the region, Chileans were the first to implement ambitious and comprehensive market reforms. Shortly after the overthrow of Allende in 1973, the Pinochet regime undertook a neoclassical economic program to replace the state-interventionist policies that characterized the socialist's tenure. As a result of the economic transformations that took place during the military regime, Chile became "one of the most open economic systems in the developing world."[78]

In the process, market orthodoxy permeated Chilean society from top to bottom, from a select group of technocrats heading key ministries in the early years of the dictatorship to the bulk of the business and middle class sectors. This contributed to reducing the spectrum of acceptable options to a narrow range within market orthodoxy. The narrowing of feasible alternatives was possible—as discussed in the previous section—given the success of market orthodoxy in bringing growth rates above the regional average.[79]

The implementation of neoliberalism during the dictatorship (1973–1990) can be divided into two main phases: the early "radical" years—when the model was first introduced—and the post-1982 or "pragmatic" years—when neoliberalism truly began to permeate society.[80] The radical period, comprising between 1975 and 1982, witnessed a "draconian economic stabilization programs—often referred to as shock therapy—and the quick liberalization of most of the economy, including prices, trade, and capital markets."[81] The implementation of the measures was extremely dogmatic, with little regard for the dislocation effects on productive sectors that had trouble adjusting to the abruptly adopted openness. During this period, the technocrats in charge of designing and executing neoliberal policies had Pinochet's unconditional support to push for radical economic change. They were effectively isolated from political pressures and only worked with a small fraction of the business sectors.

Thus, with the exception of the select group of technocrats and business leaders, neoliberalism remained a relatively foreign concept to most sectors until the 1982–1983 crisis. Following a sudden drop in GDP growth of -10 percent—due to a series of economic difficulties including excessive indebtedness, poor oversight, and the collapse of the financial system—the Pinochet government softened its pro-market dogmatism to adopt a more flexible variant dubbed "pragmatic neoliberalism."[82] As a result, the government became more involved in regulating the markets and incorporated broad sectors of the business community to participate in economic policy formulation at all levels of the bureaucracy.

A gradual process of interweaving of business actors into governmental decision making ensued, allowing the neoliberal model to influence key political and economic sectors. Before the crisis, only big business had been socialized into the neoliberal paradigm. The big business conglomerates, such as Cruzat-Larraín and Banco Hipotecario de Chile (BHC), worked with the dictatorship from the very beginning during the radical period. During the period of pragmatic neoliberalism, however, this collaboration expanded to business associations such as the Confederation for Production and Commerce—the umbrella organization of large scale business associations.[83] As part of the rapprochement between the business sectors and the government, Pinochet appointed prominent members of the business community to top bureaucratic positions right under the technocrat leadership.[84] The formal incorporation of business into government positions helped to form a network of intermediation that gradually contributed to the assimilation of the bulk of the business sectors into the neoliberal model.

This assimilation did not end with the transition to civilian governments. Instead, the Concertación governments embraced the practice and furthered the technocratization of government positions underway during the Pinochet years. Think tanks from the right, center, and left became a steady supply of technically able bureaucrats who roughly shared the same views and spoke the same language as the economic elites and business sectors. The Concertación governments appointed highly educated technocrats that emerged from specialized think tanks linked to the political parties belonging to the electoral coalition.[85] Among the most prominent think tanks are CIEPLAN, the Latin American Center for International Economics and Policy (CLEPI), the Latin American Faculty of the Social Sciences (FLACSO), the Center for Development Studies (CED), and the Latin American Center for Doctrine and Social Studies (ILADES).[86] In the words of José Jara, former director of FLACSO Chile, this well-rooted practice continued to be the norm in Chile.[87]

The long, vast assimilation of the neoliberal paradigm by different sectors had important consequences for the type of policies pursued by the different governments. The internalization of market orthodoxy in Chile resulted in the shortening of the ideological distance between political parties. By the time the Concertación reached power, a strong consensus already existed on free market economics and the central role of the private sector for economic development. If the opposition to the military regime was to have any chances of winning a majority of the vote for the presidency in 1989, it had to make very clear its embrace of orthodox economic policies. The Concertación embraced neoliberalism and fostered the communication channels that developed during the dictatorship between the government and the main economic actors. The democratically elected government and the Confederation for Production and Commerce made a habit out of the exchange of technical studies and general information about the impact of proposed economic measures.[88]

An example of the level of neoliberal consolidation in Chile is the 1999 electoral campaign between Lagos and Lavín. In that year, both candidates campaigned on the strict adherence to a market-based development model, and "in terms of policy, there was not a great deal of difference between the two leading electoral alliances."[89] Both the left and the right were entirely committed to maintaining the same economic policy. The main differences then were social issues—abortion and divorce, for example—and the extent to which certain social policies should change with respect to housing, education, and criminality.[90] According to Álvaro García Hurtado, Frei's minister of the economy, Lagos minister of the general secretariat of the presidency,[91] and member of the PPD's national directorate, what set Ricardo Lagos apart from Joaquín Lavín—the Alianza por Chile candidate and one of the "Chicago Boys"[92] that conducted neoliberal policies during the dictatorship—"was not their economic projects, but their positions on social issues."[93] In short, pro-market policies are so well rooted in Chile that it would be difficult for a serious contender to depart significantly from them.

EXECUTIVE POWERS

Chilean presidents have historically been among the strongest in Latin America, a precedent reinforced by the 1980 Constitution.[94] These formal powers of the executive survived the constitutional reforms of 1989 and 2005. Among the most important powers are the exclusive ability to introduce legislation in all matters of taxation, creation of government agencies, entitlement programs and social security, and collective bargaining procedures. The national budget automatically becomes law if Congress does not approve it within 60 days. The president may summon Congress for an extraordinary session anytime to discuss any issue the president deems a priority. These prerogatives give the executive such leverage vis-à-vis the legislature that it has been referred to as "an exaggerated presidential system."[95]

Despite executive strength, however, the existence of a highly institutionalized party system has obviated the need to rely on the president's powers.[96] Postauthoritarian presidents have consistently taken into account the views of their party, coalition, and even opposition parties to further their government program. Predictability (presidents know where the different legislators stand and how many votes they can garner), party discipline (legislators respond to programmatic issues rather than personalistic adventures), and commitment to the market-orthodox development model (the commitment that the Concertación made to respect a general pro-market framework and play by the rules of the 1980 Constitution) have been strong incentives for the president and legislature to negotiate policy and reach working consensus. Cooperation and consultation have been essential features of postauthoritarian executive-legislative relations in Chile.

Coalitional incentives function as important checks on the executive's prerogatives.[97] The need to accommodate the different interests represented in the coalition into the cabinet affect executive-legislative dynamics as well. For the sake of preserving intracoalitional harmony, the Concertación's legislative fraction relies on fluid negotiations between the president and the parties forming the coalition.[98] This practice ensures that the programmatic balance prevailing in the cabinet and ministries carries over into the legislative arena. Presidents' attempts to dominate the legislative agenda are met with pressure to respect coalition agreements.[99] In sum, the president's need to rely on his or her executive superpresidential powers is obviated because of Congress's importance to the legislative process as a result of the high institutionalization of the party system.

THE ROLE OF RESOURCES

Despite the important role of copper in the Chilean economy and the dramatic increase in the price of this commodity, this country's resource dependence did not induce exuberant statist policies. The same way that Chávez took advantage of an unprecedented influx of commodity windfalls, the Lagos administration benefited from unusually high prices of copper.[100] The average price per pound almost tripled between 2004 and 2006, increasing from US$1.30 to US$3.05. In 2006 copper revenues constituted 34 percent of the government's total revenue—much higher than Bolivia's 22 percent from natural gas—and the country's budget surplus of 7.9 percent of GDP was the largest in two decades.[101] However, the Lagos administration refrained from conducting statist policies requiring extraordinary spending. On the contrary, and in spite of the temptation that the influx of copper money represented,[102] his government furthered pro-market reforms through privatizations and more stringent government spending.

ORGANIZED LABOR

Organized labor was unsuccessful in pushing for statist policies in any of the policy spheres under study. Although Chile was the only Latin American country where labor experienced gains in unionization rates during the 1990s[103] this interest group remained significantly weak as a result of Pinochet's legacy following the 1979 labor code—known as *Plan Laboral*—that severely restricted workers' ability to bargain collectively and maintained unions under strict state control.[104] Evidence of this weakness was the inability of Chile's main workers' organization, the Unitary Workers' Central (*Central Unitaria de Trabajadores*—CUT) to push for comprehensive labor reform, which has become this interest group's top priority since Chile's labor regulation does not fully conform to International Labor Organization standards.[105] Although each of the Concertación governments promised comprehensive reform, changes to the labor code have been extremely modest, such as recognizing public employee associations and granting collective bargaining to about 12 percent of the labor force.[106]

Promising to bring the right of collective bargaining for inter-enterprise and transitory unions, and end the ban on replacing striking workers, the Lagos administration was not the exception. However, the proposed measures were quickly abandoned due to disagreement both within the Concertación and with the opposition.[107] Thus, organized labor did not enjoy enough strength to materialize its top policy priority.

Conclusion

The case of Chile illustrates how a highly institutionalized party system played an important role in sustaining the country's economic orthodoxy. Moderate economic policies are the consequence of both the temperance instilled in the candidates through the process of accommodation and consensus-building in party politics and the ability of the different forces represented in Congress to shape and moderate economic policy.

In addition to the party system, Chile's economic success and depth of market orthodoxy significantly contributed to the continuation of orthodox economic policies. There is evidence that both factors contributed to the preservation of pro-market policies during Lagos's leftist administration, although it is difficult to imagine the depth of market orthodoxy playing this role without the model's economic success. First, regarding Chile's prevailing economic conditions, there is no indication that short-term economic adversity—in an election year and during the first three years of government—affected the Lagos administration's commitment to pro-market policies. This does not mean, however, that a sustained erosion of economic conditions—such as that experienced in Venezuela for more than 20 years—would not undermine society's reliance in political parties as competent stewards of the polity and, consequently, erode the level of institutionalization in Chile's party system. Arguably, as was the case in Venezuela, the prolonged deterioration of living conditions would serve as a catalyzer for the deterioration of the party system.

Second, regarding the depth of market orthodoxy in Chile, the gradual acceptance of Pinochet's profound economic transformations was contingent upon favorable economic results. Sustained growth resulting from market-oriented reform led to a generalized acceptance of the pro-market policies, which in turn led to the narrowing of the political spectrum. However, other institutional legacies have been reversed or eliminated once a minimum consensus is reached, such as the elimination of appointed senators. The removal of such institutional legacies sheds light on how institutional constraints inherited from the dictatorship might also be altered if the required majority in Congress agrees to do so in order to respond to society's demands.

The Chilean case also illustrates how the strength of the executive vis-à-vis the legislature, the country's high resource dependence, and the strength of organized labor lack explanatory power for our purposes. A logical explanation for Chile's adherence to pro-market policies would look for a weak president who is unable to push for important transformations through executive powers and is subject to congressional authority. Instead, Chile's institutionalized party system provided disincentives to utilize presidential powers to circumvent the legislature. Similarly, this country's general adherence to pro-market policies took place in spite of the country's relatively high resource dependence. In contrast to the Venezuelan case, the Lagos administration was not encouraged by increased natural resource revenues to increase the level of state intervention in the economy. Additionally, the weakness of organized labor in Chile has resulted in this sector's inability to push for economic reforms that would materialize their long-standing demands.

Regarding the origins of Chile's institutionalized party system, several important factors have contributed toward the high levels of institutionalization in the Chilean party system. On the one hand, the party system finds its roots in the pre-Pinochet system that took shape throughout Chile's long democratic history since the early 20th century. During this time, party identities became so deeply entrenched in society that the military dictatorship's attempts to transform the political landscape failed. On the other hand, important rules, both electoral—e.g., the binomial system—and procedural—e.g., the requirement of qualified majorities to modify matters of importance—inherited from the dictatorship helped routinize practices of candidate selection and intra and intercoalition negotiation among the different political parties. The rules structured party politics in an unprecedented way in Chile and reduced further the window of opportunity for drastic economic policies, such as those of Salvador Allende's government, to occur. These factors have been supported by enviable economic conditions, which facilitate compliance with the rules of the game.

Finally, it is important to note that Chile's party system has begun to show signs of deterioration. Such signs include rising voter disenchantment—particularly among young voters—and popular demonstrations outside institutional channels.[108] If this trend continues to the point where traditional parties become unable to articulate and channel society's demands, the gradual pace of reform in post-authoritarian Chile can be expected to change as well.

The findings stemming from the Chilean case provide additional support for the hypothesized nexus between party system institutionalization and the degree of economic moderation. As the cases of Venezuela, Brazil, and Chile suggest, higher levels of institutionalization result in more moderate leftist reactions to the prevailing pro-market trend.

7   CONCLUSION

ASKED ABOUT THE significance of the arrival of the left to power, Mexican writer Carlos Fuentes remarked, "Not so long ago, this was inconceivable. The left's only recourse was through armed insurrection. [...] That is a step forward for Latin America that should not be underestimated."[1] Much less sanguine about its desirability but sharing the same fervor about the topic, Peruvian writer Álvaro Vargas Llosa characterized the arrival of the left to power as the return of "the Idiot species in the form of populist leaders who are reenacting failed policies of the past and supporters who are lending credence to them."[2] These dramatically opposed views exemplify the passion that leftist governments have generated. Although motivated by the same excitement about the left in government, this book has sought to transcend the personality centric views that have characterized the debate in policy and media circles. It has sought to advance our understanding of how the left governs and the determinants behind their government policies.

This concluding chapter is divided into three main sections. In the first part, I return to the main question posed in the introduction—what are the conditions that make the initiation and maintenance of economic transformations more likely? In this section I discuss the theoretical implications of the book's findings. In particular, I discuss its contribution regarding three main bodies of literature: the left in Latin America, party systems, and the politics of economic reforms.

The second part switches the focus of the book from the causes of the left's economic policies to their consequences from a variety of perspectives. It seeks to answer the following questions: Have the leftists' experiences in government made a difference? Does it matter whether they have implemented pro-statist or pro-market policies? Has the left performed better than the right? In order to answer these questions, this section evaluates governments' performance along three economic dimensions— economic growth, poverty, and inequality. Taking the literature on macroeconomic populism as a point of departure, the comparison of leftist governments' performance is undertaken across countries, across administrations within the same country, and vis-à-vis the right-of-center administrations in Colombia and Mexico employed as controls throughout the book. It also discusses the implications of the left's performance for democracy and for the prevalence of market orthodoxy in the region.

The third part takes the implications of party system institutionalization beyond economic policy changes and connects them with economic performance and democracy. Drawing on historical experiences and on the leftist governments' economic performance, I suggest that low levels of institutionalization have detrimental effects on the sustainability of economic growth, on the one hand, and on horizontal accountability, on the other.

Implications for Theory

This book addressed an important question of comparative political economy, namely what conditions are conducive to carrying out economic transformations? It argued that an explanation based on differences in party system institutionalization is best able to account for variation in economic policy transformations across the region. As the previous chapters showed, party systems provide important incentives and constraints shaping the behavior of relevant actors in the political arena. When institutionalized, party systems lengthen time horizons, encourage consensus seeking, and impose meaningful constraints; when in disarray, they are conducive to recalcitrant positions, executive-legislative conflict, and the concentration of presidential power. The weakness of constraints in party systems in disarray makes the election of outsider politicians without a stake in the system more likely and undermines political parties' ability to moderate the president's policies through the legislature. Conversely, institutionalized party systems discourage the election of radical leaders and provide the legislature with the muscle to effectively moderate the president's policies. Although this distinction between the two extreme types of party systems is useful for analytical purposes, the region's experiences should be understood along a continuum in order to avoid glossing over important shades of gray.

Additionally, weak party systems do not necessarily result in statist or leftist policies but tend to generate extreme policy positions away from the status quo. Instead, it is the ideology of the candidate that is likely to determine whether these changes are statist or pro-market. The rise of the left to power at the end of the 20th century in Latin America offered a range of cases showing variation between the adoption of extreme policy transformations and the generalized adherence to the prevailing framework of pro-market policies.

By focusing on leftist governments, this book made a contribution to the study of the Latin American left in two respects. Contrary to other works that have focused on taxonomical,[3] electoral,[4] political,[5] or citizenship[6] issues, this analysis is one of the first to draw attention to the left's economic policies. The few authors who have discussed the left's economic policies in specific countries have done so based on a limited number of cases and focusing mostly on performance.[7] Conversely, the systematic approach across cases followed in this book enhances the generalizability of findings and focuses on explaining the *causes* behind the left's economic policies.

Additionally, existing work in comparative politics has only anecdotally identified an association between institutions and the left.[8] Such work had focused on issues of representation rather than government policies, particularly through the analytical lens of populism. Instead, this book is the first to advance the causal logic between party systems and the left's economic policies theoretically and test it empirically. Contrary to existing studies focusing on differences within the left, this book presented a unifying theory of the left in government.[9]

Even though this book found support for the role of party systems as the most parsimonious account with the most explanatory leverage, it also challenged and revised established institutional perspectives. Stephan Haggard and Robert Kaufman broke ground with their insights that party systems matter for economic transformations. They emphasized the role of fragmentation and polarization as crucial factors in the *consolidation* of reforms. They also identified centrifugal dynamics in the party system as responsible for hindering reforms. This book built on Haggard and Kaufman's work in highlighting the importance of party systems for economic policies, but it reached different conclusions.

This study found that the problems of coordination associated with fragmentation and polarization were seldom a predictor of governments' ability to carry out economic policy changes.[10] High levels of fragmentation in Venezuela and Ecuador and polarization in Venezuela, Ecuador, and Bolivia did not impair these governments' ability to carry out economic transformations, but equally high levels of fragmentation did play a role in Brazil. Depending on whether one counts party alliances as single entities for fragmentation purposes in Chile and Uruguay, the case could be made that the number and ideological distance among parties in the system did not prevent the implementation of policy changes in these countries either.

Instead, this book highlighted the importance of institutionalization as a key dimension in explaining the role that party systems play for economic policy making more generally. Rather than limiting the analysis of the role of party systems to the consolidation of reforms, this study understood the consequences of the type of party system in the context of a longer time horizon. Instead of taking a snapshot view of the number of parties present during a particular administration, as Haggard and Kaufman did, this study focused on both the conditions leading up to the election of a particular type of candidate and the systemic dynamics that facilitate congressional bargaining and interbranch cooperation. Thus, rather than assuming that all types of candidates were equally likely to reach office at any given time regardless of the party system, or accounting for outcomes as a function of individual leadership—as other authors have[11]—the explanation advanced in this book accounted for the role of party systems both as selection mechanisms for candidates and as moderators of president's economic policy changes.

Additionally, this book's findings also call for the revision of Haggard and Kaufman's claim that centrifugal forces result in policy paralysis, thus making reforms more difficult, while centripetal forces reduce the power of forces opposed to reform, making reforms more likely.[12] Instead, the experience of the left in government in Latin America showed that centrifugal dynamics in the party system facilitate the election of antisystem candidates advocating drastic change, and then encourage the executive's circumvention of the legislature in order to carry out significant transformations by decree. Centripetal dynamics, in contrast, tend to facilitate the election of moderate leaders and the adoption of piecemeal reforms through a policy process where intra- and interparty deliberation shapes the executive's economic policies in meaningful ways.

In part, this difference in findings has to do with the context in which economic reforms took place. At the time of their writing, Haggard and Kaufman focused on cases that were undergoing or had recently undergone a democratic transition.[13] In most of their cases, the party systems were just beginning to take shape after years of authoritarian rule, and others remained authoritarian. In this context, the executive powers enjoyed by presidents served as the driving force behind many of the economic reforms in the 1980s and 1990s.

When the left arrived to power at the turn of the 21st century, however, many Latin American countries had enjoyed two decades of democratic rule, giving party systems time for their characteristic dynamics to play out. In this context, existing powers of the executive at the time leftist presidents arrived in office played an important role in some countries but provided limited explanatory leverage across

cases. Instead, relatively weak presidents turned to the expansion of their prerogatives by rewriting the rules of the game without meaningful opposition from the
political forces represented in the legislature. Thus, executive powers played a role in
facilitating economic policy changes to the extent that the disarray of the party
system contributed to making these changes possible.

In addition to revising how party systems affect governments' economic transformations, this book also contributed to the long-standing debate in comparative
political economy regarding the role that different factors play in effecting policy
changes, including economic conditions, natural resources, interest groups, executive powers, and the depth of neoliberalism.[14] To be sure, no single explanation can
account for the complexity of this phenomenon across all of our cases. Economic
conditions bring disenchantment when the economic model fails and elicit allegiance when the model brings prosperity. Natural resources significantly expand
governments' room for maneuver during commodity booms. Stronger executive offices enable presidents to carry out bolder policies. To different extents depending
on the country, many of these considerations played an important role in determining the economic policies followed by leftist governments in specific countries.

As in-depth analysis of leftist experiences in Venezuela, Brazil, and Chile showed,
different configurations of factors explain the type of economic policies observed in
each country. In the Venezuelan case, the protracted deterioration of economic conditions, corruption scandals, and rule changes promoting decentralization contributed to the dramatic deterioration of the party system throughout the 1990s. The
party system's disarray allowed Hugo Chávez to reach power via an ad hoc electoral
vehicle and an explicitly antisystem platform. Most importantly, the Venezuelan
party system lost its ability to voice and accommodate society's demands in Congress and to check the president's personalistic appeals to the population. In this
context, Chávez conducted statist measures by circumventing the legislature through
Enabling Laws and the powers conferred to him by the new Constitution. The scope
and sustainability of Chávez's statist policies depended on the massive influx of oil
revenue during most of his presidency.

In Brazil, the gradual institutionalization of the party system generated electoral
incentives contributing to the progressive moderation of Lula and the PT's government program as parties became more stable in their ideological positions, gained
access to local governments through local elections, and interacted with each other
in the context of longer time horizons. As a consequence, the chances of a radical,
antisystem candidate reaching the presidency decreased considerably. Additionally,
the progressive institutionalization of Brazil's party system has enabled the legislature to become an effective moderator of Lula's economic policies. Thus, the economic policy changes carried out by Lula's administration had to be diluted in order

to appeal to the lowest common denominator among the president's governing coalition. Market volatility leading up to Lula's presidency was a factor in crystallizing the moderation from the long process of accommodation that came with progressive institutionalization, and the president's executive powers played a supporting role in advancing Lula's agenda. The fragmentation of the Brazilian system contributed to this moderation, although fragmentation in the absence of institutionalization has failed to bring moderation, as the cases of Ecuador and Venezuela suggest.

Chile's generalized adherence to pro-market policies is the product of the country's highly institutionalized party system, depth of neoliberal reforms, and outstanding economic performance. Chile's highly institutionalized party system tends to constrain the rise of outsider, radical candidates with antisystem platforms. Its effective system of accommodation of interests within parties, within coalitions, and across coalitions has made the legislature the principal arena where society's demands are reconciled. With more stable, predictable coalitions and disciplined legislators than Brazil, political parties across the spectrum represented in the legislature have been able to directly participate in the policy making process and strongly influence economic policy outcomes. Additionally, the depth of previous market reforms was such that this paradigm became the baseline for important sectors of society, including business groups, think tanks, and academic circles by the time the left reached power. Moreover, the resounding success of Chile's orthodox economic policies provided every incentive to stay the course and continue along the pro-market path that had worked so well for more than a decade. In short, the three cases corroborated the importance of party systems for economic policy outcomes and highlighted that party systems do not provide incentives and disincentives in a vacuum. Instead, they are shaped *over time* by different economic and social forces in each country.

In contrast to alternative factors shaping economic policies in *specific* cases, however, an account based on party systems provided the most explanatory leverage, comfortably accounting for *all cases* while keeping parsimony in mind. Conversely, alternative explanations had trouble conforming to expectations in several cases. The evidence presented in this regard speaks to a number of debates in comparative political economy.

An explanation based on natural resource dependence had trouble accounting for Chile's orthodoxy in spite of unprecedented commodity windfall revenues and Argentina's statist policies despite its more diversified economy. Even in the case of Venezuela, the most oil dependent country in the hemisphere, the implementation of statist policies did not closely follow the logic of booms and busts articulated by advocates of a resource-based explanation.

This evidence supports the conclusions of scholars, such as James Robinson, Ragnar Torvik and Thierry Verdier, and Pauline Jones Luong and Erika Weinthal, who have questioned the deterministic nature of the resource curse and made the case instead for the role of institutions in determining economic policies in resource dependent countries.[15] It challenges the conclusions of those arguing that resource wealth leads governments to adopt statist policies, such as Richard Auty.[16] In the Latin American context, this study's findings side with the work of Jonathan Di John,[17] who has challenged the notion that statist policies are a byproduct of a resource curse, and goes against the works of Kurt Weyland and Manuel Hidalgo.[18] It is worth emphasizing that this contribution is about the proclivity for a certain type of policies and does not weigh in on the performance debate—i.e., whether resource dependence leads to poor economic performance—since the book focused on discussing the determinants of policy transformations rather than evaluating their success.

Similarly, a perspective based on economic conditions had difficulty accommodating Uruguay's adherence to orthodoxy following that country's severe economic crisis in 2001 through 2002, and Bolivia's and Ecuador's turn to statist policies amidst improving economic performance superior to the Latin American average at the turn of the 21st century. As the evidence from the left in government suggested, economic crises prompted leaders to make policy changes in some cases, as in Argentina when Néstor Kirchner took office, but to stay the course in others in the presence of financial instability, as in Brazil and Chile following the elections of Lula and Lagos, respectively.

While economic crises—broadly defined—played a role in effecting policy changes as Allan Drazen and Vittorio Grilli, Dani Rodrik, and Moisés Naím have argued,[19] the effect was indeterminate and it was difficult to establish what constituted a crisis ex ante, whether the prolonged deterioration of economic conditions in Venezuela, the drastic decrease of GDP in Argentina, or investors' nervousness in Brazil. These results support Michael Bruno and William Easterly's claim that poor economic performance, even if prolonged, does not generally lead to economic reforms.[20] This is because, as Anne Krueger has argued, crises may not generate change, since poor economic performance often leads to a vicious cycle: poor economic results generate the emergence of interest groups pushing for the perpetuation of current policy even if such policies are clearly suboptimal at the societal level.[21]

Instead, Bruno and Easterly's empirical test found that only crises defined as high inflation over a 40 percent threshold tend to prompt economic policy transformations.[22] This was the case of the adoption of market reforms across Latin America during the 1980s and 1990s,[23] but bouts with such high levels of inflation were absent at the time the left reached office. Even in Venezuela and Argentina, where inflation in some years spiked, yearly changes in the consumer price index have not surpassed the 31 and 25 percent marks, respectively.[24] Thus, this book's findings support the view of Javier Corrales and others who have argued that economic crises without high levels of inflation are not helpful determinants of reform in Latin America.[25]

Linking the roles of crises and executive powers, Stephan Haggard has noted that "one reason why crisis is associated with reform is not the nature of interest group conflict or changes in their policy preferences but a greater willingness during times of crises for legislators and the public to expand the discretionary authority of the president."[26] The evidence from leftist governments in Latin America provides only modest support for this proposition. As this study showed, the expansion of executive powers did not respond to crises in two out of three cases. In Bolivia and Ecuador, the new constitutional assemblies that expanded the president's prerogatives took place in a context of these two countries' best economic performance in decades. Only in Venezuela did the expansion of executive powers take place in the context of the protracted deterioration of economic conditions, although without the high levels of inflation discussed above.[27]

Finally, an explanation based on the relative strength of organized labor was unable to account for most cases. The wave of orthodox measures in the 1980s and 1990s severely undermined the political strength of organized labor,[28] making it hard for this sector to become a particularly influential player in shaping leftist governments' economic policies. This perspective had trouble accounting for statist policies in countries where organized labor was weakest, as in Bolivia and Ecuador, or where the power of organized labor had suffered most during the two decades leading up to the arrival of leftist presidents, as in Venezuela. It also had trouble accounting for pro-market policies in Brazil and Nicaragua, where the region's stronger labor organizations exist. This does not mean that organized labor's opposition was absent, but that it was not significant enough to prevent these changes from taking place. These findings support the views of Barbara Geddes, Stephan Haggard, and others authors whose works have been critical of the notion that organized labor is an influential driver of economic change.[29] Contrary to what Hector Schamis[30] and others have argued, "Democratic politicians have more autonomy from societal interests than old theories gave them credit for."[31] Having discussed the book's theoretical implications regarding a number of debates in the literature on Latin American politics, party systems, and economic reforms, the next section switches the emphasis to the left in government's performance.

Assessing the Left's Economic Performance in Latin America

A body of research on Latin America has warned about the perils of statist policies. Dubbed by scholars of Latin American political economy as "macroeconomic populism"[32] or "*facilismo económico*,"[33] the use of statist macroeconomic policy to achieve distributive goals has been associated with failed experiences "likely to end in inflationary disasters and economic collapse"[34] and even "failure, sorrow, and frustration."[35] In particular, these policies have been found to provide little relief for those sectors whose demands populist leaders claim to champion; instead, they have failed to benefit the poorest sectors of the population.[36] As a result, these policies had been predicted to become less and less common, particularly in the context of an increasingly interconnected global economy.[37]

Echoing these cautions, several scholars had warned about the arrival of the left to power in Latin America in general and the implementation of statist policies in particular. Those leftist governments following statist policies were referred to not only as macroeconomic populists,[38] but also pejoratively as "bourbon,"[39] "carnivore,"[40] and even "wrong."[41] Have leftist governments matched these expectations?

As shown in Chapter 2, the economic transformations conducted by leftist governments in the region far from constitute the abandonment of the market economy. Instead of resurrecting the revolutionary left, democratically elected leftist governments in the post-Cold War era have refrained from pursuing a generalized socialization of the means of production as was feared by many. Even in the case of Venezuela, with the highest degree of state intervention in the economy among countries in the region, Chávez's 21st century socialism has fallen short of socialist experiments in Castro's Cuba, Allende's Chile, and Ortega's revolutionary government in Nicaragua. Notwithstanding this difference in kind vis-à-vis the revolutionary left, however, it is worth evaluating how the left has fared in government and whether a relationship exists between the type of economic policies and performance indicators regarding growth, poverty, and inequality.

By and large, the leftist governments across the region have achieved economic results comparable to those of their predecessors. Most leftist governments have shown they can be as responsible economic stewards as their predecessors: passing unpopular reforms when necessary and delivering sound macroeconomic results. Furthermore, there is no discernible pattern regarding whether leftist governments following a particular policy orientation, statist or pro-market, performed better. Lastly, the left's moderate economic success is also shared by right-of-center governments.

Three indicators are illustrative in evaluating leftist governments' performance in comparative perspective: growth rates, poverty rates, and inequality. These measures are among the main tools used by the World Bank and international development agencies to assess whether government policies have an impact on the population.[42] Additionally, the amelioration of poverty and inequality has historically been among the left's main demands.[43]

Performance along the three indicators is shown in Figures 7.1, 7.2, and 7.3, respectively. Since not all governments were in office for the same number of years, performance is standardized by illustrating average yearly changes. Black bars correspond to the performance of the ten administrations—eight leftist administrations and two rightist governments—studied throughout the book. White bars reflect the performance of these governments' predecessors. Gray bars represent the difference between the two. Countries are organized based on this difference, from low to high. Leftist administrations are presented on the left-hand side and are separated from right-of-center governments by a vertical bar.

The left's record in office regarding economic growth is a far cry from the disastrous experiences of the revolutionary left. As Figure 7.1 suggests, there are differences in the extent to which governments have achieved economic growth, but all leftist governments averaged yearly growth rates above 3 percent, with the exception of Nicaragua. This means that most leftist administrations surpassed the world's average GDP growth rate of 2.5 percent for the period spanning all of these governments.[44]

With respect to their predecessors, the left in government presents a mixed picture depending on the country, but most leftist administrations have performed better. In five of the cases—Argentina, Bolivia, Brazil, Uruguay, and Venezuela—leftist governments' performance surpassed that of their predecessors. Underperformance in two of the remaining cases, Chile and Ecuador, does not mean that the left achieved poor growth. Quite the contrary, the left in these two countries performed relatively well, but their predecessors achieved growth rates of 5 percent or more.

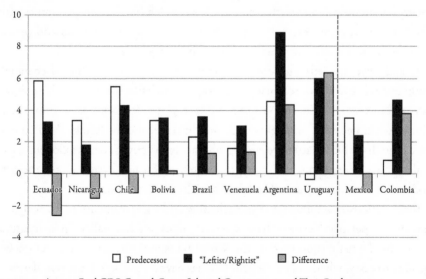

FIGURE 7.1 Average Real GDP Growth Rates, Selected Governments and Their Predecessors

NB: The Kirchner administration in Argentina is compared to the Menem administration in order to make the comparison meaningful by avoiding the 2001–2002 crisis; Dark bars correspond to governments in Bolivia (2006-present); Brazil (2003-present); Chile (2000–2006); Colombia (2002–2010); Ecuador (2007-present); Mexico (2000–2006); Nicaragua (2007-present); Uruguay (2005-present); Venezuela (1999-present).White bars correspond to their predecessors. Gray bars reflect the difference between dark and white bars.

Source: World Bank, *World Development Indicators*, 2011.

This made it difficult for leftist governments to surpass their predecessors' performance in spite of achieving respectable growth rates themselves.

High growth rates were not exclusively a left-of-center phenomenon, but they were not a generalized phenomenon either. Right-of-center administrations in Mexico and Colombia achieved very different growth rates. Colombia achieved the third largest average growth rate after Argentina and Uruguay, while Mexico achieved the second lowest next to Nicaragua. These results do not necessarily point to leftist economic policy changes as entirely responsible for growth—determining this connection is certainly a matter for a separate study—but the Figure suggests that the left should not be consigned to a reputation of economic profligacy.[45]

A second important indicator for the left is poverty reduction. Figure 7.2 reflects governments' progress in fighting poverty, defined as the percentage of the population earning less than US$2. All leftist governments have shown results in fighting poverty, with Argentina, Bolivia, and Ecuador making significant progress: more than 2 percent of the population escaped poverty every year on average. These figures are substantively significant: more than 194,000 people exited the ranks of the poor every year during the Morales administration, 336,000 people per year during Rafael Correa's administration, and one million people per year during Néstor Kirchner's administration.[46] These three governments' poverty alleviation efforts alone have certainly made a difference for the more than 6.7 million people who are no longer classified as poor in these countries.

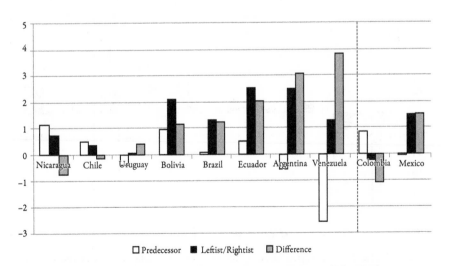

FIGURE 7.2 Average Yearly Change in Poverty Rates, Selected Governments and Their Predecessors

NB: Rates are calculated as a percentage of the total population. Annual averages were calculated to account for differences in the numbers of years in office. Positive bars reflect progress in reducing poverty, whereas negative bars reflect setbacks. The vertical line divides rightist and leftist administrations. Countries are organized based on the difference in rates between the leftist/rightist administration and its predecessor.

Source: World Bank, *World Development Indicators*, 2011.

Compared to their predecessors, leftist governments were much better able to ameliorate poverty. In all cases with the exception of Chile and Nicaragua, the leftist governments' performance surpassed that of their predecessors by far. This favorable performance bucks the trend prevailing in some countries where poverty rates increased before leftist presidents reached power, as was the case in Argentina, Uruguay, and Venezuela, or remained roughly the same, as in Brazil. As the gray bars show in Figure 7.2, the difference in average poverty alleviation rates between these countries' leftist administrations and their predecessors is significant. In contrast to Menem's presidency in Argentina, where 200,000 people joined the poor every year on average, Caldera's presidency in Venezuela, where the poor grew by half a million annually on average, or Batlle's presidency in Uruguay, where 12,000 Uruguayans fell into poverty each year, leftist governments in these countries represent a considerable improvement. The same is true for Bolivia, Brazil, and Ecuador, where, even though preceding administrations made some progress, leftist governments improved poverty abatement by at least 1 percent of the total population per year.

As with GDP growth rates, progress in fighting poverty is not exclusive to leftist governments. However, right-of-center governments presented a mixed record. Whereas the Fox administration achieved relatively high alleviation rates in Mexico, Uribe's government in Colombia was the only instance among our 10 cases where poverty indicators deteriorated. These results suggest that leftist governments have

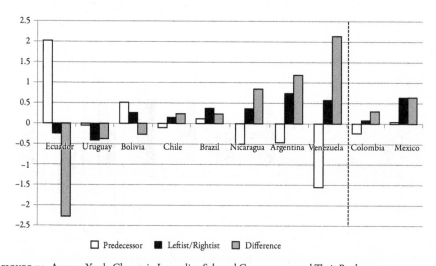

FIGURE 7.3 Average Yearly Change in Inequality, Selected Governments and Their Predecessors

NB: Change in inequality is based on Gini coefficients, ranging from 0 to 100. Annual averages were calculated to account for differences in the numbers of years in office. Positive bars reflect progress in reducing inequality, whereas negative bars reflect setbacks. The vertical line divides rightist and leftist administrations. Countries are organized based on the difference in rates between the leftist/rightist administration and its predecessor.

Source: World Bank, World Development Indicators, 2011.

been successful in reducing poverty across the region, compared both to their predecessors and to contemporaneous right-of-center administrations.

Finally, reducing inequality has historically been a third indicator of special significance for the left, although results have been more moderate compared to poverty alleviation. Figure 7.3 shows governments' progress in decreasing inequality, measured in terms of average annual changes in the Gini coefficient. Although not all leftist governments have made progress in addressing inequality—income distribution worsened in Ecuador and Uruguay—most administrations gained some ground. In particular, the Gini coefficient improved by more than half a point per year during the Kirchner administration in Argentina and the Chávez government in Venezuela.

Compared to their predecessors, progress among leftist governments is mixed. Leftist governments in Argentina, Nicaragua, and Venezuela stand out for the sharp contrast between their ability to address income inequality and their predecessors' negative results. In Brazil and Chile the record is also favorable although results are considerably more modest. In Bolivia, Ecuador, and Uruguay, leftist administrations have suffered setbacks in addressing inequality.

Compared to right-of-center governments in Colombia and Mexico, the left's record in addressing inequality appears modest. Progress addressing inequality among leftist administrations is only slightly better than in Colombia and in most cases lower than in Mexico. That the left did not clearly outperform right-of-center administrations in reducing inequality shows a disconnect between some of the left's main demands and its ability to follow through once in office.

All in all, the catastrophic economic results that prompted the abandonment of the state-interventionist ISI and the adoption of market reforms during the 1980s have not manifested themselves. Leftist governments have presided over moderately high growth rates and in most cases they have outperformed the governments they replaced. They have also made some progress in addressing inequality. However, the left's main economic success is poverty alleviation. In most cases, the difference between leftist administrations and their predecessors is noteworthy. This achievement may be the single most important accomplishment of the left in government on the economic front.

IMPLICATIONS FOR DEMOCRACY AND THE PREVALENCE OF MARKET ORTHODOXY

This general sense of economic competence has important implications for democracy and market orthodoxy as the prevailing economic model in Latin America. First, regarding implications for democratic rule, leftist governments have benefited from economic prosperity to convey an image of economic responsibility that translates into electoral viability. The reason is that the left's satisfactory performance has contributed to its establishment as a strong political alternative. Evidence of this is the consecutive election of leftist incumbents in Venezuela (2000 and 2006), Brazil (2006 and 2010), Chile (2006), Argentina (2007 and 2011), Bolivia (2009) Ecuador (2009), Uruguay (2009), and Nicaragua (2011).[47]

The left's electoral strength brings the benefit of broadening the spectrum of real electoral alternatives for voters.[48] Even if the left has had to move closer to the center of the spectrum in order to broaden its electoral support and gain electoral feasibility,[49] becoming a real contender to the presidency opened an important segment of the center-left previously unavailable or unviable. As the left enhances its economic responsibility credentials, electorates across the region become used to the idea of the alternation in power between the left and the right—a rare phenomenon until now. This alternation is a crucial aspect of a consolidated democracy.[50] In the words of Andreas Schedler, it is "the ultimate proof of any democratic electoral system."[51]

Second, regarding the implications for the prevailing market orthodoxy, leftist governments analyzed here have pushed out the boundaries set by neoliberal canons of what was possible in a globalized, post-Cold War world. As discussed in the Introduction, in the wake of the Soviet Union's collapse, the acceleration of financial interconnectedness, and the discredit of state intervention in the economy, governments seemed to be impelled to follow the playbook of market orthodoxy. Given capital's ability to move from one country to another whenever a government's economic policies—or political instability—were deemed unfavorable, policies such as nationalizations and debt defaults were seen as off-limits.[52]

Instead, the experience with leftist governments in the region at the turn of the century expanded the realm of the economically feasible within a framework of general market orthodoxy. Prominent examples are Kirchner's successful default and debt renegotiation in Argentina, and Venezuela and Bolivia's nationalizations in a variety of sectors. In the Argentine case, the move—the largest default of sovereign debt in history—became quite a success: the country secured greatly favorable terms for repayment and has regained partial access to credit markets.[53] In the case of Venezuela, the experience seems to be mixed: on the one hand, most energy companies chose to stay in spite of changes in the terms of contracts and drastic increases in royalties; on the other, that country is suffering the consequences of declining productivity and lack of technology as a result.[54] In the case of Bolivia, however, private consumption and foreign investment have increased following Morales's statist measures.[55] Difficult to imagine amidst the dominance of neoclassical economic thought among political and economic elites during the 1990s, such unorthodox policies have shown that there are viable alternatives beyond strict pro-market dogmatism.

However, the outward push of the boundaries of market orthodoxy should not be interpreted as a change in paradigm. Even in Venezuela, where the most significant statist policies have taken place, the market economy remains the prevailing mode of organization. Contrary to other studies that have emphasized differences across leftist governments,[56] this study showed that there are three ways in which their economic policies have converged. First, the privatizing trend of their predecessors was interrupted. With the exception of Chile, leftist governments put on hold the neoclassical mantra that the private sector can do things better. Instead, the idea behind the Kirchner government's claim that "the state can be as competitive as the private sector, if not more" seems to have resonated among leftist leaders.[57] Second, leftist governments emphasized the creation, reorganization, or expansion of poverty alleviation programs. These programs indicate that concern for inequality and social justice remained a priority, regardless of how moderate or drastic a government's agenda was, from Brazil's internationally acclaimed *Bolsa Família* to Venezuela's heavily criticized *Misiones*. Third, fiscal discipline remained a priority. In most cases, leftist governments tightened fiscal austerity and improved the position of the budget. As interviews with top economic decision makers in leftist governments revealed, fiscal discipline is regarded as necessary in order to create the minimum conditions to implement the government's policy agenda. In the words of Brazil's vice minister of finance, "fiscal discipline is not about ideology; it is what allows you to implement a leftist platform to begin with."[58] Or as Chile's former minister of the economy put it, "there is nothing leftist or rightist about sound economic policy, and that is what fiscal discipline is."[59] This view is strikingly similar to that of right-of-center governments. As Mexico's vice minister of the economy and former adviser to President Fox remarked, "without fiscal stringency, no government agenda will go very far."[60]

A Word on the Ends and the Means

In a region like Latin America, the unaddressed issue of extreme wealth inequality reminds us that reformism might seem glacial. On the other hand, a history plagued with regime breakdowns reminds us of the dangers of radical change. Whether the region requires more drastic economic measures or not is an important, controversial debate that raises passionate perspectives. As stated early in this study, the appropriate policy mix for a particular country might be determined by a combination of factors including its resource endowment, its capacity to carry out policies, and international factors, among other things. Thus, different countries require different combinations of pro-market and statist policies.

History has shown that extreme, dogmatic views seldom represent the best option for growth and development. Although the perception exists that Chile's faithful adoption of market orthodoxy during the Pinochet regime led to sustained economic growth, the blind adoption of market orthodoxy during the early years of the dictatorship first brought about a sharp economic crisis. It was not until the replacement of the ultra-orthodox economic cabinet and the "toning down" of neoliberalism that the country's much touted economic success took off.[61] The same can be argued for extreme state-interventionist experiences around the world, of which Allende's economic debacle constitutes a prominent example. Thus, neither extreme market orthodoxy nor extreme state-interventionism has proven to be a sound developmental alternative. This is particularly true in the long run, as extreme policy changes in either direction have been difficult to sustain in Latin America.

Regardless of where one stands in the debate, however, the findings of this study suggest that the process through which economic policy transformations are conducted matters in terms of guaranteeing the sustainability of such changes. The process of accommodation and consensus-building characteristic of highly institutionalized party systems might slow down the rate of reform, but it improves the sense of legitimacy of economic transformations and thus their chances of survival. In contrast, as party system institutionalization decreases, the rate of change can be accelerated, but the unilateral logic that prevails in party systems in disarray jeopardizes the chances of survival for drastic economic policy transformations. Even in the absence of ultimate veto players, such as the military intervening to topple a government conducting extreme transformations, the volatility that characterizes party systems in disarray makes it likely that the next president will reverse the aggressive economic policy transformations as easily as they were conducted in the first place.

HAS PARTY SYSTEM INSTITUTIONALIZATION MATTERED FOR ECONOMIC PERFORMANCE?

Most of the previous work on the effects of party systems on economic policies construed pro-market reforms as the natural path to achieve growth. These studies took for granted the correspondence between pro-market policies and economic development. Pro-market reforms were deemed as the "right type of policies." Haggard[62] and Haggard and Kaufman,[63] for example, argue that there is a correspondence between low levels of fragmentation and polarization, and economic performance. However, they reach this conclusion from a static perspective and by virtue of equating pro-market policies to desirable policies.

In the context of leftist governments in Latin America, performance does not correlate with the type of party system. As the previous sections showed, whether a party system is institutionalized or not is not a good predictor of growth, poverty alleviation, or improving income distribution (Figures 7.1, 7.2, and 7.3). However, the type of party system is a good predictor of economic *instability*. As Figure 7.4

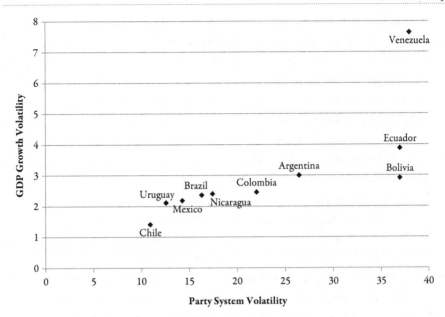

FIGURE 7.4 Party System Volatility and Economic Volatility, Selected Governments
Source: World Bank, *World Development Indicators*, 2011, and author's calculation of party system volatility. Economic volatility is measured as the standard deviation of yearly GDP growth rates for each administration.

shows, there is a correlation between party system institutionalization and volatility in economic performance, measured as the standard deviation of all yearly growth rates within an administration. Countries with high levels of party system institutionalization achieved consistent growth rates throughout the administration, whereas low levels of institutionalization correspond with large swings in economic performance. In Brazil, Chile, Nicaragua, and Uruguay, for example, leftist administrations oversaw growth rates with a standard deviation lower than 2.5 percentage points. In Argentina, Bolivia, Ecuador, and Venezuela, a typical deviation is larger than 3 percentage points. The volatility in growth rates during the Chávez administration represent an extreme case, with growth rates ranging from 18 percent to -9 percent and a typical deviation close to 8 percentage points. These results suggest that party systems in disarray may be conducive not only to economic volatility across administrations, where the succession of leaders with extreme policy positions make drastic changes likely from one administration to the next,[64] but also within administrations.

Economic volatility has been found to have negative consequences in the medium to long run, particularly regarding the sustainability of economic performance. As Ricardo Hausmann has argued, wild swings have important social, economic, and political implications.[65] They affect families, business, and political systems. Volatility prevents governments from carrying out effective long-term planning. Businesses are forced to write off investments and cancel new projects. Firms cannot offer job security since conditions are likely to change. International investors prefer to seek short-term gain through portfolio speculation and avoid channeling their money into direct investment because of uncertainty and the difficulties for decision making. As a result, people are likely to lose their jobs and families are less able to keep their children in school. Their savings may be wiped out in the next downturn, so they are likely to put their assets in hard foreign currency. Lacking insurance against these adversities, the poorest sectors of society are hit hardest. In short, even if spectacularly high growth rates are sometimes achieved, volatility inevitably shortens the time horizon of economic actors, hinders economic activity, and disproportionately affects the lives of the poor.

To the extent that poorly institutionalized party systems contribute to economic volatility, they also help to fuel these ailments. Allowing for significant economic transformations to take place without much deliberation and consensus, poorly institutionalized party systems are likely to lead to mistakes in the decision making process. Without deliberation, decisions are rushed through and poorly considered. Without taking relevant interests into account, party systems in disarray invite the abuse of power and corruption. These issues affect a country's economic growth *potential*.

Although the analysis presented here focused on economic policy changes conducted by leftist governments, the instability that results from the lack of party system institutionalization seems to hold true for other spheres as well. Governments in highly institutionalized party systems are moderate not only regarding their economic policies, but in a variety of government actions. They rely on the predictability of the different parties' positions and stake in the preservation of the system to build consensus and accommodate differing views, not only in the economic realm but also in political, social, and cultural matters. Conversely, governments with weakly institutionalized party systems tend to conduct radical policy changes by sidelining dissenting perspectives in a variety of issues beyond the economic realm. They circumvent moderating institutions, such as the legislature and the courts, to establish a direct link between the president and the population in order to implement drastic policy changes. Thus, depending on the degree of institutionalization of the party system, other aspects of the polity, such as foreign relations, executive-legislative relations, judicial independence—to name a few—are affected in a similar vein as is economic policy.

A prominent example is the executive's proclivity to rewrite the rules of the game in a party system in disarray. The combination of political outsiders reaching the presidency and parties' inability to shape the presidents' policies generated a fertile ground for the writing of new constitutions. Following through on their promise to dismantle an entrenched political class—referred to as "plunderers,"[66] or "the sewer,"[67] depending in on the country—outsider presidents in party systems in disarray convened constitutional assemblies to "refound" the republic.

Many of the provisions in the new constitutions are welcome changes: the new constitutional texts have often strengthened citizenship rights, made societies more inclusionary for minorities and indigenous groups, and protected the environment. In Venezuela, indigenous groups gained access to political representation, enjoying reserved seats in the national and local legislatures, and a series of human rights were enshrined in the 1999 Constitution.[68] In Bolivia, the 2009 Constitution recognizes a plurinational and pluricultural state, recognizes indigenous autonomies at the local level, and reserves seats in the legislature for indigenous groups.[69] In Ecuador, the 2008 Constitution granted nature the inalienable right to exist, at least on paper.[70]

However, the new texts have also contributed significantly to the concentration of power in the hands of the president. By calling for constitutional conventions, presidents have often modified executive-legislative relations in significant ways, granting the president decree powers and undermining the legislature and the judiciary's ability to check executive power.[71] This formula of election-contention-constitutional convention was followed successfully in Venezuela and later adopted by Bolivia and Ecuador.

Even though the constitutional assemblies have been convened after consulting voters through popular plebiscites, the elaboration and approval of the constitutional texts has been far from consensual.[72] Instead, these processes were characterized by high levels of contention among political forces, polarization, and in some cases low voter participation.[73] In Ecuador, the president and the legislature clashed over the appropriate way to reform the Constitution, with the legislature opposing Correa's efforts to dissolve Congress and convene a constitutional assembly in order to completely rewrite the Constitution. The disagreement over the legality of a referendum for the constitutional convention escalated into open confrontation. Correa publicly referred to legislators as "cavemen, traitors, and pseudo-representatives" and called for "popular pressure" against Congress.[74] Following riots and the takeover of Congress by pro-Correa demonstrators, the rift ended after 57 opposition legislators were sacked.[75]

In Bolivia, the opposition to the constitutional process among some sectors generated violence and even put the country at the brink of secession. Morales referred to these sectors' opposition as "responding to fascist motivations," and denounced their intention to push the country to a civil war.[76] The opposition in turn relied on racist rhetoric against the government's efforts. Even though the new Constitution was approved at the national level, the new text was rejected in the departments of Santa Cruz, Tarija, Beni, and Pando, where referendums to acquire autonomy from the national government were held.[77]

In Venezuela, the new Constitution was approved with low levels of proportionality.[78] In spite of the opposition's mustering a third of the vote to elect the Constitutional Assembly, only six out of 131 seats (5 percent) went to anti-Chavista delegates. Following the beginning of the Constitution writing in August 1999, the directorate of the Constitutional Assembly issued a decree in November restricting the extent of the debate in order to fast-track the approval of the constitutional text.[79] Supreme Court judges who expressed reservations about the legality of the process were pressured to resign, and when the National Congress, local legislatures, courts, and electoral service were officially disbanded under the new Constitution, the Constitutional Assembly appointed their replacements without elections for several months.[80]

As discussed throughout the book, the rewriting of the rules of the game in these countries gave the executives the upper hand in carrying out their economic projects by circumventing the legislature. Since political parties were unable to translate the demands of different sectors of society into shaping the executive's policy, plebiscitary rule became the avenue of choice. This way of transforming the rules of the game without a broad consensus does not bode well for the sustainability of the reforms once these governments are out of office. Thus, even if important gains were achieved in citizenship, social, and collective rights in the new constitutions, the way they were achieved jeopardizes their permanence in time.

In short, the consequences of party systems in disarray contribute to perpetuate Latin American countries' ailments regarding horizontal accountability, or what Guillermo O'Donnell has referred to as delegative democracy.[81] The election-contention-constitutional convention formula followed in party systems in disarray has contributed to undermine horizontal accountability in these countries. The legislature and the courts are less able to serve as checks and balances to the president. Presidents are able to rule by decree, they are able to stay longer in office, and the powers of the legislature are curtailed. As long as parties remain unable to represent society's demands in the political arena and enjoy enough traction to shape the executive's policies, horizontal accountability will continue to suffer.

The combination of these two considerations—that the type of party system does not correlate with economic performance but does correlate with volatility—suggests that leftist governments in party systems in disarray may be walking a tight rope. On the one hand, they have managed to improve on their predecessors' performance by presiding over moderate levels of growth, alleviating poverty, and ameliorating inequality. On the other, the volatility that characterizes patterns of interparty competition in these systems permeates into the policy sphere, translating into economic uncertainty and unrealized growth potential. Even though countries with party systems in disarray have shown comparable performance as their institutionalized counterparts, their longer-term prospects are less promising. Not only does economic activity find it more difficult to prosper in environments prone to extreme policy changes that make planning difficult, but the sustainability of leftist governments' accomplishments may be precarious. Thus, even though leftist governments have built a reputation of electoral viability regardless of the type of party system in which they rose to power, the sustainability of their project is jeopardized as long as there is no conscious effort to strengthen mediating institutions that bring horizontal accountability and that are conducive to consensual politics.

Although this is no minor task, it is not a chimera, either. All of the alternative explanations examined here are deterministic in one way or another. Although governments may seek to diversify their economies, they cannot modify their resource endowments. Although crises may contribute to effect change in some cases, it would be irresponsible to try to generate them. Although governments may attempt to undermine the influence of interest groups opposed to reform and strengthen those groups in favor, they cannot do away with interest groups or their preferences in a democracy. In short, emphasizing structure and being deterministic, these factors are generally removed from the policy maker's reach. In the words of Bhagwati, Brecher, and Srinivasan, they constitute a "determinacy paradox," where the causes of a particular phenomenon are beyond the reach of human agency and moving to action becomes a moot point.[82]

Instead, an explanation based on party systems makes room for agency in the short to medium run. Leaders of all stripes can invest in institutional development. They can invest in the party structure, training cadres and establishing rules and procedures. They can invest in giving different actors a stake in the system and allowing them to shape policy through legislative bargaining. Bringing much-needed results regarding economic growth, poverty, and inequality for the population is only half the battle. Creating the conditions for this performance to be sustainable is a much more difficult task. That is the challenge that lies ahead.

Appendix A

TABLE A.1

LEFTIST VICTORIES IN PRESIDENTIAL ELECTIONS IN LATIN AMERICA, 1998–2010

Country	Date	Winning Leftist Candidate	% of Vote	% of Vote	Difference	Main Rival
Argentina	April 27, 2003**	Néstor Kirchner (FPV)	22.0	24.4	-2.4	Carlos Menem (FPL)
	Oct. 28, 2007*	Cristina Fernández (FPV)	45.3	23.0	22.3	Elisa Carrió (Coalición Cívica)
Bolivia	Dec. 18, 2005*	Evo Morales (MAS)	53.7	28.6	25.1	Jorge Quiroga (PODEMOS)
	Dec. 6, 2009*	Evo Morales (MAS)	64.2	26.5	37.7	Manfred Villa (Plan Progreso para Bolivia / Convergencia Nacional)
Brazil	Oct. 6, 2002 (1st round)	Lula da Silva (PT)	46.4	23.2		José Serra (PSDB)
	Oct. 27, 2002		61.3	38.7	22.6	
	Oct. 1, 2006 (1st round)	Lula da Silva (PT)	48.6	41.6		Geraldo Alckmin (PSDB)
	Oct. 29, 2006		60.8	39.2	21.6	
	Oct. 3, 2010 (1st round)	Dilma Rousseff (PT)	46.9	32.6		José Serra (PSDB)
	Oct. 31, 2010		56.1	43.9	12.2	

Country	Date	Winner (party)				Runner-up (party)
Chile***	Dec. 12, 1999 (1st round)	Ricardo Lagos (PPD)	48.0	47.5		Joaquín Lavín (UDI)
	Jan. 16, 2000		51.3	48.7	2.6	Sebastián Piñera (RN)
	Dec. 11, 2005	Michelle Bachelet (PS)	46.0	25.4		
	Jan. 15, 2006		53.5	46.5	7.0	
Ecuador	Oct. 15, 2006	Rafael Correa (PAÍS)	22.8	26.8		Álvaro Noboa (PRIAN)
	Nov. 26, 2006		56.7	43.3	13.4	
	April 26, 2009*	Rafael Correa (PAÍS)	51.9	28.2	23.7	Lucio Gutiérrez (Sociedad Patriótica)
Nicaragua	Nov. 5, 2006*	Daniel Ortega (FSLN)	38.0	28.3	9.7	Eduardo Montealegre (ALN)
Uruguay	Oct. 31, 2004*	Tabaré Vázquez (FA)	51.7	35.1	16.6	Jorge Larrañaga (Partido Nacional)
	Oct. 25, 2009 (1st round)	José Mújica (FA)	47.9	29.1		Luis Alberto Lacalle (Partido Nacional)
	Nov. 29, 2009		52.4	43.5	8.9	
Venezuela	Dec. 6, 1998*	Hugo Chávez (MVR)	56.2	40.0	16.2	Henrique Salas Römer (Proyecto Venezuela)
	July 30, 2000*	Hugo Chávez (MVR)	59.8	37.5	22.3	Francisco Arias (Causa Radical)
	Dec. 3, 2006*	Hugo Chávez (MVR)	62.8	36.9	25.9	Manuel Rosales (Nuevo Tiempo)

*No need for a second round.

**There was a need for a second round, but Carlos Menem withdrew from the race.

***A leftist candidate lost in Chile's presidential elections held on Dec.13, 2009 (first round) and January 17, 2010 (second round).

Sources: Ministerio del Interior de Argentina, Corte Nacional Electoral de Bolivia, Tribunal Superior Eleitoral do Brasil, Tribunal Calificador de Chile, Tribunal Supremo Electoral de Ecuador, Consejo Supremo Electoral de Nicaragua, Tribunal Supremo Electoral de Perú, Corte Electoral de Uruguay, Consejo Nacional Electoral de Venezuela

Appendix B: Data for Hypothesis Testing in Chapter 3

PARTY SYSTEM VOTE VOLATILITY

Country	Period	Volatility
Chile	1993–2001	10.99
Uruguay	1994–2004	14.31
Brazil	1994–2002	15.12
Mexico	1994–2000	15.76
Nicaragua	1996–2006	17.42
Colombia	1994–2002	22.45
Argentina	1999–2003	26.43
Bolivia	1997–2005	37.0
Ecuador	1998–2006	37.5
Venezuela	1988–1998	38.0

Source: Author's calculations based on Pedersen's Index of Volatility, which reflects the net aggregate vote shifts from one election to another and is calculated as the sum of the absolute changes in vote share across all parties divided by two. Mogens Pedersen, "Changing Patterns of Electoral Volatility in European Party Systems, 1948–1977: Explorations in Explanation," in *Western European Party Systems: Continuity and Change*, eds. Hans Daalder and Peter Mair (London: Sage, 1983).

TABLE B.2

PARTY SYSTEM FRAGMENTATION

Country	Year	Seat Fragmentation
Bolivia	2005	2.36
Uruguay	2004	2.39
Mexico	2000	2.55
Nicaragua	2006	3.13
Argentina	2003	5.0
Ecuador	2006	5.9
Venezuela	1998	6.05
Chile	2001	6.1
Colombia	2002	7.3
Brazil	2002	8.49

Source: Author's calculations of party system fragmentation, calculated based on the Laagso and Taagapera Index of Seat Fragmentation in the legislature at the time when presidents reached office. The exception is Chile, where Ricardo Lagos became president in 2000 and legislative elections were held the following year. The formula to compute the index is $1/\Sigma_i^n (P_i^2)$, where n is the number of parties with at least one seat in the lower chamber, and P_i^2 is the square of each party's proportion of all seats.

TABLE B.3

EXECUTIVE POWERS, CA. 2004

Country	Index of Executive Power
Nicaragua	0.19
Bolivia	0.23
Mexico	0.24
Venezuela	0.3
Uruguay	0.38
Argentina	0.44
Ecuador	0.59
Colombia	0.59
Brazil	0.62
Chile	0.66

Source: United Nations Development Program, *Democracy in Latin America: Towards a Citizens' Democracy*, 2004.

TABLE B.4

PREVAILING ECONOMIC CONDITIONS

Country	Period	% Change in GDP Per Capita
Argentina	1999–2003	-24
Uruguay	2000–2004	-17
Colombia	1998–2002	-6
Venezuela	1994–1998	-1
Brazil	1998–2002	1
Bolivia	2001–2005	5
Chile	1996–2000	11
Nicaragua	2002–2006	13
Mexico	1996–2000	15
Ecuador	2002–2006	22

Source: World Bank, *World Development Indicators*, 2010.

TABLE B.5

NATURAL RESOURCE EXPORTS

Country	Period	Main Commodity Exports as a % of Total Exports	Commodity Exports as a % of Total Exports
Argentina	2003–2007	14	69
Bolivia	2006–2009	33	85
Brazil	2003–2009	12	48
Chile	2000–2006	49	85
Colombia	2002–2009	26	64
Ecuador	2007–2009	49	90
Mexico	2000–2006	14	19
Nicaragua	2007–2009	18.5	89
Uruguay	2005–2009	24	65
Venezuela	1998–2009	85	90

Source: UN Economic Commission for Latin America and the Caribbean, *Statistical Yearbook 2010* (Santiago de Chile: ECLAC, 2010). Table 2.2.2.1

TABLE B.6

DEPTH OF NEOLIBERALISM, CA. 1999

Country	Index of Neoliberal Reform
Venezuela	0.667
Colombia	0.792
Ecuador	0.801
Brazil	0.805
Mexico	0.807
Bolivia	0.816
Chile	0.843
Argentina	0.888
Uruguay	0.891

Source: Morley, Machado, and Pettinato, "Indexes of Structural Reforms in Latin America," *Serie Reformas Económicas*, UN ECLAC, January 1999. Nicaragua was not included in the Morley, Machado, and Pettinato's index as is therefore not included here.

TABLE B.7

STRENGTH OF ORGANIZED LABOR, CA. 1997

Country	Union Density as a % of Work Force
Colombia	12.1
Chile	13.1
Ecuador	13.5
Uruguay	16.3
Bolivia	16.4
Venezuela	18.0
Argentina	21.5
Mexico	22.4
Nicaragua	23.4
Brazil	24.8

Source: Inter-American Development Bank, *Good Jobs Wanted: Labor Markets in Latin America* (Washington, DC: IADB, 2004).

Notes

CHAPTER I

1. "Morales nacionaliza el negocio del gas y toma el control de 5 compañías," *La Razón* (Bolivia), May 1, 2006. Ownership was transferred to the Bolivian state, even though not all facilities were 100 percent privately owned (as was the case with those belonging to Brazilian oil company Petrobras, which has a majority state ownership).

2. "Chávez ordenó nacionalizar CANTV y el sector eléctrico," *El Universal* (Venezuela), January 9, 2007.

3. "Kirchner criticó a supermercados y salieron a responderle," *El Clarín*, November 24, 2005.

4. Throughout the book, I use the term "government" to refer specifically to the national government unless otherwise noted.

5. Jorge Castañeda, "Latin America's Left Turn," *Foreign Affairs* 85:3 (2006).

6. Sebastian Edwards op-ed, "Chile's 'New Socialist' Bids for the Presidency," *The Wall Street Journal*, June 4, 1999.

7. "O PT está preparado para a Presidência?" *Revista Veja*, September 25, 2002.

8. Speech delivered by Evo Morales in Tiahuanacu, Bolivia, on January 21, 2006.

9. All the cases are presidential, multiparty systems that transitioned to democracy and abandoned the ISI model roughly around the same period, and share features of the Iberian-Catholic tradition. Howard Wiarda, *Politics and Social Change in Latin America: Still a Distinct Tradition?* (Boulder, CO: Westview Press, 1992).

10. David Samuels, "From Socialism to Social-Democracy: Party Organization and the Transformation of the Worker's Party in Brazil," *Comparative Political Studies* 37:9 (2004). Wendy Hunter, "The Normalization of an Anomaly: The Workers Party in Brazil," *World Politics* 59:3 (2007); Jorge Lanzaro, "El Frente Amplio: Estructura y claves de desarrollo," in *La izquierda*

uruguaya entre oposición y gobierno, ed. Jorge Lanzaro (Montevideo: Editorial Fin de Siglo, 2004). Juan Pablo Luna, "Frente Amplio and the Crafting of a Social Democratic Alternative in Uruguay," *Latin American Politics and Society* 49:4 (2007).

11. Matthew Cleary, "A Left Turn in Latin America? Explaining the Left's Resurgence," *Journal of Democracy* 17:4 (2006).

12. Andy Baker and Kenneth Greene, "The Latin American Left's Mandate: Free Market Policies and Issue Voting in New Democracies," *World Politics* 63:1 (2011).

13. Teodoro Petkoff, *Las dos izquierdas* (Caracas: Alfadil, 2005); Franklin Ramírez Gallegos, "Mucho más que dos izquierdas," *Nueva Sociedad* 205 (2006); Steven Levitsky and Kenneth Roberts, "Latin America's Left Turn: A Framework for Analysis," in *The Resurgence of the Latin American Left*, ed. Steven Levitsky and Kenneth Roberts (Baltimore, MD: Johns Hopkins University Press, 2011); Maxwell Cameron, "Latin America's Left Turns: Beyond Good and Bad," *Third World Quarterly* 30:2 (2009).

14. Jorge Castañeda, *Utopia Unarmed* (New York: Knopf, 1993); Kenneth Roberts, *Deepening Democracy? The Modern Left and Social Movements in Chile and Peru*, (Stanford, CA: Stanford University Press, 1998); Hector Schamis, "A Left Turn in Latin America? Populism, Socialism, and Democratic Institutions," *Journal of Democracy* 17:4 (2006).

15. Deborah Yashar, "The Left and Citizenship Rights," in *The Resurgence of the Latin American Left*, ed. Levitsky and Roberts.

16. Two exceptions are Kurt Weyland, Raúl Madrid, and Wendy Hunter, *Leftist Governments in Latin America: Successes and Shortcomings* (New York: Cambridge University Press, 2010) and Steven Levitsky and Kenneth Roberts (eds.) *The Resurgence of the Latin American Left* (Baltimore, MD: Johns Hopkins University Press, 2011).

17. Measured in 2006 US dollars. World Bank, *World Development Indicators Online*, 2010.

18. Scott Mainwaring and Timothy Scully, "Introduction: Party Systems in Latin America," in *Building Democratic Institutions: Party Systems in Latin America*, ed. Scott Mainwaring and Timothy Scully (Stanford, CA: Stanford University Press, 1995); Joe Foweraker, "Institutional Design, Party Systems, and Governability: Differentiating the Presidential Regimes of Latin America," *British Journal of Political Science* 28 (1998); Michael Coppedge, "Party Systems, Governability, and the Quality of Democracy in Latin America" (Paper prepared for presentation at the conference on "Representation and Democratic Politics in Latin America," organized by the Department of Humanities of the Universidad de San Andrés and the Department of Political Science of the University of Pittsburgh, Buenos Aires, Argentina, June 7–8, 2001); Michelle Kuenzi and Gina Lambright, "Party System Institutionalization in 30 African Countries," *Party Politics* 7 (2001); Vicky Randall and Lars Svasand, "Party Institutionalization in New Democracies," *Party Politics* 8 (2002); Scott Mainwaring and Mariano Torcal, "Party System Institutionalization and Party System Theory after the Third Wave of Democratization" in *Handbook of Political Parties*, eds. Richard Katz and William Crotty (London: Sage Publications, 2006); Scott Mainwaring and Edurne Zoco, "Political Sequences and the Stability on Interparty Competition," *Party Politics* 13:2 (2007).

19. Haggard and Kaufman's cases are Argentina, Bolivia, Brazil, Chile, Mexico, Peru, Philippines, South Korea, Taiwan, Turkey, Thailand, and Uruguay.

20. Stephan Haggard and Robert Kaufman, *The Political Economy of Democratic Transitions* (Princeton, NJ: Princeton University Press, 1995).

21. Carol Wise, "Review of The Political Economy of Democratic Transitions, by Stephan Haggard and Robert Kaufman," *Journal of Latin American Studies* 28:3 (1996).

22. Haggard and Kaufman, *The Political Economy of Democratic Transitions*, 370.

23. Haggard and Kaufman, *The Political Economy of Democratic Transitions*, 8.

24. Haggard and Kaufman, *The Political Economy of Democratic Transitions*, 10.

25. Instead, Haggard and Kaufman point to executive authority as a determinant factor to initiate reforms. This factor is discussed along with alternative explanations in Chapter 3.

26. Haggard and Kaufman, *The Political Economy of Democratic Transitions*, 153.

27. Kurt Weyland, "The Rise of Latin America's Two Lefts: Insights from Rentier State Theory," *Comparative Politics* 41:2 (2009); Manuel Hidalgo, "Hugo Chavez's 'Petro Socialism,'" *Journal of Democracy* 20:2 (2009), 78–92; Michael Shifter, "In Search of Hugo Chávez," *Foreign Affairs* (May/June 2006); Christian Perenti, "Hugo Chávez and Petro Populism," *The Nation*, April 11, 2005.

28. Haggard and Kaufman, *The Political Economy of Democratic Transitions* (1995); Karen Remmer, "The Politics of Neoliberal Reform in South America," *Studies in Comparative International Development* 33 (1998); Kurt Weyland, "Swallowing the Bitter Pill: Sources of Popular Support for Neoliberal Reform in Latin America," *Comparative Political Studies* 31:5 (October) 1998; John Waterbury, "The Heart of the Matter? Public Enterprise and the Adjustment Process," in *The Politics of Economic Adjustment*, eds. Haggard and Kaufman (Princeton, NJ: Princeton University Press, 1992).

29. Haggard and Kaufman, *The Political Economy of Democratic Transitions* (1995). Stephan Haggard, "Interests, Institutions, and Policy Reform," in Economic Policy Reform: The Second Stage, ed. Anne Krueger (Chicago: University of Chicago Press, 2000); Stephen Holmes, "The Politics of Economics in the Czech Republic," *East European Constitutional Review* 4 (Spring 1995), 52–55.

30. Ronald McKinnon, *The Order of Economic Liberalization: Financial Control in the Transition to a Market Economy* (Baltimore: Johns Hopkins University Press, 1991); Dani Rodrik, "How Should Structural Adjustment Programs Be Designed?" *World Development* 18:7 (1990); Rudiger Dornbusch, "Credibility and Stabilization," *Quarterly Journal of Economics*, 106 (1991).

31. Schamis, *Reforming the State: The Politics of Privatization in Latin America and Europe*; Barbara Geddes, "Challenging the Conventional Wisdom," *Journal of Democracy*, 6:4 (1994); Steven Levitsky and Lucan Way, "Between a Shock and a Hard Place: The Dynamics of Labor Based Adjustment in Argentina and Poland," *Comparative Politics*, 30:2 (1998).

32. Erik Wibbels and Moisés Arce, "Globalization, Taxation, and Burden Shifting in Latin America," *International Organization* 57 (2003).

33. Barbara Stallings, *Growth, Equity, and Employment: The Impact of the Economic Reforms in Latin America* (Washington, DC: The Brookings Institution Press, 2000), 5.

34. Eduardo Silva, "From Dictatorship to Democracy: The Business-State Nexus in Chile's Economic Transformation, 1975–1994," *Comparative Politics* 28:3 (1996).

35. Albert O. Hirschman, "The Political Economy of Import-Substituting Industrialization in Latin America," *The Quarterly Journal of Economics* (1968), 5, Brian Potter, "Constricting Contestation, Coalitions, and Purpose: The Causes of Neoliberal Restructuring and Its Failures," *Latin American Perspectives* 34:3 (2007), 7.

36. Hirschman, "The Political Economy of Import-Substituting Industrialization in Latin America," 5.

37. Hirschman, "The Political Economy of Import-Substituting Industrialization in Latin America," 1–32.

38. Cuba experienced some economic opening, but the economy remained centrally planned. See Susan Eckstein, *Back from the Future: Cuba under Castro* (Princeton, NJ: Princeton University Press, 1994). For this reason, Cuba is excluded from this analysis.

39. For a classification of the timing of the adoption of structural reforms, see Sebastian Edwards, *Crisis and Reform in Latin America: from Despair to Hope* (Washington, DC: World Bank, 1995).

40. Some of the most emblematic transformers were Mexico's Miguel de la Madrid (1982–1988) and Carlos Salinas de Gortari (1988–1994), Argentina's Carlos Menem (1989–1999), Venezuela's Carlos Andrés Pérez (1989–1993), Peru's Alberto Fujimori (1990–2000), Bolivia's Gonzalo Sánchez de Lozada (1993–1997), and Brazil's Fernando Henrique Cardoso (1995–2003).

41. Kurt Weyland, "Threats to Latin America's Market Model?" *Political Science Quarterly* 119:2 (2004).

42. Evelyn Huber and Fred Solt, "Successes and Failures of Neoliberalism," *Latin American Research Review* 39:3 (2004), 3.

43. Joseph Cohen and Miguel Angel Centeno, "Neoliberalism and Patterns of Economic Performance, 1980–2006," ANNALS, AAPSS 606 (2006).

44. Jorge Domínguez, "Free Markets and Free Politics in Latin America," *Journal of Democracy* 9:4 (1998), 73.

45. Francis Fukuyama, "The End of History?" *The National Interest* (Summer 1989).

46. Andy Baker, "Why Is Trade Reform So Unpopular?" *World Politics* 55:3 (2003), 423.

47. James Cypher, "The Slow Death of the Washington Consensus in Latin America," *Latin American Perspectives* 25:6 (1998), 47.

48. Potter, "Constricting Contestation, Coalitions, and Purpose: The Causes of Neoliberal Restructuring and Its Failures," 16.

49. Dani Rodrik, "Understanding Economic Policy Reform," *Journal of Economic Literature* 34 (1996), 9.

50. Cited in Potter, "Constricting Contestation, Coalitions, and Purpose: The Causes of Neoliberal Restructuring and Its Failures."

51. In 1968, two decades after the adoption of ISI, Albert O. Hirschman denounced those who announced the loss of steam of the model as promoters of *fracasomanía*.

52. Cleary, "A Left Turn in Latin America? Explaining the Left's Resurgence," 35.

53. Castañeda, *Utopia Unarmed*; Kenneth Roberts, *Deepending Democracy? The Modern Left and Social Movements in Chile and Peru* (Stanford, CA: Stanford University Press, 1998), 21.

54. Steve Ellner, "The Changing Status of the Latin American Left," in *The Latin American Left: From the Fall of Allende to Perestroika*, ed. Steve Ellner and Barry Carr (Boulder, CO: Westview Press, 1993), 1.

55. Guillermo O'Donnell and Philippe Schmitter, *Transitions from Authoritarian Rule: Tentative Conclusions about Uncertain Democracies* (Baltimore, MD: Johns Hopkins University Press, 1986), 38–45.

56. In Chile's "protected democracy," institutional constraints included Pinochet remaining as commander in chief of Chile's armed forces, the existence of institutional senators, and the binomial electoral system. For an overview, see Jonathan Barton, "State Continuismo and Pinochetismo: The Keys to the Chilean Transition," *Bulletin of Latin American Research*, 21:3 (2002).

57. Alfred Stepan, *Rethinking Military Politics: Brazil and the Southern Cone* (Princeton, NJ: Princeton University Press, 1988).

58. Charles Gillespie, "Uruguay's Return to Democracy," *Bulletin of Latin American Research* 4:2 (1985). In both Brazil and Uruguay most of these prerogatives were gradually dismantled during the 1980s.

59. A case in point is the murder in July 1988 of two of leftist candidate Cuauhtémoc Cárdenas's close aides, Francisco Xavier Obando and Román Gil.

60. With the exception of Mexico, where the military remained loyal to the PRI regime.

61. Benjamin Rattenbach, *Sociología Militar* (Buenos Aires: Librería Perlado, 1958).

62. In Uruguay in 1992, for example, the armed forces refused to obey President Luis Alberto Lacalle's order to confront police out on strike. In 1993 rumors of a coup forced the president to cut short a trip in Europe. "Tensa situación en Uruguay por actuación de militares," *La Nación*, June 12, 1993. In Chile, Pinochet's *acuartelamiento*—when the army was called to the barracks to conduct a "readiness exercise"—on December 19, 1990, nine months after Aylwin took office, was a reminder of the risks involved in stepping on Pinochet's and the military's toes while attempting to reform the restrictions to democracy introduced in the 1980 Constitution. As Silva puts it, "It was obvious that the real goal of this show of force was to warn the government to back off." Another incident, known as *"El boinazo"* took place in May 1993 when the military's high command met in full combat clothes and "combat ready black beret elite clothes were deployed with the backing of armored vehicles" in front of the Moneda presidential palace. The incident responded to a legislative investigation "linking Pinochet to a series of irregular financial transactions." Patricio Silva, "Searching for Civilian Supremacy: The Concertación Governments and the Military in Chile," *Bulletin of Latin American Research* 21:3 (2002), 383. See also Gregory Weeks, "The Long Road to Civilian Supremacy over the Military: Chile 1990–1998," *Studies in Comparative International Development*, 35:2 (2000); Claudio Fuentes, "After Pinochet: Civilian Politics towards the Military," *Journal of Inter-American Studies and World Affairs*, 42:3 (2000). In Brazil, as Hagopian has noted, "the fear of a coup was not irrational. Security forces had attempted in 1981 to sabotage the *abertura* by planting a bomb [...] at the Riocentro complex in Rio de Janeiro during a public gathering on May Day. Once it became apparent in 1984 that Neves had the votes to triumph in the electoral college, the PMDB steeled itself for a coup expected to originate in Brasília under the command of General Newton Cruz." Frances Hagopian, "Democracy by Undemocratic Means?: Elites, Political Pacts, and Regime Transition in Brazil," *Comparative Political Studies* 23:2 (1990), 155. Similarly, Bolívar Lamounier conveys a sense of realism of the threat as late as 1993 by recounting a Brazilian senator's view that, "No more than a jeep with four soldiers would be needed, if the military really wanted to shut down the national Congress." Bolivar Lamounier, "Brazil: The Hyperactive Paralysis Syndrome," in *Constructing Democratic Governance*. ed. Jorge Domínguez and Abraham Lowenthal, (Baltimore, MD: Johns Hopkins University Press, 1996), 166.

63. Castañeda, "Latin America's Left Turn."

64. Raúl Madrid, "Laboring against Neoliberalism: Unions and Patterns of Reform in Latin America," *Journal of Latin American Studies* 35:1 (2003); Steven Levitsky, *Transforming Labor Based Parties in Latin America: Argentine Peronism in Comparative Perspective* (New York, NY: Cambridge University Press, 2003); María Victoria Murillo, "From Populism to Neoliberalism: Labor Unions and Market Reforms in Latin America," *World Politics* 52:2 (2000); Paul Almeida,

"Defensive Mobilization: Popular Movements against Economic Adjustment Policies in Latin America," *Latin American Perspectives* 34:3 (2007).

65. Murillo, "From Populism to Neoliberalism: Labor Unions and Market Reforms in Latin America," 141.

66. Murillo, "From Populism to Neoliberalism: Labor Unions and Market Reforms in Latin America," 114.

67. Murillo, "From Populism to Neoliberalism: Labor Unions and Market Reforms in Latin America," 114.

68. Steve Ellner, "The Changing Status of the Latin American Left in the Recent Past," in *The Latin American Left: From the Fall of Allende to Perestroika*, ed. Steve Ellner and Barry Carr (Boulder, CO: Westview Press, 1993), 4.

69. Castañeda, *Utopia Unarmed*, 3.

70. Roberts, *Deepending Democracy? The Modern Left and Social Movements in Chile and Peru*.

71. Examples of progress on this matter are the proliferation of Truth Commissions and trials of military officers in Argentina, Chile, and Uruguay.

72. Arturo Valenzuela, "Latin American Presidencies Interrupted," *Journal of Democracy* 15:4 (2004), 6; Tom Farer, ed., *Beyond Sovereignty: Collectively Defending Security in the Americas* (Baltimore, MD: Johns Hopkins University Press, 1996).

73. Roberts, *Deepending Democracy? The Modern Left and Social Movements in Chile and Peru*.

74. Aleida Guevara, *Chávez, Venezuela, and the New Latin America: An Interview with Hugo Chávez* (Ocean Press, 2005); Diana Raby, *Democracy and Revolution: Latin America and Socialism Today* (Ann Arbor, MI: Pluto Press, 2006).

75. Noam Chomsky, *Power over People: Neoliberalism and Global Order* (New York, NY: Seven Stories Press, 1999), 20.

76. Milton Friedman and Rose Friedman, *Capitalism and Freedom* (Chicago: University of Chicago Press, 2002).

77. "Ser de esquerda é o mesmo que ser progressista." Fernando Henrique Cardoso, *A social-democracia: O que é, o que propõe para o Brasil* (Documento elaborado pelo escritório político do senador Fernando Henrique Cardoso, São Paulo 1990).

78. Castañeda, *Utopia Unarmed*, 18.

79. Cleary, "A Left Turn in Latin America? Explaining the Left's Resurgence," 36.

80. John Williamson, *Latin American Adjustment: How Much Has Happened?* (Washington DC: IIE, 1990); Dani Rodrik, "Understanding Economic Policy Reform," *Journal of Economic Literature* 34:1 (1996),9; Kurt Weyland, "Neoliberalism and Democracy in Latin America: A Mixed Record," *Latin American Politics and Society* 46:1 (2004); Pedro-Pablo Kuczynski, "Setting the Stage" in *After the Washington Consensus*, eds. Kuczynski and Williamson (Washington, DC: IIE, 2003).

81. Jason Seawright and John Gerring, "Case Selection Techniques in Case Study Research," *Political Research Quarterly* 61:2 (2008), 301.

82. Alexander George and Andrew Bennett, *Case Studies and Theory Development in the Social Sciences* (Cambridge, MA: MIT Press, 2005).

83. George and Bennett, *Case Studies and Theory Development in the Social Sciences*, 149.

84. All interviews were conducted in Spanish or Portuguese and their translations to English are mine.

CHAPTER 2

1. "Brasil está mudando em paz. E a esperança venceu o medo. [. . .] Vamos convocar toda a sociedade brasileira, todos os homens e mulheres de bem desse país, todos os empresários, todos os sindicalistas, todos os intelectuais, todos os trabalhadores rurais, toda a sociedade brasileira, enfim, para que a gente possa construir um país mais justo, mais fraterno e mais solidário." Text of Lula's first speech as president elect, *Folha de São Paulo*, October 27, 2002.

2. Nathan Jensen and Scott Schmith, "Market Responses to Politics: The Rise of Lula and the Decline of the Brazilian Stock Market," *Comparative Political Studies* 38:10 (2005).

3. Juan Martínez and Javier Santiso, "Financial Markets and Politics: The Confidence Game in Latin American Economies," *International Political Science Review* 24:3 (2003).

4. Carlos Alberto Montaner's op-ed, "Un caudillo con la cara pintada," *El Universal*, August 9, 1998.

5. Sebastian Edwards op-ed, "Chile's 'New Socialist' Bids for the Presidency," *The Wall Street Journal*, June 4, 1999.

6. Wladimir Turianski, *El Uruguay desde la izquierda: una crónica de 50 años en la vida política y social* (Montevideo: Cal y Canto, 1997); José Molina, "The Presidential and Parliamentary Elections of the Bolivarian Revolution in Venezuela," *Bulletin of Latin American Research* 21:2 (2002); Wendy Hunter and Timothy Power, "Lula's Brazil at Midterm," *Journal of Democracy* 16:3 (2005); Dick Parker, "Chávez and the Search for an Alternative to Neoliberalism," *Latin American Perspectives* 32:2 (2005); Teodoro Petkoff, *Las dos izquierdas* (Caracas: Alfadil, 2005); Roberto Funk, *El gobierno de Ricardo Lagos: La nueva vía chilena hacia el socialismo* (Santiago: Universidad Diego Portales, 2006).

7. Two exceptions are Kurt Weyland, Raúl Madrid, and Wendy Hunter (eds.), *Leftist Governments in Latin America: Successes and Shortcomings* (New York, NY: Cambridge University Press, 2010), which focuses on economic issues in four countries, and Steven Levitsky and Kenneth Roberts (eds.), *The Resurgence of the Latin American Left* (Baltimore, MD: Johns Hopkins University Press, 2011), which discusses political, economic, and social aspects of the left in eight countries.

8. Views on democracy, human rights, the environment, health care, civil liberties, and citizenship rights are only a few examples. See Kenneth Roberts, *Deepening Democracy? The Modern Left and Social Movements in Chile and Peru* (Stanford, CA: Stanford University Press, 1999).

9. Matthew Cleary, "A Left Turn in Latin America? Explaining the Left's Resurgence," *Journal of Democracy* 17:4 (2006).

10. Huber Escaith and Igor Paunovic, "Reformas estructurales en América Latina y el Caribe en el periodo 1970–2000: Indices y notas metodológicas," CEPAL, Santiago de Chile, October 15, 2004. Samuel Morley, Roberto Machado, and Stefano Pettinato, "Indexes of Structural Reform in Latin America," *Serie de Reformas Económicas* 12 (Santiago: ECLAC, 1999).

11. Heritage Foundation, *Index of Economic Freedom 2010* (Washington, DC: The Heritage Foundation, 2010).

12. For a discussion on the importance of distinguishing between measuring outcomes and policies, see Escaith and Paunovic "Reformas estructurales en América Latina y el Caribe en el periodo 1970–2000: Indices y notas metodológicas," 4.

13. Hector Schamis, *Reforming the State: The Politics of Privatization in Latin America and Europe* (Ann Arbor, MI: University of Michigan Press, 2002).

14. Nancy Birdsall and Augusto de la Torre, *The Washington Contentious* (Washington, DC: Carnegie Endowment for International Peace and Inter-American Dialogue, 2001).

15. John Williamson, "What Washington Means by Policy Reform," in *Latin American Adjustment: How Much Has Happened?* ed. John Williamson (Washington, IIE, 1990). Robert Wade, *Governing the Market: Economic Theory and Role of Government in East Asian Development* (Princeton, NJ: Princeton University Press, 1990).

16. Birdsall and de la Torre, *The Washington Contentious*.

17. Moisés Naím, "Latin America: The Second Stage of Reform," *Journal of Democracy* 5:4 (1994), 36.

18. John Williamson, "What Washington Means by Policy Reform;" Cohen and Centeno, "Neoliberalism and Patterns of Economic Performance, 1980–2006."

19. Wade, *Governing the Market: Economic Theory and Role of Government in East Asian Development*.

20. Ernesto Stein, "Fiscal Decentralization and Government Size in Latin America" *Journal of Applied Economics* 2:2 (1999).

21. The use of the primary fiscal balance is important because governments often have little control over debt commitments inherited from previous administrations.

22. Author's interviews in Brazil, Chile, Mexico, and Venezuela with a former president, ministers and vice ministers of finance, president's chief of staff, and vice minister of the economy (Brazil's President Fernando Henrique Cardoso, Venezuela's Minister of Finance José Alejandro Rojas, Brazil's Vice Ministers of Finance Bernardo Appy, Dyogo Henrique de Oliveira, Antonio Silveira, and José Antonio Pereira, Chile's former Chief of Staff and Minister of the Economy Álvaro García Hurtado, and Mexico's Adviser to President Fox and former Vice Minister of the Economy Carlos Arce Macías).

23. Evelyn Huber and Fred Solt, "Successes and Failures of Neoliberalism," *Latin American Research Review* 39:3 (2004), 160. John Williamson, "What Washington Means by Policy Reform."

24. Huber and Solt, "Successes and Failures of Neoliberalism." Norman Loayza and Luisa Palacios, "Economic Reform and Progress in Latin America and the Caribbean," *World Bank Policy Research Paper* 1829 (June 1997). Carlos Elizondo, "Tax Reform in Mexico under the Administrations of Echeverria and Salinas," *Journal of Latin American Studies* 26:1 (1994); Delia Boylan, "The Politics of the 1990 Chilean Tax Reform," *Latin American Research Review* 31:1 (1996).

25. Jeffrey Sachs, "Poland and Eastern Europe: What Is to Be Done?" in *Foreign Economic Liberalization: Transformations in Socialist and Market Economies*, eds. Andras Koves and Paul Marer (Boulder, CO: Westview Press, 1991); Jaime Saavedra, "Labor Markets during the 1990s," in *After the Washington Consensus*, eds. Kuczynski and Williamson (Washington, DC: IIE, 2003).

26. John Williamson, *Latin American Adjustment: How Much Has Happened?* (Washington, DC: IIE, 1990). Birdsall and de la Torre, *The Washington Contentious*.

27. Roberto Bouzas and Saul Keifman, "Making Trade Liberalization Work," in *After the Washington Consensus*, eds., Pedro Pablo Kuczynski and John Williamson (Washington, DC: IIE, 2003).

28. Liliana Rojas Suárez, "Monetary Policy and Exchange Rates: Guiding Principles for a Sustainable Regime," in *After the Washington Consensus*, eds. Kuczynski and Williamson (Washington, DC: IIE, 2003).

29. David De Ferranti et al., *Inequality in Latin America: Breaking with History?* (Washington, DC: World Bank, 2003), 141.

30. Governments of all ideological stripes have implemented such programs, in the same way that there is variation regarding other policy areas such as nationalizations, central bank independence, or fiscal discipline, to name a few.

31. Castañeda, "Latin America's Left Turn."

32. Petkoff, *Las dos izquierdas.*

33. Weyland, "The Rise of Latin America's Two Lefts: Insights from Rentier Theory."

34. Weyland, Madrid, and Hunter, *Leftist Governments in Latin America: Successes and Shortcomings.*

35. Francisco Panizza, "The Social Democratization of the Latin American Left," *Revista Europea de Estudios Latinoamericanos y del Caribe* 79 (October 2005).

36. For example, social reforms, such as changes to the education and health care systems in Chile during the Lagos presidency, are beyond the scope of this study.

37. Consejo Nacional Electoral de Venezuela, *Resultados de la Elección del 6 de diciembre de 1998 para Presidente de la República* (Caracas, Venezuela, 1998).

38. Consejo Nacional Electoral de Venezuela, *Resultados de la Elección del 6 de diciembre de 1998 para Presidente de la República.*

39. For a complete list of electoral results across Latin America between 1998 and 2010 see Appendix A.

40. What Chávez has argued is a combination of Bolivarian, Marxist, and Christian values. Heinz Dietrich, *Hugo Chávez: Con Bolívar y el Pueblo.* México, DF: Editorial 21, 1999.

41. Steve Ellner, "The Radical Potential of Chavismo," *Latin American Perspectives* 28: 5 (2001).

42. The law came into effect in January 2002 and replaced the Hydrocarbons Law of 1943 and the Nationalization Law of 1975.

43. Bernard Mommer, "Subversive Oil" in *Venezuelan Politics in the Chávez Era,* eds. Steve Ellner and Daniel Hellinger (Boulder, CO: Lynn Rienner, 2003) 141.

44. Mark Sullivan and Clare Ribando, *Latin America: Energy Supply, Political Developments, and US Policy Approaches* (Congressional Research Service Report RL 33693, 2006).

45. The projects had a refining capacity of 600,000 barrels of crude oil a day and were owned by Conoco Phillips, Chevron, Exxon Mobil, BP, Statoil, and Total.

46. "Cemex velará por los intereses de sus inversores y empleados en Venezuela," *El Universal,* April 24, 2008.

47. "Nacionalización de Sidor es pilar del plan para sector siderúrgico," *El Universal,* May 2, 2008.

48. "Gobierno oficializa adquisición forzosa de café Fama de América," *El Universal,* November 11, 2009.

49. "Gobernador de Sucre anunció la expropiación de procesadora de sardinas La Gaviota," *El Nacional,* March 19, 2009.

50. "Chávez ordena expropiar Cargill y amenaza a Polar," *El Universal,* March 4, 2009.

51. "Gobierno decide expropiar el hotel Margarita Hilton," *El Universal,* October 14, 2009.

52. Julia Buxton, "Economic Policy and the Rise of Hugo Chávez" in *Venezuelan Politics in the Chávez Era,* eds. Ellner and Hellinger (Boulder, CO: Lynne Rienner, 2003), 129.

53. "Intervención de El Charcote violó acuerdo de protección de inversiones," *El Nacional,* March 26, 2005.

54. "Cronología de la implantación de la Ley de Tierras," *Agencia Bolivariana de Noticias*, December 9, 2004.

55. Buxton, "Economic Policy and the Rise of Hugo Chávez," 129; Mommer, "Subversive Oil," 141.

56. Sullivan and Ribando, *Latin America: Energy Supply, Political Developments, and US Policy Approaches*.

57. World Bank, *World Development Indicators* (2010).

58. United Nations Economic Commission for Latin America (ECLAC), *Preliminary Overview of the Economies of Latin America and the Caribbean, 2010* (Chile: UN Economic Commission for Latin America and the Caribbean, 2011).

59. "Ley de Régimen Cambiario," *Gaceta Oficial de la República Bolivariana de Venezuela* No. 4897 (extraordinaria), May 17, 1995.

60. "Decreto No. 2.302/2003 mediante el cual se crea la Comisión de Administración de Divisas," *Gaceta Oficial de la República Bolivariana de Venezuela* No. 37625, February 5, 2003.

61. "Cadenas comerciales resisten control de precios," *El Nacional*, October 15, 2005.

62. The G-3 trade agreement between Colombia, Mexico, and Venezuela was signed in 1994 and in effect since January 1995. The Andean Community is a customs union formed in 1996 by Bolivia, Colombia, Ecuador, Peru, and Venezuela, based on the former Andean Pact.

63. Venezuela's full membership was still awaiting approval of the Paraguayan Senate at the time of writing.

64. "Bolivia y Venezuela también auditarán deuda externa," *El Universal*, November 26, 2008.

65. Michael Penfold-Becerra, "Clientelism and Social Funds: Evidence from Chávez's Misiones," *Latin American Politics and Society* 49:4 (2007).

66. Penfold-Becerra, "Clientelism and Social Funds: Evidence from Chávez's Misiones," 65.

67. Ecuador adopted the US dollar as legal tender in September 2000.

68. Rafael Correa's inaugural speech, Quito, Ecuador, January 15, 2007.

69. "El discurso crítico no es todo para la imagen de Correa," *El Comercio*, February 20, 2006.

70. Alianza PAÍS, Plan de Gobierno 2007–2011 (Quito, 2006).

71. Tribunal Supremo Electoral de Ecuador, *Resultados parciales elecciones 2006, primera y segunda vueltas* (Guayaquil, 2006).

72. "El Estado embarga bienes de Odebrecht," *El Comercio*, September 24, 2008.

73. "Wilson Pástor: Ley de Hidrocarburos significa un paso radical en beneficio del país," *Noticias de Gualaquiza*, August 6, 2010.

74. "Gobierno prepara plan de toma de operaciones si alguna petrolera no logra negociar," *Hoy*, August 2, 2010.

75. "Decreto Ejecutivo 1348," *Registro Oficial de la República de Ecuador*, September 23, 2008.

76. "Decreto Ejecutivo 662," *Registro Oficial de la República de Ecuador*, October 4, 2007.

77. "París: La decisión de Quito sobre Perenco no ayuda a invertir en Ecuador," *El Tiempo*, July 21, 2009.

78. "Cinco Modificaciones a la Reforma Tributaria," *El Comercio*, December 4, 2009.

79. "El cambio del Banco Central tomó dos años," *El Comercio*, August 26, 2009.

80. "Autonomía del Banco Central del Ecuador en la cuerda floja," *El Comercio*, January 18, 2009.

81. "El Central se queda sin autonomía," *El Comercio*, July 31, 2009.

82. "Decreto Ejecutivo 846," *Registro Oficial de la República de Ecuador*, January 2, 2008; "Decreto Ejecutivo 1042," *Registro Oficial de la República de Ecuador*, April 23, 2008.

83. "Viteri anuncia para 2009 plan para renegociar deuda en mora," *Hoy*, December 23, 2008.

84. "Correa anuncia recompra de deuda externa en medio de moratoria," *Hoy*, January 15, 2009.

85. "Correa dice que muchos países quieren emular estrategia ecuatoriana de recompra de deuda," *El Comercio*, July 13, 2009.

86. Correa's term is compared with the presidencies of Lucio Gutiérrez (2003–2005) and Alfredo Palacios (2005–2007), since the first one was interrupted before the end of the constitutional period.

87. United Nations Economic Commission for Latin America (ECLAC), *Preliminary Overview of the Economies of Latin America and the Caribbean, 2010* (Chile: UN Economic Commission for Latin America and the Caribbean, 2011).

88. Decreto Ejecutivo 347, *Registro Oficial de la República de Ecuador*, May 7, 2003.

89. Decreto Ejecutivo 12, *Registro Oficial de la República de Ecuador*, January 16, 2007; Decreto Ejecutivo 1838, *Registro Oficial de la República de Ecuador*, July 20, 2009.

90. "Morales mira a la constituyente," *La Razón*, June 19, 2005.

91. "Evo Morales advierte: el movimiento popular es imparable," *La Nación*, June 8, 2005.

92. Corte Nacional Electoral de Bolivia, *Resultados de la Elección General para Presidente* (La Paz, Bolivia, 2005).

93. "Decreto Supremo de Nacionalización de Hidrocarburos 'Héroes del Chaco' 28701," *Gaceta Oficial de Bolivia*, May 1, 2006.

94. "Evo guardó el decreto, sorprendió y se movilizó para desatar una fiesta popular," *La Razón*, May 1, 2006.

95. "Morales nacionaliza el negocio del gas y toma el control de 5 compañías," *La Razón*, May 1, 2006.

96. "Decreto Supremo 29541," *Gaceta Oficial de Bolivia*, May 1, 2008.

97. Telecom Italia sought international arbitration before the World Bank's International Center for Settlement of Investment Disputes (ICSID), from which the Bolivian government formally withdrew on May 1, 2007, as a result. "Gobierno revierte 47 por ciento de acciones de Entel al Estado," *El Diario*, April 24, 2007; "Euro Telecom inicia arbitraje contra Bolivia," *La Razón*, October 24, 2007.

98. "Decreto Supremo 29888," *Gaceta Oficial de Bolivia*, January 23, 2009.

99. "Decreto Supremo 0111," *Gaceta Oficial de Bolivia*, May 1, 2009.

100. "Decreto Supremo 0493," *Gaceta Oficial de Bolivia*, May 1, 2010.

101. "Ley 065/2010 (Ley de Pensiones)," *Gaceta Oficial de Bolivia*, December 10, 2010.

102. Retirement age for miners is 56. Women are able to retire at 55 if they have more than three children.

103. "El gobierno expropiará 180 mil has. en Chuquisaca," *La Razón*, December 3, 2008.

104. "Decreto Supremo de Nacionalización de Hidrocarburos 'Héroes del Chaco' 28701," *Gaceta Oficial de Bolivia*, May 1, 2006.

105. "El control de precios da sus primeros resultados," *La Razón*, August 21, 2007. As of December 2011, only price controls on sugar had been lifted.

106. For an overview of shock therapy liberalization see Jeffrey Sachs, "Poland and Eastern Europe: What Is to Be Done?"

107. During President Hugo Banzer's administration (1997–2001), Bonosol was renamed Bolivida and its benefits curtailed. Sánchez de Lozada reinstated Bonosol in 2002 during his second presidency.

108. Katharina Mullner, "Contested Universalism: From Bonosol to Renta Dignidad," *International Journal of Social Welfare* 18:2 (2009), 163.

109. "Morales entrega Renta Dignidad e inicia su distribución a nivel nacional," *Agencia Boliviana de Información*, February 1, 2008.

110. Decreto Supremo 28899, *Gaceta Oficial de Bolivia*, October 26, 2006.

111. Juancito Pinto was modeled after Bono Esperanza, a local program operating in El Alto between 2003 and 2005. Bono Esperanza granted 50 bolivianos and benefited 14,000 students. "Niños recibieron primer Bono Esperanza," *El Diario*, September 19, 2003.

112. Decreto Supremo 29321, *Gaceta Oficial de Bolivia*, October 24, 2007.

113. "Bono Juancito Pinto: Un buen paso," *La Prensa*, November 8, 2010.

114. United Nations Economic Commission for Latin America (ECLAC), *Preliminary Overview of the Economies of Latin America and the Caribbean, 2010*.

115. "Una decisión entre dudas y discusiones," *La Nación*, May 15, 2003.

116. Ministerio del Interior de Argentina, *Escrutinio definitivo de las elecciones generales 2003* (Buenos Aires: Ministerio del Interior de Argentina, 2003).

117. By 2008 Líneas Aéreas Federales had employees and funds appropriated in the national budget, but had not flown a single plane. "Hay más empresas del Estado," *La Nación*, May 4, 2008.

118. Enarsa was created with 53 percent of federal government ownership, 12 percent of provincial governments' ownership, and the remainder corresponding to private equity. "El ABC de Enarsa," *Pagina 12*, September 19, 2005.

119. "El Estado puede ser más eficiente que un privado," *La Nación*, November 30, 2003.

120. "La relación con París quedó bajo el agua," *Página 12*, March 24, 2006.

121. "Con críticas a Suez, Kirchner lanzó el plan de inversions de AySA," *La Nación*, October 12, 2006.

122. "Decreto No. 798," *Boletín Oficial de la República Argentina*, June 23, 2004.

123. "El gobierno reestatizó el astillero naval Tandanor," *La Nación*, March 31, 2007.

124. "The Dark Horse Who's about to Be President," *Businessweek*, May 26, 2003.

125. "Puntapié inicial para la salida del default," *Página 12*, October 8, 2004.

126. "Obligan a los supermercados a informar precios al gobierno," *La Nación*, November 28, 2003.

127. "El FMI critica la política del gobierno contra la inflación," *La Nación*, June 10, 2006.

128. "Rechazó Kirchner las críticas sobre la inflación," *La Nación*, February 6, 2007.

129. World Bank, *World Development Indicators* 2011.

130. Heritage Foundation, *Index of Economic Freedom* (Washington, DC: The Heritage Foundation, 2010).

131. "Decreto No. 1506," *Boletín Oficial de la República Argentina*, October 26, 2004.

132. World Bank, *Argentina: Income Support Policies toward the Bicentennial* (Washington, DC: The World Bank, 2009), 19–21.

133. Presidencia de la República de Argentina, "Anuncios para el area social," Press conference with Alicia Kirchner, minister of social development. (Buenos Aires, Argentina, October 27, 2005).

134. World Bank, *Argentina: Income Support Policies towards the Bicentennial*.

135. The average fiscal surplus becomes 0.8 percent if the years 2001 and 2002 are included.

136. United Nations Economic Commission for Latin America (ECLAC), *Preliminary Overview of the Economies of Latin America and the Caribbean, 2010*.

137. Ortega selected former "Contra" Jaime Morales Carazo as his running mate. The term "Contra" refers to the US-backed guerrilla movement that attempted to overthrow the Sandinista movement during the 1980s.

138. Consejo Supremo Electoral de Nicaragua, *Escrutinio General de la Elección Presidencial* (Managua, 2006).

139. "Eduardo presenta su plan de gobierno en Atlántico Norte y Sur," *La Jornada* (Nicaragua), October 11, 2006.

140. "Caricom y Centroamérica negociarán TLC," *El Nuevo Diario*, May 12, 2007.

141. "El TLC entre Panamá y Nicaragua entrará en vigor en treinta días," *La Prensa*, October 23, 2009.

142. "Nicaragua y Canadá retoman las negociaciones para un TLC," *La Prensa*, November 2, 2010.

143. The date for the official signing of the agreement was pending at the time of writing. See "Nicaragua y Chile estrechan lazos comerciales," *El Nuevo Diario*, August 8, 2010.

144. "Europa y Centroamérica llegan a un acuerdo sobre un tratado de libre comercio," *AFP*, May 17, 2010.

145. United Nations Economic Commission for Latin America (ECLAC), *Preliminary Overview of the Economies of Latin America and the Caribbean, 2010*.

146. "Ley No. 713, Ley Anual de Presupuesto General de la República," *La Gaceta Diario Oficial* 240, December 18, 2009.

147. Ministerio Agropecuario y Forestal, *Programa Productivo Alimentario*, Managua, Nicaragua.

148. Even though the PSDB was generally considered a center-left party in the late 1980s and early 1990s, it has since drifted toward the center-right of the political spectrum. See Wendy Hunter, "The Normalization of an Anomaly: The Workers' Party in Brazil," *World Politics* 59:3 (2007), 458; Timothy Power, "Centering Democracy? Ideological Cleavages and Convergence in the Brazilian Political Class," in *Democratic Brazil Revisited*, ed. Kinston and Power (Pittsburgh, PA: University of Pittsburgh Press, 1998), 58. It is worth mentioning that the official documents of the party still describe it as a center-left political party. The PSDB's gradual shift over time is discussed in Chapter 5.

149. Tribunal Superior Eleitoral do Brasil, *Relatório das eleições* (Brasilia: TSE, 2003).

150. Lula was succeeded by PT candidate Dilma Rousseff.

151. Paulo Paiva, "Lula's Political Economy: Changes and Challenges," *ANNALS of the American Academy of Political and Social Science* 606:1 (2006).

152. "Banco Central mantém Selic a 26,5%" *Época*, May 21, 2003.

153. Maria de Lourdes Mollo and Alfredo Saad-Filho, "Neoliberal Economic Policies in Brazil (1994–2005): Cardoso, Lula, and the Need for a Democratic Alternative," *New Political Economy* 11:1 (2006).

154. United Nations Economic Commission for Latin America (ECLAC), *Preliminary Overview of the Economies of Latin America and the Caribbean, 2010*.

155. The Lula administration did increase its stake in Petrobras from 57.5 to 64.25 percent of common stock. "Petrobras capta R$ 115 bilhões em oferta pública," *Fohla de São Paulo*, September 30, 2010. On Collor's, Franco's, and Cardoso's privatizations see BNDES (Banco Nacional de Desenvolvimento), *Privatizations in Brazil: Results and Agenda* (Brasilia, Brazil: Ministry of Development, Industry, and Trade—Federal Privatization Office, 2002); BNDES, *Privatizations in Brazil: 1990–1994 and 1995–2002* (Brasilia, Brazil: Ministry of Development, Industry, and Trade 2002); Gesner Oliveira and Federico Turolla, "Política econômica no segundo governo FHC: mudança em condições adversas," *Tempo Social* 15 (2003); Rex Hudson, *Brazil: A Country Study* (Washington, DC: GPO for the Library of Congress, 1997).

156. Banco Central do Brasil, "Inauguration speech of the new governor of Brazil's Central Bank," (Brasilia, Brazil: Banco Central do Brasil, 2003).

157. "Lula diz que autonomia do Banco Central se dá na relação com o presidente," *O Globo*, October 10, 2008.

158. PricewaterhouseCoopers, *Worldwide Summary: Corporate Taxes* (John Wiley & Sons, 2000–2006).

159. Oliveira and Turolla, "Política econômica no segundo governo FHC: mudança em condições adversas."

160. Chapter 5 provides details about Lula's attempts to pass fiscal reform through Congress.

161. "Lei 10.836, que cria o Programa Bolsa Família, e dá outras providências," *Diário Oficial da União*, January 9, 2004.

162. "Decreto No. 5.209, que regulamenta a Lei no 10.836," *Diário Oficial da União*, January 9, 2004.

163. Mark Weisbrot and Luis Sandoval, *Brazil's Presidential Election: Background on Economic Issues*, CEPR Issue Brief (2006).

164. World Bank, "Bolsa Familia: Scaling Up Cash Transfers for the Poor," *Emerging Good Practice in Managing for Development Results* (Washington, DC: World Bank, 2007).

165. Vázquez was succeeded by José Mújica, the Broad Front candidate and former guerrilla.

166. Investment protection agreements do not require congressional approval to come into force.

167. USTR, *US-Uruguay Trade Investment Protection Agreement* (Washington, DC: Office of the United States Trade Representative, 2005).

168. "Gobierno definió negociación con Estados Unidos," *El País* (Uruguay), September 28, 2006.

169. "Se firmó el Tifa: Uruguay y EEUU abrieron la puerta a mayor acercamiento commercial," *La República*, January 26, 2007.

170. "Indefinición en el Frente sobre acuerdo con EEUU," *El País* (Uruguay), January, 25, 2007.

171. "Tras áspera discusión, el Parlamento aprobó creación de nuevo Ministerio," *La República*, March 19, 2005.

172. "Casi 25.000 solicitudes en primera jornada del Plan de Emergencia," *El País* (Uruguay), April 2, 2005.

173. Organization of American States, *National Reports on the Implementation of the Commitments from the Fourth Summit of the Americas: Uruguay* (Washington, DC: OAS, 2008).

174. World Bank, *Del PANES al Plan de Equidad: Nota Técnica* (Washington, DC: World Bank, 2008).

175. World Bank, *World Bank's Privatization Database* (Washington, DC: World Bank: 2011).

176. This reform was mandated by a referendum in tandem with Vázquez's election and is therefore not coded as the leftist government's policy. "Fue aprobada reforma constitucional del agua," *El País* (Uruguay), November 1, 2004.

177. "Ley 18.083, Reforma al Sistema Tributario," *Diario Oficial de la República Oriental de Uruguay*, January 18, 2007.

178. Jorge Lanzaro, for example, estimates the overall effect of the new tax law as a reduction in government revenue by as much as 1 percent of GDP. Jorge Lanzaro, "Uruguay: A Social Democratic Government in Latin America."

179. United Nations Economic Commission for Latin America (ECLAC), *Preliminary Overview of the Economies of Latin America and the Caribbean, 2010*.

180. Tribunal Calificador de Chile, *Resultados de Presidente 2000* (Santiago, Chile: TCC, 2000).

181. Lagos was succeeded by Socialist Party candidate Michelle Bachelet.

182. Sebastian Edwards, "Chile's 'New Socialist' Bids for the Presidency," *The Wall Street Journal*, June 4, 1999.

183. World Bank, *World Bank's Privatization Database*.

184. "Ad portas que finalice venta de bases de la licitación," *La Tercera*, September 2, 2002; "José Miguel Insulza reafirmó venta de Essbío," *El Mercurio*, August 24, 2000.

185. Claudio Fuentes, "La apuesta por el poder blando. La política exterior de la Concertación durante 2000–2006" in *El gobierno de Ricardo Lagos*, ed. Roberto Funk (Santiago: Universidad Diego Portales, 2003).

186. "Gobierno destaca TLC con Nueva Zelanda, Singapur y Brunei," *La Tercera*, June 3, 2005.

187. USTR, *The US-Chile Free Trade Agreement: An Early Record of Success* (Washington, DC: Office of the United States Trade Representative, 2004).

188. Fuentes, "La apuesta por el poder blando. La política exterior de la Concertación durante 2000–2006," 111.

189. "Impuestos a la importación de Chile sufrirán nuevas bajas en 2003," *El Mercurio*, November 11, 2002.

190. "Nicolás Eyzaguirre: además de economista, artista e irónico," *El Mercurio*, February 2, 2000.

191. "Amplían cobertura de Sistema Chile Solidario para las familias más pobres del país," Ministry of Planning (MIDEPLAN) Press Release, Reñaca Alto, Viña del Mar, February 1, 2006.

192. Ariel Fiszbein and Norbert Schady, *Conditional Cash Transfers* (Washington, DC: World Bank Press, 2009), 246.

193. Eduardo Silva, "Capitalist Regime Loyalties and Redemocratization in Chile," *Journal of Interamerican Studies and World Affairs*, 34:4 (1993); Felipe Aguero, "Chile: Unfinished Transition and Increased Political Competition" in *Constructing Democratic Governance in Latin America*, eds. Dominguez and Shifter (Baltimore: Johns Hopkins University Press, 2003).

194. "Consequences of the US-Chile Free Trade Agreement," *MercoPress*, June 10, 2003.

195. United Nations Economic Commission for Latin America (ECLAC), *Preliminary Overview of the Economies of Latin America and the Caribbean, 2010*.

196. Santiago Levy, *Progress against Poverty: Sustaining Mexico's Progresa-Oportunidades Program* (Washington, DC: Brookings Institution Press, 2006). Judith Teichman, "Multilateral Lending Institutions and Transnational Policy Networks in Mexico and Chile," *Global Governance* 13 (2007).

197. Author's interview with Gabriela Hernández, former assistant secretary for communications, Ministry of Communications and Transportation, and former deputy attorney-general for consumer protection, July 2004.

198. World Bank, *World Bank's Privatization Database*.

199. Author's interview with Carlos Arce Macías, former assistant secretary for international trade, Ministry of the Economy, former PAN deputy, and former legal council for President Fox, August 2008.

200. Author's interview with Eduardo Javier Ramos Avalos, chief negotiator for international trade, Ministry of the Economy. August 25, 2010.

201. United Nations Economic Commission for Latin America (ECLAC), *Preliminary Overview of the Economies of Latin America and the Caribbean, 2010*.

202. Author's interview with Margarita de Lourdes Guerra, director-general for social programs, Ministry of Social Development, July 2007.

203. Santiago Levy and Evelyne Rodríguez, *Sin Herencia de Pobreza: El Programa Progresa Oportunidades en México* (Mexico, DF: Inter American Development Bank, 2005).

204. Manuel Pastor and Carol Wise, "The Politics of Second-Generation Reform," *Journal of Democracy* 10:3 (2005).

205. Fiszbein and Schady, *Conditional Cash Transfers*, 269.

206. World Bank, *World Bank Privatizations Database*. See also "Uribe Cocina la Segunda Face de Reestructuración," *El Tiempo*, September 3, 2006; "Rediseño del Estado le ahorró al país $18 billones," *El Espectador*, February 22, 2008.

207. "Presidente Álvaro Uribe anuncia que no venderá Ecopetrol sino que la capitalizará para fortalecerla," *El Tiempo*, November 14, 2006.

208. "Congreso aprobó venta del 20 por ciento de Ecopetrol a socios privados," *El Tiempo*, December 13, 2006.

209. Author's interviews with Santiago Castro, Partido Conservador deputy, and president of the House of Representatives' Third Commission, which focuses on economic issues, and Augusto Posada, Partido de la U deputy, and member of the Third Commission, March 26 and 24, 2010, respectively.

210. Ley 1111 (Ley por la cual se modifica el estatuto tributario de los impuestos administrados por la dirección de impuestos y aduanas nacionales), *Diario Oficial 46.494*, December 27, 2006.

211. Author's interviews with Fernando Jiménez Rodríguez, director-general for budgets and planning, and Rutty Paola Ortiz, director for budgets, Ministry of Finance, March 26, 2010.

212. United Nations Economic Commission for Latin America (ECLAC), *Preliminary Overview of the Economies of Latin America and the Caribbean, 2010*.

213. "Arranca TLC con Estados Unidos," *El Tiempo*, November 13, 2003.

214. "Congreso aprobó con pupitrazo el Tratado de Libre Comercio con Estados Unidos," *El Tiempo*, June 14, 2007.

215. Ministerio de Comercio, Industria y Turismo, "Rueda de Prensa de Mincomercio sobre el TLC con Estados Unidos," Press Release, Bogotá, Colombia, April 6, 2008.

216. Ministerio de Comercio, Industria y Turismo, "Cierre de Negociaciones TLC Colombia con AELC y Canadá," Press Release, Bogotá, Colombia, July 3, 2008.

217. Inter-Regional Inequality Facility, "Familias en Acción," Policy Brief 2 (London, UK, 2006).

218. Castañeda, "Latin America's Left Turn."

219. Susan Stokes, *Mandates and Democracy: Neoliberalism by Surprise in Latin America* (New York, NY: Cambridge University Press, 2001).

CHAPTER 3

1. I thank an anonymous reviewer for making this observation. Without developing a causal logic or conducting systematic testing, some authors have suggested the importance of party systems for democracy in the context of the left or populist leaders. For example, in an exploratory essay in *Journal of Democracy*, Hector Schamis organizes what he calls "populist" and "leftist leaders" into the categories of institutionalized politics, disjointed politics, and the petro-left. In

doing so, he suggests that "looking at the operation of party systems offers a deeper insight into the left and the quality of democracy more generally." See Schamis, "Populism, Socialism, and Democratic Institutions," 22. In another exploratory essay, Jorge Lanzaro attributes the moderation of leftist parties in Brazil, Chile, and Uruguay to the "democratic process" and "republican normalcy." See Lanzaro, "La socialdemocracia criolla," *Revista Nueva Sociedad* 217 (2008), 49–50. Pointing to the origins of the crisis of representation in the region, Scott Mainwaring has warned about "plebiscitarian forms of representation in which populist presidents displace parties as the primary vehicles for expressing the popular will." See Mainwaring, "The Crisis of Representation in the Andes," *Journal of Democracy* 17:3 (2006), 18. Kenneth Roberts has also argued that "the revived populist parties and the new political movements in Venezuela and Bolivia reflect not the maturation of democracy, but rather its crisis." Kenneth Roberts, "Repoliticizing Latin America: The Revival of Populist and Leftist Alternatives," *Woodrow Wilson Center Update on the Americas* 28 (November 2007), 12.

2. Centripetal incentives are those that motivate politicians to take positions closer to the ideological center, while centrifugal incentives have the opposite effect. Gary Cox, "Centrifugal and Centripetal Incentives in Electoral Systems," *American Journal of Political Science* 34:4 (1990).

3. Stephan Haggard and Robert Kaufman (eds.), *The Politics of Economic Adjustment* (Princeton, NJ: Princeton University Press, 1992); John Waterbury, "The Heart of the Matter? Public Enterprise and the Adjustment Process" in *The Politics of Economic Adjustment*, eds. Haggard and Kaufman (Princeton, NJ: Princeton University Press, 1992); Anne Krueger, *Political Economy of Policy Reform in Developing Countries* (Cambridge, MA: MIT Press, 1993); Stephan Haggard and Steven B. Webb, "Introduction" in *Voting for Reform: Democracy, Political Liberalization, and Economic Adjustment*, eds. Haggard and Webb (Washington, DC: World Bank, 1994). Haggard and Kaufman, *The Political Economy of Democratic Transitions*, (Princeton, NJ: Princeton University Press, 1995); Kurt Weyland, "Risk Taking in Latin American Economic Restructuring: Lessons from Prospect Theory," *International Studies Quarterly*, 40 (1996); Javier Corrales, "Do Economic Crises Contribute to Economic Reform? Argentina and Venezuela in the 1990s," *Political Science Quarterly* 112:4 (1997); Karen Remmer, "The Politics of Neoliberal Reform in South America, 1980–1994," *Studies in Comparative International Development* 33:2 (1998); Steven Levitsky and Lucan Way, "Between a Shock and a Hard Place: The Dynamics of Labor Based Adjustment in Argentina and Poland," *Comparative Politics*, 30:2 (1998); Hector Schamis, *Reforming the State: The Politics of Privatization in Latin America and Europe* (Ann Arbor, MI: University of Michigan Press, 2002).

4. Schamis, "A Left Turn in Latin America? Populism, Socialism, and Democratic Institutions"; Lanzaro, "La socialdemocracia criolla"; Weyland, "The Rise of Latin America's Two Lefts: Insights from Rentier State Theory"; Hidalgo, "Hugo Chavez's 'Petro Socialism.'"

5. Giovanni Sartori, *Parties and Party Systems* (New York, NY: Cambridge University Press, 1976); Robert Dix, "Democratization and the Institutionalization of Latin American Political Parties," *Comparative Political Studies* 24:4 (January 1992); Scott Mainwaring and Timothy Scully, "Introduction: Party Systems in Latin America," in *Building Democratic Institutions: Party Systems in Latin America*, eds. Scott Mainwaring and Timothy Scully (Stanford, CA: Stanford University Press, 1995); Scott Mainwaring, "Party Systems in the Third Wave," *Journal of Democracy* 9:3 (1998).

6. Mainwaring and Scully, "Introduction: Party Systems in Latin America."

7. Pipa Norris, "Recruitment" in *Handbook of Party Politics*, eds. Katz and Crotty (London: Sage, 2006).

8. Angelo Panebianco, *Political Parties: Organization and Power* (New York, NY: Cambridge University Press, 1988).

9. Vicky Randall and Lars Svasand, "Party Institutionalization in New Democracies," *Party Politics* 8:1 (2002), 19.

10. Mainwaring and Torcal, "Party System Institutionalization and Party System Theory after the Third Wave of Democratization."

11. Sartori, *Parties and Party Systems*, 135.

12. Guillermo O'Donnell, "Delegative Democracy," *Journal of Democracy* 5:1 (1994).

13. George Mailath and Larry Samuelson, *Repeated Games and Reputations: Long-Run Relationships*, (New York, NY: Oxford University Press, 2006).

14. Alberto Alesina and Stephen Spear, "An Overlapping Generations Model of Electoral Competition," *Journal of Public Economics* 37 (1998); See also Susan Stokes, "Political Parties and Democracy," *Annual Review of Political Science* 2 (June 1999).

15. It is worth emphasizing the probabilistic nature of the relationship. A notable case where consensual dynamics ceased to play out was Chile between 1965 and 1973, to the point where democracy broke down. As is discussed in the next section, the combination of institutionalization and extreme polarization contributed toward this outcome.

16. George Tsebelis, *Veto Players* (Princeton, NJ: Princeton University Press, 2002), 58.

17. Steven Levitsky, "Organization and Labor-based Party Adaptation."

18. Guillermo O'Donnell, "Horizontal Accountability in New Democracies," *Journal of Democracy* 9:3 (1998), 112.

19. Francisco Flores-Macías, "Electoral Volatility in 2006" in *Consolidating Mexico's Democracy: The 2006 Presidential Campaign in Comparative Perspective*, eds. Jorge Domínguez, Chappell Lawson, and Alejandro Moreno (Baltimore, MD: Johns Hopkins University Press, 2009).

20. Anthony Downs, *An Economic Theory of Democracy* (New York, NY: Harper, 1957); Andy Baker and Kenneth Greene, "The Latin American Left's Mandate: Free Market Policies and Issue Voting in New Democracies," *World Politics* 63:1 (2011).

21. Alexander Todorov et al., "Inferences of Competence from Faces Predict Election Outcomes," *Science* 308 (2005); Gabriel Lenz and Chappell Lawson, "Looking the Part: Television Leads Less Informed Citizens to Vote Based on Candidates' Appearance," MIT Department of Political Science Working Paper (2008).

22. This consideration is probabilistic. Not every president elected on a leftist platform pursues a leftist agenda once in power, nor does every president elected on a rightist platform pursue a rightist agenda. The presidencies of Carlos Menem in Argentina, Alberto Fujmori in Peru, Carlos Andrés Pérez in Venezuela, and Lucio Gutiérrez in Ecuador, are cases in point. However, presidents' platforms can be considered a general indication of leftist government's programs, as discussed in Chapter 2. For an account of the adoption of market reforms that did not follow ideological lines see Susan Stokes, *Mandates and Democracy: Neoliberalism by Surprise in Latin America* (New York, NY: Cambridge University Press, 2001).

23. Diego Abente, "The Political Economy of Tax Reform in Venezuela," *Comparative Politics* 22:2 (1990).

24. Mainwaring and Scully, "Introduction: Party Systems in Latin America"; Eduardo Gamarra and James Malloy, "The Patrimonial Dynamics of Party Politics in Bolivia" in *Building Democratic Institutions: Party Systems in Latin America*, eds. Mainwaring and Scully (Stanford, CA: Stanford University Press, 1995).

25. For an analysis on the economic policy differences between Collor's and Cardoso's presidencies see Peter Kingston, *Crafting Coalitions for Reform: Business Preferences, Political Institutions, and Neoliberal Reform in Brazil* (University Park, PA: Penn State University Press, 1999).

26. By the 2003 election, when Néstor Kirchner reached office, the Radicals' share of the vote had dropped to 2 percent. Steven Levitsky and María Victoria Murillo, "Argentina: From Kirchner to Kirchner," *Journal of Democracy* 19:2 (2008). On the erosion of Argentina's party system see Michael Coppedge, "The Dynamic Diversity of Latin American Party Systems," *Party Politics* 4:4 (1998).

27. Stokes, *Mandates and Democracy*.

28. The index is a commonly used measure of party system volatility. It reflects the net aggregate vote shifts from one election to another and is calculated as the sum of the absolute changes in vote share across all parties divided by two. Mogens Pedersen, "Changing Patterns of Electoral Volatility in European Party Systems, 1948–1977: Explorations in Explanation," in *Western European Party Systems: Continuity and Change*, eds. Hans Daalder and Peter Mair (London: Sage, 1983).

29. Kenneth Roberts and Erik Wibbels, "Party Systems and Electoral Volatility in Latin America: A Test of Economic, Institutional, and Structural Explanations," *American Political Science Review* 93:3 (1999); Scott Mainwaring and Mariano Torcal, "Party System Institutionalization and Party System Theory after the Third Wave of Democratization" in *Handbook of Political Parties*, eds. Katz and Crotty (London: Sage Publications).

30. Mainwaring and Torcal, "Party System Institutionalization and Party System Theory after the Third Wave of Democratization," 208.

31. The volatility index can be found in table format in Appendix B. The scores are generally consistent with Mainwaring and Scully's seminal classification (1995), and update it to reflect the gradual institutionalization of Brazil's party system since the end of military rule in the mid 1980s, as well as the drastic deterioration of Venezuela's party system throughout the 1990s. On Brazil's institutionalization see Leslie Armijo, Philippe Faucher, and Magdalena Dembinska, "Compared to What? Assessing Brazilian Political Institutions," *Comparative Political Studies* 39:6 (2006). On Venezuela's deterioration see Henry Dietz and David Myers, "From Thaw to Deluge: Party System Collapse in Venezuela and Peru," *Latin American Politics and Society* 49:2 (2007).

32. The deinstitutionalization of Venezuela's party system before Chavez's arrival to power is further discussed in Chapter 4.

33. Kurt Weyland identifies a status quo bias in favor of preserving the prevailing pro-market trend due to a sunk cost mentality. In his words, "The status quo bias helps explain persistent support for free-market principles." Kurt Weyland, "Threats to Latin America's Market Model?" *Political Science Quarterly* 119: 2 (2004), 301.

34. The dominance of the pro-market paradigm before the arrival of the left to power was discussed in Chapter 1.

35. When Chávez became president of Venezuela, he controlled only one third of Congress. In Bolivia, Morales won 50 percent of the seats in the lower house, but the opposition remained in control of the Senate. In Ecuador, Correa's party did not field any candidates to the legislature.

36. Steven Levitsky and María Victoria Murillo, "Argentina: From Kirchner to Kirchner," 23.

37. "Dígale SÍ al nuevo partido opositor," *Página 12*, May 18, 2008.

38. The recent political rise of businessmen Mauricio Maccri and Francisco de Narváez are two prominent examples.

39. "Los piquetes en las estaciones dispararon el cruce de acusaciones," *Página 12*, March 14, 2005.

40. Levitsky and Murillo, "Argentina: From Kirchner to Kirchner."

41. Presidencia de Nicaragua, *Proyecto de Ley de Concertación Tributaria*, Managua, Nicaragua, October 15, 2009.

42. "Ley No. 713, Ley Anual de Presupuesto General de la República," *La Gaceta Diario Oficial* 240, December 18, 2009.

43. Shelley McConnell, "Nicaragua's Turning Point," *Current History* 106:697 (2007).

44. Wendy Hunter, "The Normalization of an Anomaly: The Workers' Party in Brazil," *World Politics* 59:3 (2007).

45. The PT's gradual moderation is discussed in Chapter 5.

46. Jeffrey Cason, "Electoral Reform, Institutional Change, and Party Adaptation in Uruguay," *Latin American Politics and Society* 44:3 (2002).

47. Jorge Lanzaro, "Uruguay: A Social Democratic Government in Latin America," in *The Resurgence of the Latin American Left*, ed. Levitsky and Roberts; Daniel Chasquetti, "Uruguay 2006: éxitos y dilemas del gobierno de izquierda," *Revista de Ciencia Política* 27 (2007).

48. Lanzaro, "Uruguay: A Social Democratic Government in Latin America."

49. Lanzaro, "Uruguay: A Social Democratic Government in Latin America."

50. As Senator Carlos Ominami, vice president of the Socialist Party and Lagos's former minister of the economy, pointed out in an interview, there is a system of rewards in place to accommodate losing candidates into positions in the executive branch. Author's interview, June 6, 2009.

51. Stephan Haggard and Steven B. Webb, "Introduction," in *Voting for Reform: Democracy, Political Liberalization, and Economic Adjustment*, eds. Haggard and Webb (Washington, DC: World Bank, 1994), 9.

52. Eduardo Lora and Mauricio Oliviera, "What Makes Reform Likely: Political Economy Determinants of Reforms in Latin America," *Journal of Applied Economics* 8:1 (2004), 102.

53. Mainwaring, "Party Systems in the Third Wave," 283.

54. Haggard and Kaufman, *The Political Economy of Democratic Transitions*, 170.

55. Mainwaring, "Party Systems in the Third Wave," 286.

56. Haggard and Kaufman, *The Political Economy of Democratic Transitions*, 170.

57. Although Alesina conflates populist with leftist, the quote is useful in illustrating the role attributed to polarization. Alberto Alesina, "Political Models of Macroeconomic Policy and Fiscal Reform," in *Voting for Reform: Democracy, Political Liberalization, and Economic Adjustment*, eds. Haggard and Webb (Washington, DC: World Bank, 1994), 47.

58. Sartori, *Parties and Party* Systems, 132–37; G. Bingham Powell, *Contemporary Democracies: Participation, Stability, and Violence* (Cambridge, MA: Harvard University Press, 1982), 99.

59. Haggard and Kaufman, *The Political Economy of Democratic Transitions*, 167.

60. Mark Jones, "Political Parties and Party Systems in Latin America," Paper prepared for the symposium "Prospects for Democracy in Latin America," Department of Political Science, University of North Texas, Denton, Texas, (April 5–6, 2007), 34.

61. An alternative approach would be to focus on the fragmentation of the vote rather than the fragmentation of the seats in the legislature. Vote fragmentation tends to be slightly higher than seat fragmentation across countries and the results presented here do not change in any meaningful way.

62. Sartori, *Parties and Party Pystems*, 132–37; Powell, *Contemporary Democracies: Participation, Stability, and Violence*, 99.

63. Haggard and Kaufman use the share of the left vote as an indicator of polarization in society. This approach was a plausible approximation of polarization when the left was in opposition, but it is problematic to study polarization in the context of leftist candidates winning a plurality of the vote in order to reach power. Haggard and Kaufman, *The Political Economy of Democratic Transitions*.

64. Anne Krueger, "Introduction," in *Economic Policy Reform: The Second Stage*, ed. Anne Krueger (Chicago, IL: University of Chicago Press, 2000), 3.

65. Rudiger Dornbusch and Sebastian Edwards, "The Macroeconomics of Populism," in *The Macroeconomics of Populism in Latin America*, eds. Dornbusch and Edwards (Chicago: University of Chicago Press, 1991); Haggard and Kaufman, *The Political Economy of Democratic Transitions*, 160; Stephan Haggard and Mathew McCubbins, "Politics, Institutions and Macro-Economic Adjustment: Hungarian Fiscal Policy-Making in Comparative Perspective," in *Reforming the State: Fiscal and Welfare Reform in Post-Socialist Countries*, eds. János Kornai, Stephan Haggard and Robert Kaufman (New York, NY: Cambridge University Press, 2001); Weyland, "Neoliberalism and Democracy in Latin America: A Mixed Record."

66. Allan Drazen and Vittorio Grilli, "The Benefit of Crises for Economic Reform," *American Economic Review* 83:3 (1993); Krueger, *Political Economy of Policy Reform in Developing Countries*, 109; Robert Bates and Anne Krueger, "Generalizations Arising from the Country Studies," in *Political and Economic Interactions in Economic Policy Reform*, eds. Bates and Krueger (Oxford: Basil Blackwell, 1993); Haggard and Kaufman, *The Political Economy of Democratic Transitions*, 159.

67. Peter Evans, "The State as a Problem and a Solution: Predation, Embedded Autonomy, and Structural Change," in *The Politics of Economic Adjustment*, eds., Haggard and Kaufman (Princeton, NJ: Princeton University Press, 1992); John Waterbury, "The Heart of the Matter? Public Enterprise and the Adjustment Process," in *The Politics of Economic Adjustment*, eds., Haggard and Kaufman (Princeton, NJ: Princeton University Press, 1992).

68. Schamis, *Reforming the State: The Politics of Privatization in Latin America and Europe*; Barbara Geddes, "Challenging the Conventional Wisdom," *Journal of Democracy*, 6:4 (1994); Steven Levitsky and Lucan Way, "Between a Shock and a Hard Place: The Dynamics of Labor Based Adjustment in Argentina and Poland."

69. Ronald McKinnon, *The Order of Economic Liberalization: Financial Control in the Transition to a Market Economy* (Baltimore, MD: Johns Hopkins University Press, 1991); Dani Rodrik, "How Should Structural Adjustment Programs Be Designed," *World Development* 18:7 (1990); Rudiger Dornbusch, "Credibility and Stabilization," *Quarterly Journal of Economics* 106:3 (1991).

70. Rudiger Dornbusch and Sebastian Edwards, "The Macroeconomics of Populism," in *The Macroeconomics of Populism in Latin America*, eds. Dornbusch and Edwards (Chicago, IL: University of Chicago Press, 1991). The claim that differences in regime type lead to differences in the type of economic policies has not remained uncontested. For a critique see Barbara Geddes, "The Politics of Economic Reform," *Latin American Research Review* 30:2 (1995).

71. The exception may be Venezuela, whose status as a democracy has been questioned. See Javier Corrales, "The Repeating Revolution: Chavez's New Politics and Old Economics," in *Leftist Governments in Latin America: Successes and Shortcomings*, ed. Weyland, Madrid, and Hunter (New York, NY: Cambridge University Press, 2010).

72. Evans, "The State as a Problem and a Solution: Predation, Embedded Autonomy, and Structural Change"; Waterbury, "The Heart of the Matter? Public Enterprise and the Adjustment Process."

73. Weyland, "The Rise of Latin America's Two Lefts: Insights from Rentier State Theory"; Hidalgo, "Hugo Chavez's 'Petro Socialism'"; Christian Perenti, "Hugo Chávez and Petro Populism," *The Nation*, April 11, 2005.

74. Michael Shafer, *Winners and Losers: How Sectors Shape the Developmental Prospects of States* (Ithaca, NY: Cornell University Press, 1994); Terry Karl, *The Paradox of the Plenty: Oil Booms and Petro-States* (Berkeley: University of California Press, 1997); Michael Ross, "The Political Economy of the Resource Curse," *World Politics* 51:2 (1999); Prateek Goorha, "The Political Economy of the Resource Curse in Russia," *Demokratizatsiya* 14 (2006); Weyland, "The Rise of Latin America's Two Lefts: Insights from Rentier State Theory."

75. Ross, "The Political Economy of the Resource Curse."

76. Weyland, "Neoliberal Populism in Latin America and Eastern Europe."

77. Michael Ross, *Timber Booms and Institutional Breakdown in South East Asia* (New York, NY: Cambridge University Press, 2001).

78. Karl, *The Paradox of the Plenty: Oil Booms and Petro-States.*

79. Goorha, "The Political Economy of the Resource Curse in Russia."

80. Helene Norberg and Magnus Blomström, "Dutch Disease and Management of Windfall Gains in Botswana," in *Economic Crisis in Africa: Perspectives on Policy Responses*, eds. Blomström and Lundahl (New York, NY: Routledge, 1993).

81. According to this view, Mexico and Colombia are also likely candidates to experience statist policies due to the importance of oil in both countries, particularly in the former where oil accounts for 40 percent of government revenue. However, they are not included in this analysis due to the rightist ideology of their respective governments. In other words, the assumption is that the interaction between leftist ideology and natural resources would prompt statist policies.

82. United Nations Economic Commission for Latin America (ECLAC), *Preliminary Overview of the Economies of Latin America and the Caribbean, 2010.*

83. Ross, "The Political Economy of the Resource Curse," 310.

84. Crucial cases are those "that must closely fit a theory if one is to have confidence in the theory's validity." Harry Eckstein, "Case Studies and Theory in Political Science," in *Handbook of Political Science*, Vol. 7, eds. Fred Greenstein and Nelson Polsby, *Handbook of Political Science: Scope and Theory* (Reading, MA: Addison-Wesley, 1975), 118.

85. His early inclination for statist policies—such as the nationalization of the oil industry—is evident in the manifestos and government programs of the MBR-200, the MVR, and the Polo Patriótico. For further discussion see Chapter 4.

86. "El Congreso Considerará Observaciones del Ejecutivo," *El Universal*, April, 7, 1999. See also Julia Buxton, "Economic Policy and the Rise of Hugo Chavez," in *Venezuelan Politics in the Chavez Era*, eds. Ellner and Hellinger (Boulder, CO: Lynn Rienner, 2003), 129.

87. For a more detailed discussion on the role of natural resources in Venezuela see Chapter 4. In particular Figure 4.2 shows a comparison of Chavez's statist policies along a timeline with oil prices.

88. The time period covered in Figures 3.4 and 3.5 spans the administrations of the leftist and rightist governments under study.

89. United Nations Economic Commission for Latin America (ECLAC), *Preliminary Overview of the Economies of Latin America and the Caribbean, 2010.*

90. The rentier state literature attributes the same effects to minerals, hydrocarbons, and any point-source extraction resource. Jeffrey Sachs and Andrew Warner, "The Big Rush, Natural

Resource Booms and Growth," *Journal of Development Economics*, 59:1 (1999); Jeffrey Frankel, *The Natural Resource Curse: A Survey*, Kennedy School Faculty Research Working Paper Series RWP10-005 (February 2010).

91. This measure is the most frequently used in resource dependence literature. See, for example, Jeffrey Frankel, *The Natural Resource Curse: A Survey*; Jeffrey Sachs and Andrew Warner, "The Curse of Natural Resources," *European Economic Review* 45 (2001).

92. Allan Drazen and Vittorio Grilli, "The Benefit of Crises for Economic Reform," *American Economic Review* 83:3 (1993); Krueger, *Political Economy of Policy Reform in Developing Countries*, 109; Robert Bates and Anne Krueger, "Generalizations Arising from the Country Studies" in *Political and Economic Interactions in Economic Policy Reform*, eds. Bates and Krueger (Oxford: Basil Blackwell, 1993); Moisés Naím, "Latin America: The Second Stage of Reform," *Journal of Democracy* 5:4 (1994), 35; Haggard and Kaufman, *The Political Economy of Democratic Transitions*, 159; Dani Rodrik, "Understanding Economic Policy Reform," *Journal of Economic Literature* 34:1 (1996); Andrés Velasco, "A Model of Endogenous Fiscal Deficits and Delayed Fiscal Reforms," in *Fiscal Institutions and Fiscal Performance*, eds. James Poterba and Jürgen von Hagen (Chicago, IL: University of Chicago Press, 1999).

93. However, Rodrik notes the difficulty in establishing a threshold that determines what effectively constitutes a crisis. Dani Rodrik, "Understanding Economic Policy Reform," 28–29. For a critique of crisis-driven economic transformations in Latin America see Javier Corrales, "Do economic crisis contribute to economic reform? Argentina and Venezuela in the 1990s," *Political Science Quarterly* 112 (Winter 1997/1998).

94. Karen Remmer, "The Politics of Neoliberal Reform in South America, 1980–1994," *Studies in Comparative International Development* 33:2 (1998), 10.

95. Haggard and Kaufman, *The Political Economy of Democratic Transitions*, 14.

96. Waterbury, "The Heart of the Matter? Public Enterprise and the Adjustment Process."

97. Javier Corrales, "Do Economic Crises Contribute to Economic Reform? Argentina and Venezuela in the 1990s."

98. Glen Biglaiser and Karl DeRouen Jr., "The Expansion of Neoliberal Economic Reforms in Latin America," *International Studies Quarterly*, 48:3 (2004).

99. Kurt Weyland, "Growing Sustainability in Brazil's Democracy," in *The Third Wave of Democratization in Latin America*, eds. Francis Hagopian and Scott Mainwaring (New York, NY: Cambridge University Press, 2005).

100. Moisés Naím, *Paper Tigers and Minotaurs* (Washington, DC: Carnegie Endowment for International Peace, 1993).

101. The source of all statistics presented in this section, unless otherwise noted, is World Bank, *World Development Indicators*, 2011.

102. Dani Rodrik, "Understanding Economic Policy Reform"; Corrales, "Do Economic Crises Contribute to Economic Reform? Argentina and Venezuela in the 1990s."

103. Juan Martínez and Javier Santiso, "Financial Markets and Politics: The Confidence Game in Latin American Economies," *International Political Science Review* 24: 3 (2003), 373.

104. As will be discussed in Chapter 5 financial instability leading to Lula's election played a role in shaping the leftist government's economic policies in Brazil.

105. Birdsall and de la Torre, *The Washington Contentious*, 6; Eduardo Lora, Ugo Panizza, Myriam Quispe-Agnoli, "Reform Fatigue: Symptoms, Reasons, and Implications," *Economic Review* (Federal Reserve of Atlanta) (Second Quarter 2004).

106. Miles Kahler, "External Influence, Conditionality, and the Politics of External Adjustment," in *The Politics of Economic Adjustment*, eds. Kaufman and Haggard (Princeton, NJ: Princeton University Press, 1992).

107. Ronald McKinnon, *The Order of Economic Liberalization: Financial Control in the Transition to a Market Economy* (Baltimore, MD: Johns Hopkins University Press, 1991); Dani Rodrik, "How Should Structural Adjustment Programs Be Designed," *World Development* 18:7 (1990); Rudiger Dornbusch, "Credibility and Stabilization," *Quarterly Journal of Economics*, 106:3 (1991).

108. Sebastian Edwards, *Crisis and Reform in Latin America: From Despair to Hope* (New York, NY: Oxford University Press, 1995); Samuel Morley, Roberto Machado, and Stefano Pettinato, "Indexes of Structural Reform in Latin America," *Serie Reformas Económicas* 12 (Santiago, Chile: ECLAC, 1999).

109. John Williamson, "An Agenda for Growth and Reform," in *After the Washington Consensus*, eds. Kuczynski and Williamson (Washington, DC: IIE, 2003).

110. Moisés Naím, "The Real Story Behind Venezuela's Woes," *Journal of Democracy* 12:2 (2001).

111. Morley, Machado, and Pettinato's (1999) index of market reform is constructed based on measures of privatizations, trade liberalization, financial liberalization, and tax reform. The lowest value of the index is 0—indicating no reform—and the highest is 1. The conclusions presented here remain unchanged when using earlier classifications of neoliberal depth characterizing Argentina, Bolivia, Chile, and Mexico as countries experiencing a dramatic liberalization process, and Brazil, Colombia, Uruguay, and Venezuela as countries with limited liberalizing efforts. See, for example, Geddes, "Challenging the Conventional Wisdom," 108.

112. Schamis, *Reforming the State: The Politics of Privatization in Latin America and Europe*; Geddes, "Challenging the Conventional Wisdom"; Levitsky and Way, "Between a Shock and a Hard Place: The Dynamics of Labor Based Adjustment in Argentina and Poland."

113. Schamis, *Reforming the State: The Politics of Privatization in Latin America and Europe*, 4.

114. Currency substitution is defined as residents of one country preferring to hold foreign currency to adapt to adverse domestic economic conditions, particularly during inflationary times.

115. Erik Wibbels and Moisés Arce, "Globalization, Taxation, and Burden Shifting in Latin America," *International Organization* 57:1 (2003).

116. Some authors suggest that interest groups fail to account altogether for the initiation of economic transformations. See Krueger, *Political Economy of Policy Reform in Developing Countries*. This view claims that business demands were largely ignored in some cases, such as in Brazil in the late 1970s. In the case of Chile, one argument suggests that Pinochet's change of economic model preceded the involvement of business. See Silva, "From Dictatorship to Democracy: The Business-State Nexus in Chile's Economic Transformation, 1975–1994." Consistent with this perspective, Geddes suggests that societal interests hurt by globalization, even when numerically large and well-organized (e.g., labor in comparison with other groups) have often failed to force policy change at all. She argues that scholars tend to wrongly rely on interest groups or classes as explanatory variables, without considering whether these groups are politically influential. See Geddes, "Challenging the conventional wisdom," 109.

117. Geddes, "Challenging the conventional wisdom"; Murillo, "From Populism to Neoliberalism: Labor Unions and Market Reforms in Latin America;" Richard Roman and Edur Velasco, "Neoliberalism, Labor Market Transformation, and Working-Class Responses," *Latin American Perspectives* 28:4 (2001); Schamis, *Reforming the State: The Politics of Privatization in Latin*

America and Europe; Wibbels and Arce, "Globalization, Taxation, and Burden Shifting in Latin America."

118. Wibbels and Arce, "Globalization, Taxation, and Burden Shifting in Latin America."

119. Cohen and Centeno, "Neoliberalism and Patterns of Economic Performance, 1980–2006," 35; Saavedra, "Labor Markets during the 1990s," 246.

120. Geddes, "Challenging the Conventional Wisdom," 110.

121. The Inter-American Development Bank reports unionization rates circa 1997, i.e., a year before Hugo Chávez was elected president of Venezuela. While this indicator does not allow us to know exactly the unionization rate at the time each leftist president reached power in each country, it provides a good approximation given that unionization rates are generally slow moving. Inter-American Development Bank, *Good Jobs Wanted: Labor Markets in Latin America* (Washington, DC: IADB, 2004).

122. Haggard and Kaufman, *The Political Economy of Democratic Transitions*, 160; Stephan Haggard and Mathew McCubbins, "Politics, Institutions and Macro-Economic Adjustment: Hungarian Fiscal Policy-Making in Comparative Perspective," in *Reforming the State: Fiscal and Welfare Reform in Post-Socialist Countries*, eds. János Kornai, Stephan Haggard and Robert Kaufman (New York, NY: Cambridge University Press, 2001); Weyland, "Neoliberalism and Democracy in Latin America: A Mixed Record"; Mark Jones, "Legislator Behavior and Executive-Legislative Relations in Latin America," *Latin American Research Review* 37:3 (2002), 182.

123. Joan Nelson, "The Politics of Economic Transformation: Is Third World Experience Relevant in Eastern Europe?" *World Politics* 45:3 (1993), 436.

124. Stephen Holmes, "The Politics of Economics in the Czech Republic," *East European Constitutional Review* 4 (Spring 1995), 52–55.

125. Haggard and Kaufman, *The Political Economy of Democratic Transitions*, 9.

126. Alejandro Foxley, *Latin American Experiments in Neoconservative Economics* (Berkeley, CA: University of California Press, 1983).

127. Delia Ferreira Rubio and Matteo Goretti, "When the President Governs Alone: The Decretazo in Argentina 1989–1993," in *Executive Decree Authority*, eds. John Carey and Matthew Shugart (New York, NY: Cambridge University Press, 1998); Murillo, "From Populism to Neoliberalism: Labor Unions and Market Reforms in Latin America."

128. Brian Crisp, "Lessons from Economic Reform in the Venezuelan Democracy," *Latin American Research Review* 33:1 (1996).

129. Programa de Naciones Unidas para el Desarrollo, *La democracia en América Latina* (New York, NY: UNDP, 2004). This classification ranks countries based on whether presidents have package veto, item veto, power of decree, the exclusive authority to introduce legislation, and the ability to pass legislation through plebiscites. It reflects changes in executive powers in Venezuela as a result of the 1999 Constitution. An alternative index reflecting executive powers before all leftist presidents reached power is Shugart and Haggard's index of presidential powers. The conclusions presented in this discussion do not change in any meaningful way when this alternative index is used. See Shugart and Haggard, "Institutions and Public Policy in Presidential Systems," 80.

130. "Decreto Supremo de Nacionalización de Hidrocarburos 'Héroes del Chaco' 28701," *Gaceta Oficial de Bolivia*, May 1, 2006.

131. "El control de precios da sus primeros resultados," *La Razón*, August 21, 2007.

132. "Decreto Supremo 29541," *Gaceta Oficial de Bolivia*, May 1, 2008.

133. "Decreto Supremo 29888," *Gaceta Oficial de Bolivia*, January 23, 2009.

134. "Decreto Ejecutivo 662," *Registro Oficial*, October 4, 2007.

135. "Decreto Ejecutivo 846," *Registro Oficial*, January 2, 2008. "Decreto Ejecutivo 1042," *Registro Oficial*, April 23, 2008.

136. "Decreto Ejecutivo 1348," *Registro Oficial*, September 23, 2008.

137. In Venezuela, opposition parties had a majority in the Chamber of Deputies and the Senate. In Bolivia, the opposition had a majority in the Senate. Although not a case of a weak executive, Ecuador is another example where the opposition dominated both houses of Congress; Correa's party did not field a single candidate to the legislature.

138. Ricardo Combellas, "El proceso constituyente y la Constitución de 1999," *Politeia* 30:30 (2003); Javier Corrales, "Origins of Constitutions and Degrees of Presidentialism in Latin America 1987–2009," unpublished ms., Amherst College (2009).

139. In Bolivia the presidential term remained unchanged at five years with reelection, but consecutive election is now allowed. In Ecuador, the new Constitution maintained the existing prerogatives of the executive to issue decrees and veto legislation, but changed the reelection provision from one interim period to consecutive reelection. For a discussion of Ecuador's reforms, see Santiago Basabe-Serrano, "Ecuador: Reforma Constitucional, Nuevos Actores Políticos y Viejas Prácticas Partidistas," *Revista de Ciencia Política* (Santiago, Chile), 29:2 (2009), 388.

140. Mainwaring, *Rethinking Party Systems in the Third Wave of Democratization: The Case of Brazil*, 5; Adam Przeworski, "Institutions Matter?" *Government and Opposition* 39:4 (Autumn 2004).

141. Paul Pierson and Theda Skocpol, "Historical Institutionalism in Contemporary Political Science," in *Political Science: The State of the Discipline*, eds. Ira Katznelson and Helen Millner (New York, NY: Norton, 2002); Kathleen Thelen, "Historical Institutionalism in Comparative Politics," *Annual Review of Political Science* 2 (June 1999).

CHAPTER 4

1. Speech given in the ceremony to swear in his new cabinet, January 8, 2007.

2. Speech given in the ceremony to swear in his new cabinet, January 8, 2007.

3. As will be discussed later in the chapter, the 1999 Constitution altered executive-legislative relations to strengthen the powers of the president. These transformations were a product of Chávez's presidency and were possible due to the disarray of the party system.

4. Miriam Kornblith and Daniel Levine, "Venezuela: The Life and Times of the Party System" in *Building Democratic Institutions: Party Systems in Latin America*, eds. Scott Mainwaring and Timothy Scully (Stanford, CA: Stanford University Press, 1995); Mainwaring and Scully, "Introduction: Party Systems in Latin America."

5. The Pact's objective was to avoid the unilateral rule that sparked the coup ending the democratic rule of the *Trienio* (1945–1948) and gave way to a decade of military rule under Marcos Pérez Jiménez.

6. Jennifer McCoy, "Chávez and the End of 'Partyarchy' in Venezuela," *Journal of Democracy* 10:3 (1999).

7. María Antonia Moreno and Cameron A. Shelton, "Sleeping in the Bed One Makes: The Venezuelan Fiscal Policy Response to the Oil Boom" in *Anatomy of a Collapse: Venezuela*, eds.

Ricardo Hausmann and Francisco Rodríguez (unpublished ms., Harvard University and Wesleyan College, 2010).

8. Espinasa served as PDVSA's former chief economist. Ramón Espinasa, "Petróleo, economía e historia," in Luis Pedro España, *Democracia y Renta Petrolera* (Caracas: Universidad Católica Andrés Bello, 1989).

9. Ricardo Villasmil, Francisco Monaldi, Germán Ríos, and Marino González, "The Difficulties of Reforming an Oil Dependent Economy: The Case of Venezuela," in *Understanding Market Reforms in Latin America*, ed. José María Fanelli (New York, NY: Palgrave, 2007).

10. Steve Ellner, *Rethinking Venezuelan Politics* (Boulder, CO: Lynne Rienner, 2008).

11. Ricardo Villasmil, Francisco Monaldi, Germán Ríos, and Marino González, "The Difficulties of Reforming an Oil Dependent Economy: The Case of Venezuela," 273.

12. Thad Dunning, *Crude Democracy* (New York, NY: Cambridge University Press, 2008), 177.

13. Francisco Monaldi, Rosa Gonzalez, Richard Obuchi, and Michael Penfold, "Political Institutions, Policymaking Processes, and Policy Outcomes in Venezuela," Inter American Development Bank, Research Network Working Paper R-507 (2006); Dunning, *Crude Democracy*, 178.

14. Aníbal Romero, "Rearranging the Deck Chairs on the Titanic: The Agony of Democracy in Venezuela," *Latin American Research Review*, 32:1 (1997).

15. World Bank, *World Development Indicators*, 2011.

16. Measured in Purchasing Power Parity (PPP) dollars of 2000.

17. Kenneth Roberts, "Social Correlates of Party System Demise and Populist Resurgence in Venezuela," *Latin American Politics and Society* 45:3 (2003).

18. López Maya, "The Venezuelan Caracazo of 1989: Popular Protest and Institutional Weakness," 117. In a slightly different view, former COPEI congressional leader Gustavo Tarre emphasizes that the protests were not as much a reaction to the neoliberal reforms announced by Pérez, which had not been implemented yet, as to the escalation of violence due to the slow, inefficient response of young, inexperienced soldiers and their perplexed leadership (author's interview, March 14, 2007, Caracas, Venezuela).

19. López Maya, "The Venezuelan Caracazo of 1989: Popular Protest and Institutional Weakness."

20. Although the Ministry of Defense officially reported 277 deaths and approximately 1,800 wounded, López Maya assembles evidence from different sources that the actual toll approximated 400 dead people and a considerably higher number of wounded people. López Maya, "The Venezuelan Caracazo of 1989: Popular Protest and Institutional Weakness."

21. Romero, "Rearranging the Deck Chairs on the Titanic: The Agony of Democracy in Venezuela"; Daniel Levine, "Good-bye to Venezuelan Exceptionalism," *Journal of Inter-American Studies and World Affairs* 36:4 (1994).

22. Edgardo Lander, "The Impact of Neoliberal Adjustment in Venezuela, 1983–1993," *Latin American Perspectives* 23:3 (1996).

23. Brian Crisp, "Lessons from Economic Reform in the Venezuelan Democracy," *Latin American Research Review* 33:1 (1996), 23.

24. Levine, "Good-bye to Venezuelan Exceptionalism," 148.

25. The deterioration of the party system has been extensively documented. See Kornblith and Levine, "Venezuela: The Life and Times of the Party System" in *Building Democratic Institutions: Party Systems in Latin America, eds.* Mainwaring and Scully (Stanford, CA: Stanford University Press, 1995); Aníbal Romero, "Rearranging the Deck Chairs on the Titanic: The Agony of Democracy in Venezuela"; José Molina and Carmen Pérez, "Evolution of the Party System in

Venezuela 1946–1993," *Journal of Interamerican Studies and World Affairs* 40:3 (1998); Jennifer McCoy, "Chávez and the End of 'Partyarchy' in Venezuela," *Journal of Democracy* 10:3 (1999); Roberts, "Social Correlates of Party System Demise and Populist Resurgence in Venezuela"; Jennifer McCoy and David Myers (eds.), *The Unraveling of Representative Democracy in Venezuela* (Baltimore, MD: Johns Hopkins University Press, 2004); Levine, "Good-bye to Venezuelan Exceptionalism." Some authors have even referred to this deterioration as collapse. See Henry Dietz and David Myers, "From Thaw to Deluge: Party System Collapse in Venezuela and Peru," *Latin American Politics and Society* 49: 2 (2007), 61.

26. Mainwaring and Scully, "Introduction: Party Systems in Latin America."

27. Michael Coppedge, "The Dynamic Diversity of Latin American Party Systems," *Party Politics* 4:4 (1998).

28. Romero, "Rearranging the Deck Chairs on the Titanic: The Agony of Democracy in Venezuela," 14.

29. Steve Ellner and Miguel Tinker Salas, "The Venezuelan Exceptionalism Thesis: Separating Myth from Reality," *Latin American Perspectives* 32: 5 (2005), 10.

30. José Molina, "The Presidential and Parliamentary Elections of the Bolivarian Revolution in Venezuela: Change and Continuity (1998–2000)," *Bulletin of Latin American Research* 21:2 (2002), Table 3.

31. Conciencia 21, *Estudio de Valores del Venezolano*, Caracas, Venezuela, June 1995, 217.

32. Michael Coppedge, "The Rise and Fall of Partyarchy," in *Constructing Democratic Governance: South America in the 1990s*, ed. Jorge Domínguez and Abraham Lowenthal (Baltimore, MD: Johns Hopkins University Press, 1996).

33. Molina, "The Presidential and Parliamentary Elections of the Bolivarian Revolution in Venezuela."

34. Levine, "Good-bye to Venezuelan Exceptionalism," 148.

35. Romero, "Rearranging the Deck Chairs on the Titanic: The Agony of Democracy in Venezuela," 28.

36. Steve Ellner and Miguel Tinker Salas, "The Venezuelan Exceptionalist Thesis: Separating Myth from Reality," 10.

37. Giovanni Sartori, *Parties and Party Systems: A Framework for Analysis.*

38. Javier Corrales, "The Backlash against Market Reforms in Latin America in the 2000s," in *Constructing Democratic Governance in Latin America*, ed. Domínguez and Shifter (Baltimore, MD: Johns Hopkins University Press, 2008), 64.

39. Margarita López Maya, "Venezuela after the Caracazo: Forms of Protest in a Deinstitutionalized Context," *Bulletin of Latin American Research* 21:2 (2002); Charles Tilly and Sidney Tarrow, *Contentious Politics* (Boulder, CO: Paradigm Publishers, 2007).

40. Michael Coppedge, "The Rise and Fall of Partyarchy," in *Constructing Democratic Governance: South America in the 1990s*, ed. Jorge Domínguez and Abraham Lowenthal (Baltimore, MD: Johns Hopkins University Press, 1996), 15.

41. Jennifer McCoy and William Smith, "Desconsolidación o reequilibrio democrático en Venezuela," *Nueva Sociedad* 140 (1995), 10.

42. Polo Patriótico, *Programa de Gobierno* (Caracas, Venezuela, 1998).

43. Henry Dietz and David Myers, "From Thaw to Deluge: Party System Collapse in Venezuela and Peru".

44. The MVR, for example, was formed in July 1997 and registered officially on October 21, 1997. See Richard Gott, *Hugo Chávez and the Bolivarian Revolution* (London: Verso, 2005), 137; Valia Pereira-Almao, "Movimiento V República" in *Partidos políticos de América Latina*, eds. Manuel Alcántara and Flavia Freidenberg (Salamanca, Spain: Universidad de Salamanca Press, 2001), 587.

45. "Irene Sáez: las encuestas suben y bajan pero las preferencias se mantienen," *Notitarde de Valencia*, March 28, 1998.

46. Author's interview with president of COPEI, Luis Ignacio Planas, March 15, 2007.

47. Deborah Norden, "The Rise of the Lieutenant Colonels: Rebellion in Argentina and Venezuela," *Latin American Perspectives*, 23:3 (1996), 78.

48. Author's interview with former COPEI congressional leader Gustavo Tarre, March 14, 2007.

49. As further evidence that the support for democratic institutions was eroding, Caldera, who was a senator at the time of the coup, gave a famous speech sympathizing with Chávez's reasons for staging a coup. In justifying Chávez's motives he stated that, "It is difficult to expect from people unconditional support for freedom and democracy when people know that freedom and democracy are incapable of feeding them." Transcript of Caldera's congressional speech on February 4, 1992.

50. Valia Pereira-Almao, "Movimiento V República."

51. Roberts, "Social Correlates of Party System Demise and Populist Resurgence in Venezuela."

52. Weyland, "Economic Voting Reconsidered: Crisis and Charisma in the Election of Hugo Chavez."

53. Kirk Hawkins, *Venezuela's Chavismo and Populism in Comparative Perspective* (New York, NY: Cambridge University Press, 2010), 99–110.

54. Hugo Chávez, *Agenda Alternativa Bolivariana*, (Caracas, Venezuela: MBR, 1996), 4.

55. Damarys Canache, "Urban Poor and Political Order," in *The Unraveling of Venezuelan Democracy*, eds. McCoy and Myers (Baltimore, MD: Johns Hopkins University Press, 2004), 46.

56. Javier Corrales, "In Search of a Theory of Polarization: Lessons from Venezuela, 1999–2005," *Revista Europea de Estudios Latinoamericanos y del Caribe* 79 (October 2005), 106.

57. As is the case in any free and fair election, the outcome of the 1998 election was by no means certain beforehand. However, only personalistic candidates with recently created electoral vehicles participated in that election.

58. Congreso de la República de Venezuela, *Ley orgánica que autoriza al presidente de la república para dictar medidas extraordinarias en material económica y financiera requeridas por el interés público (Ley Habilitante)*, Caracas, Venezuela, April 1999.

59. "Congreso considerará observaciones del Ejecutivo," *El Universal*, April 7, 1999.

60. "Chávez rechazó Habilitante que le aprobó el Congreso," *Notitarde*, April 7, 1999.

61. McCoy, "Chávez and the End of 'Partyarchy' in Venezuela."

62. "Fracciones repudiaron decisión del Ejecutivo," *El Universal*, April 8, 1999.

63. "El Congreso Nacional se está autodisolviendo," *Notitarde*, April 15, 1999.

64. "Nuevas amenazas ameritan intervención de la OEA," *El Universal*, April 12, 1999.

65. "En una semana aprobarán Ley Habilitante," *El Universal*, April 8, 1999.

66. The election of 27-year-old Capriles Radonski, a first-time representative (diputado), as the president of the Chamber of Deputies reflects the disarray of the established parties and the exodus of more seasoned cadres.

67. Interview with Henrique Capriles Radonski in *Notitarde*, "Congreso Nacional plantea entendimiento con Hugo Chávez," April 8, 1999.

68. "Comisión Bicameral de Finanzas Aprobó Reformas a la Habilitante," *Notitarde*, April 22, 1999.

69. Thaís Maingón, Carmen Pérez, and Heinz Sonntag, "La batalla por una nueva Constitución para Venezuela," *Revista Mexicana de Sociología* 62:4 (2000), 109.

70. Although pro-Chávez candidates garnered 60 percent of the total vote, the government's electoral rules designed for the Constitutional Convention granted Chavista candidates 95 percent of the seats. Michael Coppedge, "Venezuela: Popular Sovereignty versus Liberal Democracy," in *Constructing Democratic Governance in Latin America*, ed. Jorge Domínguez and Michael Shifter (Baltimore, MD: Johns Hopkins University Press, 2003).

71. The 1961 Constitution mandated a 10-year ban for reelection after a president had been in office.

72. Previously, Leyes Habilitantes granted the president powers related to financial matters, but the 1999 Constitution expanded the scope of the powers granted by Congress.

73. Kurt Weyland, "Will Chávez Lose His Luster?" *Foreign Affairs* 80:6 (2001).

74. Asamblea Nacional de la República Bolivariana de Venezuela, *Ley que autoriza al Presidente de la República para dictar decretos con fuerza de ley en materias que se delegan (Ley Habilitante)*, Caracas, Venezuela, November, 11, 2000.

75. "Ley Habilitante permite un cambio estructural," *Notitarde de Valencia*, November 14, 2000; "Ley Habilitante: Vía directa al socialismo," *Agencia Bolivariana de Noticias*, February 7, 2007.

76. Luis Lander and Margarita López Maya, "Venezuela: La hegemonía amenazada," *Revista Nueva Sociedad* 167 (2000), 23.

77. World Bank, *World Development Indicators*, 2011.

78. Author's interview with Venezuela's Vice President Adina Bastida (2000–2002), May 10, 2011.

79. Author's interview with Bernardo Álvarez, Venezuela's ambassador to the United States, former vice minister of hydrocarbons at the Ministry of Energy and Mines, and former deputy to the National Assembly, December 5, 2006.

80. Author's interview with Luis Ignacio Planas, COPEI's secretary-general and later president, March 15, 2007.

81. This was the last election before the MVR and other pro-Chávez parties merged into the Partido Socialista Unido de Venezuela (United Socialist Party of Venezuela—PSUV) with the exceptions of the Partido Comunista de Venezuela (Communist Party of Venezuela—PCV), Patria Para Todos (Fatherland for All—PPT), and Por la Democracia Social (For Social Democracy—PODEMOS). The PSUV held its founding Congress in January 2008 and formally participated for the first time in the November 2008 regional elections.

82. Asamblea Nacional de la República Bolivariana de Venezuela, *Ley que autoriza al Presidente de la República para dictar Decretos con Rango, Valor y Fuerza de Ley, en las Materias que se Delegan, Gaceta Oficial 38.617*, Caracas, Venezuela, February 1, 2007.

83. "Decreto 5.229," *Gaceta Oficial* 38.638, March 6, 2007.

84. "Decreto 5.200," *Gaceta Oficial* 38.632, February 26, 2007.

85. "Decreto 5.197," *Gaceta Oficial* 38.629, February 21, 2007. Chávez's statist measures were described in detail in Chapter 2.

86. Asamblea Nacional de la República Bolivariana de Venezuela, *Ley que autoriza al Presidente de la República para dictar Decretos con Rango, Valor y Fuerza de Ley en las materias que se delegan, Gaceta Oficial (Extraordinaria) 6.009*, Caracas, Venezuela, December 20, 2010.

87. "TSJ declara constitucional el primer decreto ley de Chávez en marco habilitante," *Noticias 24 de Zulia*, January 7, 2011.

88. Weyland, "The Rise of Latin America's Two Lefts: Insights from Rentier State Theory"; Raúl Madrid, "The Origins of the Two Lefts in Latin America," *Political Science Quarterly* 125:4 (Winter 2010–11).

89. Luis Gómez Calcaño and Margarita López Maya, *El tejido de Penélope: La reforma del Estado en Venezuela (1984–1988)*. Caracas: Cendes-APUCV-IPP (1990).

90. Jennifer McCoy and William Smith, "Desconsolidación o reequilibrio democrático en Venezuela," 5.

91. Coppedge, "The Rise and Fall of Partyarchy," 8–19.

92. Jorge Domínguez, "Constructing Democratic Governance in Latin America," in *Constructing Democratic Governance in Latin America*, ed. Domínguez and Shifter (Baltimore, MD: Johns Hopkins University Press, 2003), 364.

93. Di John, *From Winfall to Course? Oil and Industrialization in Venezuela, 1920 to the Present*, 21.

94. Julia Buxton, "Economic Policy and the Rise of Hugo Chávez," in *Venezuelan Politics in the Chávez Era*, ed. Steve Ellner and Daniel Hellinger (Boulder, CO: Lynne Rienner, 2003).

95. Michael Penfold-Becerra, "Clientelism and Social Funds: Evidence from Chávez's Misiones," *Latin American Politics and Society* 49:4 (2007).

96. Penfold-Becerra, "Clientelism and Social Funds: Evidence from Chávez's Misiones."

97. Dubbed as "Agenda Venezuela," Caldera's stabilization policies included measures to rein in the fiscal deficit, introduce a value-added tax, allow private investment in the energy sector, and secure an IMF credit line.

98. Hugo Chávez, *Agenda Alternativa Bolivariana* (Caracas, Venezuela: MBR, 1996).

99. Polo Patriótico, *Programa de Gobierno*.

100. Author's interview with Teodoro Petkoff, March 13, 2007.

101. All of the oil prices included here are rounded to the nearest dollar and expressed in real terms (January 2009 dollars). Source: Inflation Data, available at http://inflationdata.com/inflation/Inflation_Rate/Historical_Oil_Prices_Table.asp.

102. "El Congreso considerará observaciones del Ejecutivo," *El Universal*, April, 7, 1999.

103. The 1999 Constitution is explicit about the state's obligations regarding industrial policy; the promotion of manufacturing, agriculture, and tourism; and ownership of PDVSA, inter alia, in its Title IV, Chapter 1: Del Régimen Socio Económico y la Función del Estado en la Economía.

104. Bernard Mommer, "Subversive Oil" in *Venezuelan Politics in the Chávez Era*, ed. Steve Ellner and Daniel Hellinger (Boulder, CO: Lynn Rienner, 2003).

105. Buxton, "Economic Policy and the Rise of Hugo Chávez."

106. "Cronología de la implantación de la Ley de Tierras," *Agencia Bolivariana de Noticias*, December 9, 2004.

107. Ellner, *Rethinking Venezuelan Politics*.

108. Janet Kelly and Pedro Palma, "Economic Decline and the Quest for Change," in *The Unraveling of Representative Democracy in Venezuela*, ed. Jennifer McCoy and David Myers (Baltimore, MD: Johns Hopkins University Press, 2004), 220.

109. Fiscal stringency remained a priority in the face of Congress' rejection of the 1999 budget, which meant that the country operated on the previous year's budget, based on higher oil prices calculated in 1997. Ministerio de Finanzas de la República Bolivariana de Venezuela, *Presupuesto Reconducido 1999 y Modificaciones* (Caracas, Venezuela, January 31, 2000).

110. Author's interview with José Alejandro Rojas, Hugo Chavez's finance minister (1999–2001), September 27, 2010.

111. Decreto 2.308, *Gaceta Oficial* 38.638, February 5, 2003.

112. "Nacionalización de Sidor es pilar del plan para sector siderúrgico," *El Universal*, May 2, 2008; "Cemex velará por los intereses de sus inversores y empleados en Venezuela," *El Universal*, April 24, 2008.

113. "Otorgan fondos para el avalúo del Banco de Venezuela," *El Universal*, December 19, 2008.

114. "Venezuela y Rusia explotarán el gran yacimiento de oro de Las Cristinas," *Tal Cual Digital*, January 14, 2009.

115. "Gobierno oficializa adquisición forzosa de café Fama de América," *El Universal*, November 11, 2009.

116. "Gobernador de Sucre anunció la expropiación de procesadora de sardinas La Gaviota," *El Nacional*, March 19, 2009.

117. "Chávez ordena expropiar Cargill y amenaza a Polar," *El Universal*, March 4, 2009.

118. "Gobierno decide expropiar el hotel Margarita Hilton," *El Universal*, October 14, 2009.

119. Author's interview with José Vicente Rangel, former vice president, minister of defense, and minister of foreign affairs. Caracas, Venezuela, March 15, 2007.

120. Weyland, "Will Chávez Lose His Luster?" Javier Corrales and Michael Penfold, "Venezuela: Crowding Out the Opposition," *Journal of Democracy* 18: 2 (2007).

121. Author's interview with Teodoro Petkoff, Caracas, Venezuela, March 13, 2007.

122. Raúl Madrid, "Laboring against Neoliberalism: Unions and Patterns of Reform in Latin America," *Journal of Latin American Studies* 35:1 (2003); Murillo, "From Populism to Neoliberalism: Labor Unions and Market Reforms in Latin America."

123. Steve Ellner, "Organized Labor Movement and the Challenge of *Chavismo*," in *Venezuelan Politics in the Chavez Era: Class, Polarization, and Conflict*, ed. Steve Ellner and Daniel Hellinger (Boulder, CO: Lynn Rienner, 2003).

124. Steve Ellner, "Organized Labor Movement and the Challenge of Chavismo."

125. Ángel Álvarez, "Venezuela 2007: los motores del socialismo se alimentan con petróleo," *Revista de Ciencia Política* (Santiago) 27, Special Volume (2007).

126. Haggard and Shugart, "Institutions and Public Policy in Presidential Systems," 80. UNDP, *La democracia en América Latina*; Gabriel Negretto, "Political Parties and Institutional Design: Explaining Constitutional Choice in Latin America," *British Journal of Political Science* 39:1 (2009).

127. United Nations Development Program, *La democracia en América Latina* (New York, NY: UNDP, 2004); Ricardo Combellas, "El proceso constituyente y la Constitución de 1999," *Politeia* 30:30 (2003); Javier Corrales, "Origins of Constitutions and Degrees of Presidentialism in Latin America 1987–2009," unpublished ms., Amherst College (2009); Negretto, "Political Parties and Institutional Design: Explaining Constitutional Choice in Latin America."

128. The Constitutional Assembly also found resistance in the legal arena. However, federal judges expressing reservations about the legality of the process were first intimidated by pro-Chávez supporters and then formally removed. Combellas "El proceso constituyente y la

Constitución de 1999"; Corrales, "Origins of Constitutions and Degrees of Presidentialism in Latin America 1987–2009."

129. Morley, Machado, and Pettinato, "Indexes of Structural Reform in Latin America."

130. Author's interview with Eleazar Díaz Rangel, Caracas, Venezuela, March 14, 2007.

131. Dubbed "The Great Turnaround," the reform included privatizations, the reduction of government spending, trade, financial, and monetary liberalization, tax reform, and general macroeconomic stabilization. See Crisp, "Lessons from Economic Reform in the Venezuelan Democracy," 22.

CHAPTER 5

1. Lula da Silva's "Carta ao povo brasileiro," (Letter to the Brazilian People) São Paulo, June 22, 2002.

2. "A reforma agrária está para nós assim como o oxigênio está para a humanidade." 1989 Presidential debate between Fernando Collor de Mello and Lula da Silva.

3. "E preciso que aqueles que ganharam muito durante os ultimos 30 anos deixem de ganhar o que estão ganhando para poder redistribuir em forma do salario. Sem que alguém perda não é possível alguém ganhar." 1989 Presidential debate between Fernando Collor de Mello and Lula da Silva.

4. Scott Mainwaring, "Brazilian Party Underdevelopment in Comparative Perspective," *Political Science Quarterly* 107:4 (1992); Scott Mainwaring and Timothy Scully, "Introduction: Party Systems in Latin America," in *Building Democratic Institutions: Party Systems in Latin America*, ed. Mainwaring and Scully (Stanford, CA: Stanford University Press, 1995); Kurt Weyland, "Neoliberal Populism in Latin America and Eastern Europe," *Comparative Politics* 31:4 (1999); Timothy J. Power, "Political Institutions in Democratic Brazil: Politics as a Permanent Consitutional Convention," in *Democratic Brazil*, ed. Timothy Power and Peter Kingstone (Pittsburgh, PA: University of Pittsburgh, 2000).

5. Francisco Panizza, "Is Brazil Becoming a Boring Country?" *Bulletin of Latin American Research* 19:4 (2000).

6. Leslie Armijo et al., "Compared to What? Assessing Brazilian Political Institutions," *Comparative Politial Studies* 39:6 (2006).

7. Bolívar Lamounier and Rachel Meneguello, *Partidos políticos e consolidacão democrática* (São Paulo: Brasilense, 1986); Bolívar Lamounier, "Estrutura institucional e governabilidade na década de 1990," in *O Brasil e as reformas políticas*, ed. João Paulo dos Reis Velloso (Rio de Janeiro: José Olympio, 1992). Scott Mainwaring, "Brazil: Weak Parties, Feckless Democracy," in *Building Democratic Institutions: Party Systems in Latin America*, ed. Mainwaring and Scully (Stanford, CA: Stanford University Press, 1995).

8. Mainwaring and Scully, "Introduction: Party Systems in Latin America."

9. Such electoral rules required straight party voting (known as *voto vinculado*), prohibited electoral coalitions, prevented a candidate from withdrawing unless the entire party was also withdrawing, and required parties to present candidates for all offices. See Timothy J. Power, *The Political Right in Post-Authoritarian Brazil: Elites, Institutions, and Democratization* (University Park, PA: Penn State University Press, 2000), 65.

10. Barry Ames, *The Deadlock of Democracy in Brazil* (Ann Arbor, MI: University of Michigan Press, 2002).

11. Riordan Roett, *Brazil: Politics in a Patrimonial Society*,(Westport, CT: Praeger, 1999).

12. Efforts to address this issue have been unsuccessful. Electoral rules introduced in October 2006 included 5 percent national thresholds (*cláusula de barreira*) and 2 percent across nine different states for a party to obtain recognition as a party fraction. Candidates that failed to reach these thresholds could still hold on to their seat, but they would not receive public funding for the next election. However, in December 2006, Brazil's top federal tribunal (*Supremo Tribunal Federal*) struck down the measure. "Fim da cláusula de barreira divide opiniões no Congresso," *Agencia Brasil*, December 7, 2006.

13. Mainwaring, "Brazil: Weak Parties, Feckless Democracy," 375.

14. Panizza, "Is Brazil Becoming a Boring Country?"

15. In spite of these parties' dominance in presidential races, these parties do not always command the two largest party fractions in Congress.

16. Bolívar Lamounier, *Partidos e utopias: o Brasil no limiar dos anos 90* (São Paulo: Loyola, 1989).

17. Margaret Keck, *The Workers' Party and Democratization in Brazil* (New Haven, CT: Yale University Press, 1992).

18. Brazil's electoral rules give a legislator the right to appear on the ballot for reelection, regardless of political behavior or party switching. This prerogative is known as *candidato nato*. Octavio Amorim Neto, "Critical Debates: The Puzzle of Party Discipline in Brazil," *Latin American Politics and Society* 44:1 (2002), 135.

19. Fabiano Santos and Márcio Grijó Vilarouca, "Political Institutions and Governability from FHC to Lula," in *Democratic Brazil Revisited*, ed. Kingstone and Power (Pittsburgh, PA: University of Pittsburgh Press, 2008), 77.

20. Senator Heloisa Helena and three representatives were expelled from the PT after opposing the party line on Lula's pension reforms. "Após expulsão, PT adverte os outros rebeldes," *Agência Estado*, December, 14, 2003.

21. The PDS replaced ARENA in 1979 following the military regime's provision (Decree 6.767, December 20, 1979) that parties had to include the word "party" as part of their name. Keck, *The Workers' Party and Democratization in Brazil*, 40–55.

22. "Quanto riso, oh, quanta alegria," *Veja*, August 27, 2003.

23. "Tiririca é o deputado federal mais votado no Brasil," *O Globo*, October 3, 2010.

24. In Portuguese, "*Pior do que tá não fica, vote Tiririca*" and "*Se eleito prometo ajudar todas as famílias brasileiras, especialmente a minha.*"

25. Yan de Souza Carreirão and Maria D'Alva Kinzo, "Partidos Políticos, Preferência Partidária e Decisão Eleitoral no Brasil (1989–2002)," *Dados* 47:1 (2004).

26. Recognition levels according to results from a survey conducted in 2002. Maria D'Alva Kinzo, "Parties in the electorate: Public Perceptions and Party Attachments in Brazil," *Revista Brasileira de Ciências Sociais* 2 (2006). The PFL became Democratas in 2007.

27. Some authors have characterized the PT's gradual shift from the left to the center-left as the erosion of its ideological consistency. See João Machado Borges Neto, "Um governo contraditório," *Revista da Sociedade Brasileira de Economia Política* 12 (June 2003); Hunter "The Normalization of an Anomaly: The Workers' Party in Brazil," *World Politics* 59:3 (2007). As will be discussed later, the PT and the PSDB have gradually shifted their positions over time.

28. "O PMDB é a essência do fisiologismo. Tem bons quadros, mas vive de troca de favores. Ignora concepção programática, visão doutrinária, tudo para acomodar os interesses dos seus

parlamentares, que só querem assegurar suas reeleições." Interview with PT Senator Tião Viana by Sandra Brasil, *Veja*, July 8, 2009.

29. Author's interview with former President Fernando Henrique Cardoso, April 6, 2010.

30. Rachel Meneguello, *PT: A formacão de um partido (1979–1982)* (São Paulo: Paz e Terra, 1989).

31. José Genoino, *Entre o sonho e o poder: a trajetória da esquerda brasileira através das memórias de José Genoino* (São Paulo: Geração Editorial, 2006), 111.

32. Michael Lowy, "A New Type of Party: The Brazilian PT," *Latin American Perspectives* 14:4 (1987), 454.

33. Luis Felipe Miguel, "Transformations in the Discourse of the Workers Party in the 2002 Elections," *Latin American Perspectives*, 33:4 (2006).

34. Luiz Inácio "Lula" da Silva, *Discurso na 1a Convenção Nacional do Partido dos Trabalhadores*, São Paulo, August 8, 1981.

35. Partido dos Trabalhadores, *Resolução do 4° Encontro Nacional do PT*, São Paulo, May–June 1986.

36. Three was also the PT's position on the ballot during the 1980s. Genoino, *Entre o sonho e o poder: a trajetória da esquerda brasileira através das memórias de José Genoino*, 121.

37. Genoino, *Entre o sonho e o poder: a trajetória da esquerda brasileira através das memórias de José Genoino*, 121.

38. Partido dos Trabalhadores, *Regulamentação das Tendencias Internas*, Brasília, December 1987.

39. Alan Daniel Freire de Lacerda, "O PT e a unidade partidária como problema," *Dados* 45:1 (2002), 50.

40. Partido dos Trabalhadores, *Resolução 5° Encontro Nacional do PT*, Brasília, December 1987.

41. Partido dos Trabalhadores, *Brasil, Urgente! Lula Presidente! Carta Aberta ao Povo Brasileiro*, Brasilia, December 6, 1987.

42. Partido dos Trabalhadores, *Resolução 5° Encontro Nacional do PT, Brasília*, December 1987.

43. Partido dos Trabalhadores, *Resolução 6° Encontro Nacional do PT*, São Paulo, June 1989.

44. Partido dos Trabalhadores, *Resolução 7° Encontro Nacional do PT*, São Paulo, May–June, 1990.

45. The National Congress has a similar format as an Encounter but is attended by a greater number of delegates and intends to elaborate more ambitious programmatic lines for the party's future.

46. Partido dos Trabalhadores, *Resolução I Congresso Nacional do PT*, São Bernardo do Campo, November–December 1991.

47. The following year the group founded the United Socialist Workers Party (*Partido Socialista dos Trabalhadores* Unificado—PSUT).

48. Freire de Lacerda, "O PT e a unidade partidária como problema," 61.

49. Clovis Bueno de Azevedo, *PT: A estrela Partida ao Meio* (Sao Paulo: Entrelinhas, 1995), 153.

50. Democracia Radical favored an alliance with PSDB for the 1994 election. In contrast, the tendencias on the left of the party's spectrum supported electoral alliances with ideologically like-minded parties, such as the PC do B and PSB. Genoino, *Entre o sonho e o poder: a trajetória da esquerda brasileira através das memórias de José Genoino*, 127.

51. Samuels, "From Socialism to Social-Democracy: Party Organization and the Transformation of the Worker's Party in Brazil," *Comparative Political Studies* 37:9 (2004), 1002. For a similar argument based on the moderating influence of local government but in the context of the

Uruguayan left, see David Altman, Rossana Castiglioni, and Juan Pablo Luna, "Uruguay: A Role Model for the Left?" in *Leftovers: Tales of the Two Latin American Lefts*, ed. Jorge Castañeda and Marco Morales (New York, NY: Routledge, 2008).

52. Author's interview with Glauco Arbix, October 20, 2010.

53. Other cities governed by the PT in the early 1990s include Santos, Campinas, Santo André, São Bernardo, Diadema and Piracicaba in São Paulo state; Angra dos Reis in Rio de Janeiro state; Ipatinga, João Monlevado, and Timoteo in Minas Gerais. Bueno de Azevedo, *PT: A Estrela Partida ao Meio*, 34.

54. Cláudio Gonçalves Couto, *O desafio de ser governo: O PT na prefeitura de São Paulo, 1989–1992* (São Paulo: Paz e Terra, 1995), 104.

55. Diretório Municipal do PT—São Paulo, *Resolução da Reunião do Diretório Municipal, November 26, 1988*, cited in Gonçalves Couto, *O desafio de ser governo: O PT na prefeitura de São Paulo, 1989–1992*, 134.

56. Gilson Menezes and Maria Luiza Fontenelle, respectively.

57. Gonçalves Couto, *O desafio de ser governo: O PT na prefeitura de São Paulo, 1989–1992*, 109.

58. Benjamin Goldfrank and Brian Wampler, "From Petista Way to Brazilian Way: How the PT Changes in the Road," *Revista Debates* (Porto Alegre) 2:2 (July–December 2008), 253–54.

59. Pedro Ribeiro, *Um partido em mutação: A transformação do PT e seus reflexos sobre as campanhas presidenciais (1989, 2002)* (PhD diss., Universidad Federal de São Carlos, 2004), 127.

60. Freire de Lacerda, "O PT e a unidade partidária como problema," 64.

61. Some of Articulação de Esquerda's most prominent leaders have been Arlindo Chinaglia, José Fritsch, Sonia Hypólito, Valter Pomar, Adão Pretto, and Luciano Zica.

62. Pere Petit and Pep Valenzuela, *Lula, ¡dónde vas!: Brasil entre la gestión de la crisis y la prometida transformación social* (Barcelona: Editorial Icaria, 2004), 107.

63. Bueno de Azevedo, *PT: A Estrela Partida ao Meio*, 157.

64. The PT's 1994 coalition, *Frente Brasil Popular*, included the Brazilian Socialist Party (*Partido Socialista Brasileiro*—PSB), Popular Socialist Party (*Partido Popular Socialista*—PPS), Communist Party of Brazil (*Partido Comunista do Brasil*—PC do B), United Socialist Workers Party (*Partido Socialista dos Trabalhadores Unificado*—PSUT), and the Green Party (*Partido Verde*—PV).

65. Partido dos Trabalhadores, *Bases do Programa de Goberno: Lula Presidente, Uma Revolução Democrática no Brasil*, 1994.

66. Bueno de Azevedo, *PT: A Estrela Partida ao Meio*, 158.

67. Even though Cardoso became president in the first round, a second round was held to decide some governorships.

68. Freire de Lacerda, "O PT e a unidade partidária como problema," 66–69.

69. Nova Democracia would be incorporated into Articulação Unidade na Luta by the PT's Second National Congress in 1999.

70. Freire de Lacerda, "O PT e a unidade partidária como problema," 69.

71. Samuels, "From Socialism to Social-Democracy: Party Organization and the Transformation of the Worker's Party in Brazil."

72. Hunter, "The Normalization of an Anomaly: The Workers Party in Brazil," 24.

73. "De 3 ao 13, do socialismo ao pragmatismo" *Folha de São Paulo*, October, 28, 2002.

74. Partido dos Trabalhadores, *Resolução do 12° Encontro Nacional do PT*, December 2001.

75. Partido dos Trabalhadores, *Resolução do Diretório Nacional sobre a Política de Alianças* (São Paulo, 2002), 1.

76. "Pedro Simon diz que aliança entre o PT e o PMDB daria vitória a Lula," *Universo Juridico*, June 1st, 2002. See also Matthew Flynn, "Alliances Key in the Scramble to Win Brazil's Presidency," Americas Program News Feature (Silver City, NM: Interhemispheric Resource Center, June 14, 2002).

77. Hunter, "The Normalization of an Anomaly: The Workers' Party in Brazil," 454.

78. Leoncio Martins Rodrigues, *Quem é quem na Constituinte: Uma análise sócio-política dos partidos e deputados* (São Paulo: OESP-Maltese, 1987).

79. Timothy J. Power, "Centering Democracy? Ideological Cleavages and the Convergence of Brazil's Political Class," in *Democratic Brazil Revisited*, ed. Kingstone and Power (Pittsburgh, PA: University of Pittsburgh Press, 2008), 93.

80. Peter Kingstone, *Crafting Coalitions for Reform: Business Preferences, Political Institutions, and Neoliberal Reforms in Brazil* (University Park, PA: Penn State University Press, 1999), 157.

81. Evidence of the difficulty to sustain such diverse alliances was the PL's opposing the government's position on the vote on minimum wages on June 17, 2004. "Planalto libera R$135,8 milhões en 20 dias," *Folha de São Paulo*, June 18, 2004.

82. Lula explicitly selected Liberal Party's José Alencar to become part of his ticket as vice president in order to appeal to conservative sectors of society who were concerned about Lula's leftist credentials. In 2005 Alencar left the Liberal Party and joined the new Brazilian Republican Party (PRB).

83. Author's interview with former President Fernando Henrique Cardoso, April 6, 2010.

84. Lee Alston and Bernardo Mueller, "Pork for Policy: Executive and Legislative Exchange in Brazil," *Journal of Law, Economics, and Organization* 22:1 (2005).

85. "Reformas tributária e da Previdência são prioridade," *O Estado do Paraná*, February 11, 2003.

86. This was the case not only for the PMDB as a swing party, but also for Lula's PT party, which was unable to guarantee 100 percent of support among its legislators. Additionally, guaranteeing a majority was complicated by party switching: 69 legislators had switched parties between the legislative election in October 2002 and May 2003. "Migração de deputados," *Correio Braziliense*, May 12, 2003.

87. "Megaoperação para votar reforma da Previdência: Verbas e nomeações em troca de votos," *Diario de Pernambuco*, August 4, 2003.

88. "Reforma da previdência é uma farsa, acusa Helena," *O Estado do Paraná*, June 11, 2003.

89. "Oposição e Governo negociam Reforma Previdenciária," *Agência Câmara*, July 10, 2003.

90. "Previdência terá novas mudanças," *Correio Braziliense*, September 17, 2003.

91. "Berzoini: Governo pode mudar pontos da reforma previdenciaria," *Correio do Brasil*, July 7, 2003.

92. Testimony by PSDB Representative Ronaldo Dimas, Chamber of Deputies, Congressional Session Transcript 199.3.52.O, August 8, 2005.

93. The CPMF was created in 1997 and renewed in 1999 and 2001 by Fernando Henrique Cardoso. In 2003 Lula renewed it in what was dubbed as a *minireforma tributaria*, or mini-tax reform. The Lula government was forced to break up his intended tax reform into several pieces, with the CPMF being one of them, in order to improve changes of approval.

94. Agência Brasil, "Oposição derrubou CPMF para ganhar de mim as eleições de 2010, diz Lula," March 3, 2008.

95. "Considerando diretamente, acaba o Bolsa Família." Interview with Patrus Ananias, minister of social development, in *Agência Brasil*, "Para ministro, fim da CPMF poderia acabar com o Bolsa Família," September 4, 2007.

96. Interview with PMDB Senator Gérson Camata, member of the Economic Affairs Committee (CAE) in *O Globo Online*, "Oposicão derruba a prorrogacão da CPMF no Senado," December 13, 2007.

97. *Café com o Presidente* (Lula's weekly radio address), "Para Lula, rejeição da CPMF pelo Senado não é o fim do mundo," December 17, 2007.

98. "Agora, PT vai propor lei de BC autônomo," *Fohla de São Paulo*, October 28, 2002; "Palocci anuncia projeto de autonomia para o Banco Central," *Época*, January 3, 2003.

99. *Folha de São Paulo*, "Governo retoma projeto de autonomia do BC," March 5, 2005; "Palocci defende aprofundamento de discussões sobre autonomia do Banco Central," *Época*, March 30, 2005.

100. The administration's efforts ended when Guido Mantega replaced Palocci as finance minister in March 2006. "Guido Mantega assume e acalma mercados," *O Estado do Paraná*, March 29, 2006.

101. "Lula defende reforma tributária ainda neste ano," *O Globo*, December 2, 2008.

102. Lula's attempt to reorganize the power industry was approved by the lower chamber, but proved unable to work its way through the Senate. "Critics put paid to Lula's Power Bill," *FT*, February 6, 2004.

103. "Lula pede ajuda na aprovação do PAC, mas admite racha na base," *Folha de São Paulo*, January 30, 2007.

104. Author's interview with Eduardo Melo, special adviser to the President's Chief of Staff, in charge of overseeing the PAC, November 11, 2010.

105. The 1997 Asian crisis contributed to Brazil's meager growth, but its consequences are hardly comparable to the severe contraction of the Argentine and Uruguayan economies due to the 2001–2002 crisis.

106. The rest of the BRICS, Russia, India, and China, were growing above 7 percent annually. World Bank, *World Development Indicators*, 2011.

107. Maria de Lourdes Mollo and Alfredo Saad-Filho, "Neoliberal Economic Policies in Brazil (1994–2005): Cardoso, Lula, and the Need for a Democratic Alternative," *New Political Economy*, 11:1 (2006), 107.

108. World Bank, *World Development Indicators*, 2011.

109. Mollo and Saad-Filho, "Neoliberal Economic Policies in Brazil (1994–2005): Cardoso, Lula, and the Need for a Democratic Alternative," 108.

110. Hunter and Power, "Lula's Brazil at Midterm," 128.

111. Martínez and Santiso, "Financial Markets and Politics: The Confidence Game in Latin American Economies," 369.

112. "Man of the Year: Arminio Fraga, The Man Who Saved Brazil," *Latin Finance* 135, March 2002.

113. Nathan Jensen and Scott Schmith, "Market Responses to Politics: The Rise of Lula and the Decline of the Brazilian Stock Market," *Comparative Political Studies* 38:10 (2005), 1247; Goldfrank and Wampler, "From Petista Way to Brazil Way," 259.

114. Martínez and Santiso, "Financial Markets and Politics: The Confidence Game in Latin American Economies," 372.

115. Some authors point to Lula's candidacy as the source of instability. Others point to the uncertainty that historically has accompanied presidential elections in Brazil. Yet others point to the generalized slide in markets across the world as a result of a global economic downturn. For the first view see Martínez and Santiso, "Financial Markets and Politics: The Confidence Game in Latin American Economies"; Jensen and Schmith, "Market Responses to Politics: The Rise of Lula and the Decline of the Brazilian Stock Market." For the second view see Iain Hardie, "The Power of Markets? The International Bond Markets and the 2002 Elections in Brazil," *Review of International Political Economy* 13: 1 (2006). For the third perspective see Barry Eichengreen, "A Temporary Respite for Brazil," UC Berkeley Working Paper, August 9, 2002.

116. "Carta ao povo brasileiro" (Letter to the Brazilian People), Luiz Inácio Lula da Silva, São Paulo, June 22, 2002.

117. Jensen and Schmith, "Market Responses to Politics: The Rise of Lula and the Decline of the Brazilian Stock Market," 1250.

118. "Um liberal no PT," *Isto É Gente*, July 1st, 2010. Staub's quote reads: "Não entendo as resistências absurdas a Lula, provocam críticas de um radicalismo absolutamente incompreensível."

119. "Business Likes Lula, but Wall Street Doesn't," *Businessweek*, October 14, 2002. For an account of industrialists' discontent with Cardoso's economic policies see José Fiori. *Brasil no espaço* (Petrópolis, Vozes, 2001).

120. For a study of campaign finance in Brazil see David Samuels, "Money, Elections, and Democracy in Brazil," *Latin American Politics and Society* 43:2 (2001).

121. Tribunal Superior Eleitoral do Brasil, *Prestação de Contas dos Candidatos* (Brasilia: TSE, 2002). Historic levels of campaign contributions allowed Lula to hire Duda Mendonça, one of the top political marketing consultants, for his campaign. Mendonça was responsible for Lula's popular campaign slogan "*Lula, paz e amor*," or "Lula, peace and love."

122. As Guido Mantega put it, "the PT had credibly shown its economic prudency much before the election through its actions while governing five states and 186 cities, including São Paulo." Interview with Guido Mantega, minister of planning and budget (2003–2004), head of the National Development Bank (BNDES) (2004–2006), and minister of finance (2006–2010), in *El País*, "El eterno candidato del Partido de los Trabajadores suaviza su discurso para optar con garantías a la presidencia de Brasil," June 9, 2002.

123. Author's interview with Bernard Appy, deputy minister of finance at the time the ministry was headed by Antônio Palocci (2003–2006). November 16, 2010.

124. Nelson Barbosa and José Antônio Pereira de Souza, "A inflexão do governo Lula: política econômica, crescimento e distribuição da renda," In *Brasil entre o Passado e o Futuro*, ed. Emir Sader and Marco Aurélio Garcia (Editora Fundação Perseu Abramo e Boitempo Editorial, 2010).

125. The Brazilian stock market began a steep climb right after the second round of the 2002 election and recuperated all of its losses and returned to its pre-instability levels seven months after Lula's election. See Hardie, "The Power of Markets? The International Bond Markets and the 2002 Elections in Brazil."

126. Barbosa and Pereira de Souza, "A inflexão do governo Lula: política econômica, crescimento e distribuição da renda."

127. Author's interview with Julio Alexandre Menezes da Silva, deputy vice minister of finance, November 29, 2010.

128. Author's interview with Antônio Henrique Silveira, head of the Finance Ministry's Secretariat for Economic Monitoring (Secretário de Acompanhamento da Receita Econômica), October 21, 2010.

129. Matthew Shugart and Stephan Haggard, "Institutions and Public Policy in Presidential Systems," in *Presidents, Parliaments, and Policy*, ed. Haggard and McCubbins (New York, NY: Cambridge University Press, 2001), 80.

130. Carlos Pereira, Timothy Power, and Lucio Rennó, "Agenda Power, Executive Degree Authority, and the Mixed Results of Reform in the Brazilian Congress," *Legislative Studies Quarterly* 33:1 (2008).

131. In 2001, Constitutional Amendment 32 allowed the president to reissue provisional decrees once for another 60-day period if Congress has not voted on the measure. However, if no vote is held 45 days after the decree's publication, the measure goes to the top of the legislative agenda and no other issue can be discussed until the vote is held. Fabiano Santos and Márcio Grijó Vilarouca, "Political Institutitions and Governability from FHC to Lula," in *Democratic Brazil Revisited*, ed. Kingstone and Power (Pittsburgh, PA: University of Pittsburgh Press, 2008), 70; Armijo, Faucher, and Dembinska, "Compared to What? Assessing Brazilian Political Institutions," 762.

132. These restrictions are particularly salient vis-à-vis the provisions in the previous Constitution, which gave the president the right to pass decree laws that remained legally binding without congressional approval.

133. Author's interview with Deputy Vice Minister of Finance Dyogo Henrique de Oliveira, November 29, 2010.

134. Author's interview with Deputado José Carlos Aleluia, leader of the Democratas (former PFL) faction in the House of Representatives and sponsor of several bills to limit the prerogative of executive decrees, October 27, 2010.

135. The rest of the members of the council are the ministers of finance, planning, industry and foreign trade, social security, labor, environment, and foreign relations.

136. "Para Mantega, atual status do Banco Central é adecuado," *Reuters*, August 23, 2006.

137. Among the main challenges brought up by the opposition parties were that the executive decree did not meet the "urgent" character reserved for Medidas Provisórias in the Constitution.

138. This was in part due to how controversial the measure was, since voting age in Brazil is 16. The change was seen by the opposition as an electoral strategy. "Medida Provisória estende Bolsa Família a jovens de 16 e 17 anos de idade," *Agência Brasil*, March 1, 2008.

139. "Câmara aprova medida provisória que altera o Projovem," *Agência Brasil*, April 15, 2008.

140. Interview with Antonio Henrique Silveira, secretary for economic monitoring at the Ministry of Finance, October 21, 2010.

141. Rudiger Dornbusch and William Cline, "Brazil's Incomplete Stabilization and Reform," *Brookings Papers on Economic Activity*, No. 1 (1997).

142. Mostly during the administrations of Menem, Sánchez de Lozada, and Pinochet in Argentina, Bolivia, and Chile, respectively.

143. The official name of the market reform package was New Brazil Plan (Plano Brasil Novo). For a detailed description of the Plan, see John Crabtee, "The Collor Plan: Shooting the Tiger," *Bulletin of Latin American Research* 10:2 (1991).

144. Edmund Amann and Werner Baer, "Neoliberalism and its Consequences in Brazil," *Journal of Latin American Studies* 34:4 (2002), 947.

145. Under the National De-statization Program (*Programa Nacional de Desestatização*), created by Law 8.031/90 an initial list of state-owned enterprises to be privatized was created. The executive was granted the authority to modify the list.

146. Amann and Baer, "Neoliberalism and its Consequences in Brazil," 947.

147. Author's interterview with Deputy Minister of Finance Bernard Appy, November 16, 2010.

148. Author's interview with former President Fernando Henrique Cardoso, April 6, 2010.

149. Author's interview with Deputy Vice Minister of Finance Dyogo Henrique de Oliveira, November 29, 2010.

150. Mollo and Saad-Filho, "Neoliberal Economic Policies in Brazil (1994–2005): Cardoso, Lula, and the Need for a Democratic Alternative."

151. Rosa Maria Marques and Áquilas Mendes, "O Governo Lula e a Contra-Reforma Previdenciaria," *São Paulo em Perspectiva*, 18:3 (2004), 12.

152. CONLUTAS is associated with the PSUT and the P-SOL. "Metalúrgicos de São José Aprobam Saída da CUT," *Folha de São Paulo*, August 20, 2004.

153. CONLUTAS, "Concepção, Princípios e Programa," (São Paulo, Brazil: Coordenação Nacional de Lutas, 2005).

154. Intersindical is associated with the Partido Comunista Brasileiro and the CTB is associated with the Partido Comunista do Brasil.

155. Wendy Hunter and Timothy Power, "Lula's Brazil at Midterm," *Journal of Democracy* 16:3 (2005).

156. João Machado Borges Neto, "Governo Lula: Una opcão neoliberal," in *Adeus ao Desenvolvimento*, ed. Joao Antonio de Paula (Belo Horizonte: Editora *Autêntica, 2005*); Mollo and Saad-Filho, "Neoliberal Economic Policies in Brazil (1994–2005): Cardoso, Lula, and the Need for a Democratic Alternative."

157. "Meirelles toma posse e destaca estabilidade como principal objetivo econômico," *Época*, January 7, 2003.

158. Author's interview with Bernard Appy, former deputy minister of finance. November 16, 2010.

159. Ministério do Trabalho e Emprego, *Evolução do Salário Mínimo*, February 2010.

160. Reiner Radermacher and Waldeli Melleiro, "Mudanças no cenário sindical brasileiro sob o governo de Lula," *Nueva Sociedad* 211 (September–October 2007).

161. Michael Hall, "The Labor Policies of the Lula Government," in *Brazil under Lula: Economy, Politics, and Society under the Worker-President*, ed. Joseph Love and Werner Baer (New York, NY: Palgrave, 2009).

162. Hunter and Power, "Lula's Brazil at Midterm," 130; Mollo and Saad-Filho, "Neoliberal Economic Policies in Brazil (1994–2005): Cardoso, Lula, and the Need for a Democratic Alternative," 112.

163. Juan Pablo Jiménez and Varinia Tromben, "Política fiscal y bonanza: impacto del aumento de los precios de los productos no renovables en América Latina y el Caribe," *Revista de la CEPAL* 90 (2006).

164. "Petrobras capta R$115 bilhões em oferta pública," *Fohla de São Paulo*, September 30, 2010.

165. According to Almir Barbassa, chief financial officer and investor relations officer at Petrobras, the company's public share offering was necessary because its debt had reached 34 percent of its total liquid assets, close to the 35 percent required to maintain investment grade. "Endividamento no limite motivou capitalização de Petrobras," *Fohla de São Paulo*, September 13, 2010.

166. "Petrobras vende todo o lote de ações e capitalização atingue R$120 bilhões," *Fohla de São Paulo*, October 1, 2010.

167. "Entenda a capitalização de Petrobras," *Fohla de São Paulo*, September 13, 2010.

168. I am indebted to Oswaldo Guerra, adviser to Petrobras and economics professor at the Universidade Federal da Bahia for pointing this out. Author's interview with Oswaldo Guerra, October 30, 2010.

169. "Lei 9478, Que dispõe sobre a política energética nacional, as atividades relativas ao monopólio do petróleo, institui o Conselho Nacional de Política Energética e a Agência Nacional do Petróleo e dá outras providências," *Diario Oficial da União* 9478 August 6, 1997.

170. "Nova reserva de petróleo pode ser maior que Tupi," *Estado de São Paulo*, June 13, 2008.

171. "Petróleo já representa 8% do PIB do Brasil," *Folha de São Paulo*, January 3, 2007.

172. "Petrobrás se expande em várias áreas e já movimenta 10% do PIB," *Estadão de São* Paulo, January 30, 2010.

173. The source of this comparative data is US Energy Information Administration, *International Energy Statistics 2010* (Washington, DC: EIA, 2010).

174. On the PSDB see Celso Roma, "A institucionalização do PSDB entre 1988 e 1999," *Revista Brasileira de Ciências Sociais* 17:49 (2002). On the PT see Hunter, "The Normalization of an Anomaly: The Workers' Party in Brazil."

CHAPTER 6

1. "Teníamos que ser muy realistas con los límites impuestos por la herencia institucional de la dictadura y la necesidad de mantener la cohesión entre los distintos partidos en el gobierno. Sin lugar a dudas, el paso de las reformas económicas de la Concertación se ha visto disminuido por la necesidad de buscar acuerdos entre todas las fuerzas políticas, tanto de la izquierda como de la derecha." Author's interview, June 5, 2009.

2. For a discussion of the recurrent tension caused by differences in statist and pro-market views within the Concertación see the op-ed "El retorno de las dos almas," by Patricio Navia, *La Tercera*, April 25, 2006.

3. Matthew Shugart and Stephan Haggard, "Institutions and Public Policy in Presidential Systems," in *Presidents, Parliaments, and Policy*, ed. Haggard and McCubbins (New York, NY: Cambridge University Press, 2001); *UNDP, La democracia en América Latina* (New York, NY: UNDP, 2004); Gabriel Negretto, "Political Parties and Institutional Design: Explaining Constitutional Choice in Latin America," *British Journal of Political Science* 39:1 (2009).

4. Alan Angell, "Party Change in Chile in Comparative Perspective," *Revista de Ciencia Politica* (Santiago) 23:2 (2003); Mainwaring and Scully, "Introduction: Party Systems in Latin America, " in *Building Democratic Institutions: Party Systems in Latin America*, ed. Scott Mainwaring and Timothy Scully (Stanford, CA: Stanford University Press, 1995); Samuel Valenzuela and Timothy Scully, "Electoral Choices and the Party System in Chile," *Comparative Politics*, 29:4 (1997).

5. Timothy Scully, "Reconstituting Party Politics in Chile," in *Building Democratic Institutions: Party Systems in Latin America*, ed. Scott Mainwaring and Timothy Scully (Stanford, CA: Stanford University Press, 1995), 102.

6. Scully, "Reconstituting Party Politics in Chile," 123.

7. Scully, "Reconstituting Party Politics in Chile."

8. Valenzuela and Scully, "Electoral Choices and the Party System in Chile," 511.

9. The Gremialista movement was a typically Catholic University student union, with some resemblance to the Integrist movement in Franco's Spain. Rossana Castiglioni, "Pensions and Soldiers: The Role of Power, Ideas, and Veto Players under Military Rule in Chile and Uruguay," 21.

10. Arturo Valenzuela, "Government and Politics," in *Chile: A Country Study*, ed. Rex Hudson (Washington, DC: Library of Congress, 1994).

11. Pamela Constable and Arturo Valenzuela, *A Nation of Enemies: Chile under Pinochet* (New York, NY: Norton, 1991).

12. Many of the most prominent UDI cadres emerged from the gremialistas of the Universidad Católica. They were led by Jaime Guzmán, who became a prominent founder and leader of the party.

13. Arturo Valenzuela, "The Breakdown of Authoritarian Regimes: Chile," in *The Breakdown of Democratic Regimes*, ed. Juan Linz and Alfred Stepan (Baltimore, MD: Johns Hopkins University Press, 1991).

14. Valenzuela, "Government and Politics."

15. J. Samuel Valenzuela, "Orígenes y transformaciones del sistema de partidos en Chile," *Estudios Públicos* 58 (Fall 1995).

16. Although the PC reached 5 percent of the vote in the 2005 parliamentary elections, its support has not translated into congressional seats due to Chile's binomial electoral system (discussed in the following pages).

17. J. Samuel Valenzuela, "Reflexiones sobre el presente y futuro del paisaje político chileno a partir de su pasado," *Estudios Públicos* 75 (Winter 1999), 275.

18. The index was calculated based on each individual party's share of the vote. A calculation based on alliances instead of parties results in an even lower volatility score.

19. Valenzuela and Scully, "Electoral Choices and the Party System in Chile," 515.

20. Angell, "Party Change in Chile in Comparative Perspective."

21. Valenzuela and Scully, "Electoral Choices and the Party System in Chile," 520.

22. Biblioteca del Congreso Nacional de Chile, Reseña biográfica parlamentaria de Francisco Javier Errázuriz (Santiago, Chile: Biblioteca del Congreso Nacional de Chile, 2008).

23. David Altman, "Political Recruitment and Candidate Selection in Chile (1990–2003): The Executive Branch," in *Pathway to Power in Latin America*, ed. Scott Morgenstern and Peter Siavelis (University Park, PA: Penn State University Press, 2008).

24. UDI and RN presented a single candidacy in a right-wing coalition known as Unión por el Progreso de Chile. Gerardo Munck, "Democratic Stability and Its Limits: An Analysis of Chile's 1993 Elections," *Journal of Inter-American Studies of World Affairs* 36: 2 (1994), 3.

25. "Marco Enríquez-Ominami abre la puerta a su renuncia del PS," *La Nación*, January 19, 2009.

26. The Concertación leadership closed ranks behind Frei, in spite of Enríquez-Ominami's lineage: he is the biological son of Miguel Enríquez—the leader of the Movimiento de Izquierda Revolucionaria (MIR) and key actor in the underground resistance to the dictatorship until his murder. Enríquez-Ominami is also the adoptive son of former Socialist Party notable, Senator Carlos Ominami.

27. Valenzuela and Scully, "Electoral Choices and the Party System in Chile."

28. Valenzuela, "Government and Politics."

29. Valenzuela and Scully, "Electoral Choices and the Party System in Chile," 524.

30. Valenzuela, "Government and Politics."

31. Scully, "Reconstituting Party Politics in Chile," 122.

32. Ley Orgánica Constitucional sobre Votaciones Populares y Escrutinios (Ley No. 18.700) May 6, 1988.

33. Claudia Heiss and Patricio Navia, "You Win Some, You Lose Some: Constitutional Reforms in Chile's Transition to Democracy," *Latin American Politics and Society*, 49:3 (2007).

34. John Carey and Peter Siavelis, "Insurance for Good Losers and the Survival of Chile's Concertación," *Latin American Politics and Society*, 47:2 (2005), 4.

35. Carmen Fariña, "Génesis y significación de la Ley de Partidos Políticos," *Estudios Públicos* 27 (1987).

36. Timothy Scully, "Chile: The Political Underpinnings of Economic Liberalization," in *Constructing Democratic Governance*, ed. Domínguez and Lowenthal (Baltimore, MD: Johns Hopkins University Press, 1996), 111.

37. "El Congreso Pleno aprobó las 58 reformas constitucionales," *El Mercurio*, August 21, 2005.

38. Scully, "Chile: The Political Underpinnings of Economic Liberalization," 112.

39. David Altman, "Political Recruitment and Candidate Selection in Chile (1990–2003): The Executive Branch," in *Pathway to Power in Latin America*, ed. Scott Morgenstern and Peter Siavelis (University Park, PA: Penn State University Press, 2008).

40. In 2005 the withdrawal of candidates initially intending to run against Michelle Bachelet obviated the need for an open primary.

41. Hess and Navia, "You Win Some, You Lose Some: Constitutional Reforms in Chile's Transition to Democracy."

42. Carey and Siavelis, "Insurance for Good Losers and the Survival of Chile's Concertación," 4.

43. In the context of the Concertación's governments, Carey and Siavelis have made reference to the *partido transversal* (transversal party) as an "informal, though well recognized, cadre of supra-party elites whose loyalty lies as much with the Concertación coalition as with their individual parties." Carey and Siavelis, "Insurance for Good Losers and the Survival of Chile's Concertación," 7.

44. Author's interview with former Minister of the General Secretariat of the President, Álvaro García Hurtado, June 10, 2009.

45. Arturo Valenzuela and Lucía Dammert, "Problems of Success in Chile," *Journal of Democracy*, 17:4 (2006), 70.

46. Author's interview with Pamela Figueroa, director of the office of governability, Ministry of the Interior, June 19, 2009.

47. Heiss and Navia, "You Win Some, You Lose Some: Constitutional Reforms in Chile's Transition to Democracy."

48. Rossana Castiglioni, "Cambios y continuidad en política social," in *Gobierno de Ricardo Lagos*, ed. Roberto Funk (Santiago, Chile: Universidad Diego Portales, 2006).

49. Author's interview with Senator Carlos Ominami, June 5, 2009.

50. This view was reiterated in interviews with fomer Minister Álvaro García Hurtado, former Minister and Senator Carlos Ominami, and by Jorge Frei Toledo, former adviser to Lagos between 2003 and 2006 and deputy minister of justice under President Bachelet.

51. Designated senators were eliminated following a constitutuional reform that came into force on March 11, 2006, the last day of Lagos's presidency.

52. Author's interview with Francisco Javier Díaz, office of the president's director of public policy, member of the Socialist Party's Directorate, and speech writer and adviser to Michelle Bachelet, June 5, 2009.

53. Scully, "Chile: The Political Underpinnings of Economic Liberalization," 103.

54. In the 1989 Senate election, Andrés Zaldívar beat Lagos by less than 1 percent as the Concertación candidate. Lagos would beat Zaldívar in a primary for the presidential nomination in 1999.

55. Before serving in this capacity, he became the minister of education (1990–1992) in Patricio Aylwin's administration.

56. Alvear withdrew her candidacy before the primary could take place. "Precandidata Soledad Alvear abandonó la carrera presidencial," El Mercurio, May 24, 2005.

57. The predictability of the opposition is a crucial distinction between the Chilean and Brazilian systems. In Chile, the policy positions of the opposition are extremely predictable, compared to more fluid legislative positions in Brazil.

58. Scully, "Chile: The Political Underpinnings of Economic Liberalization," 111.

59. Valenzuela and Dammert, "Problems of Success in Chile," 70.

60. Aguero, "Chile: Unfinished Transition and Increased Political Competition," 51.

61. "Lagos promulga TLC con Estados Unidos," El Mercurio, December 4, 2003.

62. "Debate en el Senado: ni panacea ni tragedia," El Mercurio, October 23, 2003.

63. Transcript of the 48th Ordinary Session, Chilean Senate, April 13, 2004.

64. "Congreso aprueba ley que crea programa Chile Solidario," La Tercera, April 15, 2004.

65. Volker Frank, "Politics without Policy: The Failure of Social Concertation in Democratic Chile 1990–2000," in Victims of the Chilean Miracle, ed. Peter Winn (Durham, NC: Duke University Press, 2004), 91.

66. In a significantly watered down version of his labor reform bill, Lagos faced difficulty in getting the Christian Democrats on board. "Senado aprobó finalmente ayer el proyecto en su último trámite constitucional," La Tercera, September 12, 2001.

67. Fernando Durán-Palma, Adrian Wilkinson, and Marek Korcynski "Labour Reform in a Neo-Liberal 'Protected' Democracy: Chile 1990–2001," International Journal of Human Resource Management 16:1 (2005), 72–73.

68. Author's interview with Francisco Javier Díaz, office of the president's director of public policy, member of the Socialist Party, and President Bachelet's adviser and speechwriter, June 5, 2009.

69. In May 1983, amid discontent among the middle and working classes because of the economic crisis, national protests erupted. The protest was led by the copper workers union and resulted in massive demonstrations. Subsequent protests were organized on a monthly basis.

70. Eduardo Silva, "Capitalist Regime Loyalties and Redemocratization in Chile," Journal of Interamerican Studies and World Affairs, 34:4 (1993), 96.

71. Silva, "Capitalist Regime Loyalties and Redemocratization in Chile," 96.

72. Author's interview with Jorge Frei Toledo, adviser to Ricardo Lagos and former deputy minister of justice, June 30, 2009.

73. Patricio Meller, "Consideraciones económicas en torno al gobierno de Ricardo Lagos," in El Gobierno de Ricardo Lagos, ed. Robert Funk (Santiago, Chile: Universidad Diego Portales, 2006).

74. World Bank, World Development Indicators, 2011.

75. United Nations Economic Commission for Latin America (ECLAC), *Preliminary Overview of the Economies of Latin America and the Caribbean, 2010* (Chile: UN Economic Commission for Latin America and the Caribbean, 2011).

76. Patricio Navia, "La aprobación presidencial en el sexenio de Lagos," in *El gobierno de Ricardo Lagos: La nueva vía chilena hacia el socialismo*, ed. Roberto Funk, (Santiago: Universidad Diego Portales, 2006), 23; Valenzuela and Dammert, "Problems of Success in Chile," 66.

77. For the right's account of the Concertación's declining average growth rates across presidencies see Andrés Allamand, *El Desalojo: Por qué la Concertación debe irse en el 2010*, (Santiago de Chile: Aguilar, 2007).

78. Arturo Valenzuela, "Government and Politics."

79. It must be noted that wealth inequality increased along with GDP growth throughout the Pinochet regime.

80. Eduardo Silva, "From Dictatorship to Democracy: The Business-State Nexus in Chile's Economic Transformation, 1975–1994," *Comparative Politics*, 28:3 (1996): 304.

81. However, exchange rates were fixed between 1979 and 1982 in an attempt to achieve stability. Eduardo Silva, "Capitalist Regime Loyalties and Redemocratization in Chile," *Journal of Interamerican Studies and World Affairs*, 34:4 (1992–1993), 84.

82. Silva, "From Dictatorship to Democracy: The Business-State Nexus in Chile's Economic Transformation, 1975–1994," 305.

83. Eduardo Silva, "Capitalist Coalitions, the State, and Neoliberal Economic Restructuring: Chile, 1973–88," *World Politics*, 45:4 (1993); Silva, "From Dictatorship to Democracy: The Business-State Nexus in Chile's Economic Transformation, 1975–1994."

84. For example, Modesto Collados was president of the construction chamber and later became finance minister.

85. Alejandro Foxley former director of the CIEPLAN, and later Patricio Aylwin's finance minister, constitutes a prominent example. Patricio Silva, "Technocrats and Politics in Chile: From the Chicago Boys to the CIEPLAN Monks," *Journal of Latin American Studies* 23: 2 (1991).

86. Jeffrey Puryear, *Thinking Politics: Intellectuals and Democracy in Chile* (Baltimore, MD: Johns Hopkins University Press, 1994).

87. Author's interview with José Jara, Director of FLACSO Chile, June 3, 2009.

88. Silva, "From Dictatorship to Democracy: The Business-State Nexus in Chile's Economic Transformation, 1975–1994."

89. Jonathan Barton, "State Continuismo and Pinochetismo: The Keys to the Chilean Transition," *Bulletin of Latin American Research*, 21:3 (2002), 370.

90. Barton, "State Continuismo and Pinochetismo: The Keys to the Chilean Transition."

91. This office was created by President Aylwin and performs similar functions as the US president's chief of staff.

92. *Chicago Boys* is the name given to the team of University of Chicago-educated economists appointed to key economic positions during the Pinochet government.

93. Author's interview with Álvaro García Hurtado, June 18, 2009. For a comparison of Lagos's and Lavin's campaigns see "Lavín vs Lagos," *El Mercurio* (Chile), October 9, 1999.

94. Matthew Shugart and John Carey, *Presidents and Assemblies* (New York, NY: Cambridge University Press, 1992); Peter Siavelis, "Exaggerated Presidentialism and Moderate Presidents: Executive Legislative Relations in Chile," in *Legislative Politics in Latin America*, ed. Morgenstern and Nacif (New York, NY: Cambridge University Press, 2002); John Carey, "Parties and Coalitions in

Chile in the 1990s," in *Legislative Politics in Latin America*, ed. Morgenstern and Nacif (New York, NY: Cambridge University Press, 2002).

95. Siavelis, "Exaggerated Presidentialism and Moderate Presidents: Executive Legislative Relations in Chile," 81.

96. Author's interview with Pamela Figueroa, June 19, 2009.

97. Peter Siavelis, "La lógica oculta de la selección de candidatos en las elecciones parlamentarias chilenas," *Estudios Públicos* 98 (Fall 2005).

98. Author's interview with Francisco Javier Díaz, office of the president's director of public policy, member of the Socialist Party, and President Bachelet's adviser and speechwriter, June 5, 2009.

99. Siavelis, "Exaggerated Presidentialism and Moderate Presidents: Executive Legislative Relations in Chile," 106.

100. Chile's state-owned enterprise, Corporación Nacional del Cobre de Chile (CODELCO), is the world's largest copper producer, controlling 20 percent of the world's total reserves.

101. DIPRES, "Director de Presupuestos Informa sobre Ejecución Presupuestaria del Gobierno Central y Activos Financieros del Tesoro Público de 2006," Press Release, January 31, 2007.

102. Although the extraction of copper could have different effects on policy makers than the extraction of other natural resources, there is no distinction made in the resource dependence literature. See for example Sachs and Werner, "The Curse of Natural Resources."

103. Helia Henríquez Riquelme, "Las Relaciones Laborales en Chile" in *El modelo chileno*, eds. Paul Drake and Ivan Jaksic (Santiago de Chile: LOM Ediciones, 1999).

104. Volker Frank, "The Elusive Goal in Democratic Chile: Reforming the Pinochet Labor Legislation," *Latin American Politics and Society* 44:1 (2002).

105. Daniel Nuñez and Antonio Aravena, "El gobierno de Ricardo Lagos ¿avanzan los trabajadores?" *Revista Laboral ICAL*, Instituto de Ciencias Alejandro Lipschutz, Santiago, Chile (April–June 2005).

106. Frank, "The Elusive Goal in Democratic Chile: Reforming the Pinochet Labor Legislation."

107. *El Mercurio*, "Las áreas pendientes de Lagos en leyes económicas," May 16, 2005.

108. Juan Pablo Luna and David Altman, "Uprooted but Stable: Chilean Parties and the Concept of Party System Institutionalization," *Latin American Politics and Society* 53:2 (2011).

CHAPTER 7

1. Carlos Fuentes, "Latin America's New Left," *New Perspectives Quarterly* 23:2 (2006), 57.

2. Álvaro Vargas Llosa, "The Return of the Idiot," *Foreign Policy* (May/June 2007), 56.

3. Teodoro Petkoff, *Las dos izquierdas* (Caracas: Alfadil, 2005); Franklin Ramírez Gallegos, "Mucho más que dos izquierdas," *Nueva Sociedad* 205 (September–October 2006).

4. Andy Baker and Kenneth Greene, "The Latin American Left's Mandate: Free-Market Policies and Issue Voting in New Democracies" *World Politics* 63:1 (2011); María Victoria Murillo, Virginia Oliveros, and Milan Vaishnav, "Voting for the Left or Governing on the Left," in *The Resurgence of the Latin American Left*, ed. Levitsky and Roberts (Baltimore, MD: Johns Hopkins University Press, 2011).

5. Steven Levitsky and Kenneth Roberts, "Latin America's Left Turn: A Framework for Analysis," in *The Resurgence of the Latin American Left*, ed. Levitsky and Roberts.

6. Deborah Yashar, "The Left and Citizenship Rights," in *The Resurgence of the Latin American Left*, ed. Levitsky and Roberts (Baltimore, MD: Johns Hopkins University Press, 2011).

7. Kurt Weyland, Raúl Madrid, and Wendy Hunter (eds.) *Leftist Governments in Latin America: Successes and Shortcomings* (New York, NY: Cambridge University Press, 2010); Maxwell Cameron and Eric Hershberg (eds.) *Latin America's Left Turns: Politics, Policies, and Trajectories of Change* (Boulder, CO: Lynne Rienner, 2010); Levitsky and Roberts (eds.), *The Resurgence of the Latin American Left*.

8. Hector Schamis, "Populism, Socialism, and Democratic Institutions," *Journal of Democracy* 17:4 (2006); Jorge Lanzaro, "La Socialdemocracia Criolla" *Revista Nueva Sociedad* 217 (September–October 2008); Scott Mainwaring, "The crisis of representation in the Andes" *Journal of Democracy* 17:3 (2006).

9. I am indebted to Kenneth Roberts for sharing this observation.

10. Stephan Haggard, "Interests, Institutions, and Policy Reform," in *Economic Policy Reform: The Second Stage*, ed. Anne Krueger (Chicago, IL: University of Chicago Press, 2000), 45.

11. Jorge Castañeda, "Latin America's Left Turn," *Foreign Affairs* 85:3 (2006); Jorge Castañeda and Marco Morales (eds.), *Leftovers: Tales of the Latin American Left* (New York, NY: Routledge, 2008).

12. Stephan Haggard and Robert Kaufman, *The Political Economy of Democratic Transitions* (Princeton, NJ: Princeton University Press, 1995), 153.

13. Two exceptions among their cases were Mexico and Taiwan, with single party rule at the time.

14. See, inter alia, Anne Krueger (ed.), *Economic Policy Reform: The Second Stage.* (Chicago, IL: University of Chicago Press, 2000).

15. James Robinson, Ragnar Torvik, and Thierry Verdier, "Political Foundations of the Resource Curse," *Journal of Development Economics* 79 (April 2006); Pauline Jones Luong and Erika Weinthal, *Oil is Not a Curse: Ownership Structure and Institutions in Soviet Successor State* (New York, NY: Cambridge University Press, 2010).

16. Richard Auty, "Conclusion," in *Resource Abundance and Economic Development*, ed. Richard Auty (New York, NY: Oxford University Press, 2001).

17. Jonathan Di John, *From Windfall to Curse? Oil and Industrialization in Venezuela, 1920 to the Present* (University Park, PA: Penn State University Press, 2009).

18. Kurt Weyland, "The Rise of Latin America's Two Lefts: Insights from Rentier State Theory," *Comparative Politics* 41:2 (2009); Manuel Hidalgo, "Hugo Chávez's 'Petro Socialism,'" *Journal of Democracy* 20:2 (2009).

19. Allan Drazen and Vittorio Grilli, "The Benefits of Crisis for Economic Reform," *American Economic Review* 83:3 (1993), 598–607; Dani Rodrik, "Understanding Economic Policy Reform," *Journal of Economic Literature.* 34:1 (1996), 9–41; Moisés Naím, "Latin America: The Second Stage of Reform," *Journal of Democracy* 5:4 (1994).

20. Michael Bruno and William Easterly, "Inflation's Children: Tales of Crises that Beget Reforms," *American Economic Review* 86:2 (1996), 213–17.

21. Anne Krueger, "The Political Economy of Rent-Seeking," *American Economic Review* 64:3 (1974), 291–303; Anne Krueger, *Economic Policy Reform in Developing Countries* (Blackwell Publishers 1992); James Cassing, Timothy McKeown, and Jack Ochs, "The Political Economy of the Tariff Cycle," *American Political Science Review* 80:3 (1986).

22. Michael Bruno and William Easterly, "Inflation's Children: Tales of Crises that Beget Reforms," 213–17.

23. Kurt Weyland, "Swallowing the Bitter Pill: Sources of Popular Support for Neoliberal Reforms in Latin America," *Comparative Political Studies* 31: 5 (1998).

24. The Argentine government's changes in the way inflation is calculated may mask some of the country's true inflation rate.

25. Javier Corrales, "Do Economic Crises Contribute to Economic Reform? Argentina and Venezuela in the 1990s," *Political Science Quarterly* 112 (Winter 1997–1998), 617–44.

26. Stephan Haggard, "Interests, Institutions, and Policy Reform," in *Economic Policy Reform: The Second Stage*, ed. Anne Krueger (Chicago, IL: University of Chicago Press, 2000), 41.

27. Following a spike in 1996, Venezuela's inflation rate showed significant improvement during the second half of the 1990s.

28. María Victoria Murillo, "From Populism to Neoliberalism: Labor Unions and Market Reforms in Latin America," *World Politics* 52:2 (2000); Raúl Madrid, "Laboring against Neoliberalism: Unions and Patterns of Reform in Latin America," *Journal of Latin American Studies* 35:1 (2003).

29. Barbara Geddes, "Challenging the Conventional Wisdom," *Journal of Democracy* 5:4 (1994); Stephan Haggard, "Interests, Institutions, and Policy Reform."

30. Hector Schamis, *Reforming the State: The Politics of Privatization in Latin America and Europe* (Ann Arbor, MI: University of Michigan Press, 2002).

31. Barbara Geddes, "Challenging the Conventional Wisdom," 111.

32. Rudiger Dornbusch and Sebastian Eduards (eds.) *The Macroeconomics of Populism in Latin America* (Chicago, IL: University of Chicago Press, 1991).

33. José Antonio Ocampo, *Reconstruir el futuro: globalización, desarrollo y democracia en América Latina* (Bogotá, Colombia: Grupo Editorial Norma, 2004).

34. Martín Ardanaz, Carlos Scartascini, and Mariano Tommasi, *Political Institutions, Policymaking, and Economic Policy in Latin America*, Inter-American Development Bank Working Paper Series No. IDB-WP-158 (March 2010), 5.

35. Dornbusch and Edwards, "Introduction," in *The Macroeconomics of Populism in Latin America*, ed. Dornbusch and Edwards (Chicago, IL: University of Chicago Press, 1991), 2.

36. Eliana Cardoso and Anne Helwege, "Populism, Profligacy, and Redistribution," in *The Macroeconomics of Populism in Latin America*, ed. Dornbusch and Edwards (Chicago, IL: University of Chicago Press, 1991).

37. Robert Kaufman and Barbara Stallings, "The Political Economy of Latin American Populism," in *The Macroeconomics of Populism in Latin America*, ed. Dornbusch and Edwards (Chicago, IL: University of Chicago Press, 1991).

38. Francisco Panizza, "The Social Democratization of the Latin American Left," *Revista Europea de Estudios Latinoamericanos y del Caribe* 79 (October 2005); Sebastian Edwards, *Left Behind: Latin America and the False Promise of Populism* (Chicago, IL: University of Chicago Press, 2010).

39. Petkoff, *Las dos izquierdas*.

40. Álvaro Vargas Llosa, "The Return of the Idiot."

41. Castañeda, "Latin America's Left Turn."

42. In the context of Latin America see, for example, Guillermo Perry, Luis Serven, William Maloney, Humberto Lopez, and Omar Arias, *Poverty Reduction and Growth: Virtuous and Vicious Cycles* (Washington, DC: World Bank, 2006).

43. Jorge Castañeda, *Utopia Unarmed* (New York: Knopf, 1993); Matthew Cleary, "A Left Turn in Latin America? Explaining the Left's Resurgence," *Journal of Democracy* 17:4 (2006).

44. The period begins with Hugo Chávez's first year in office and ends in 2009, the last year for which GDP growth data were available at the time of writing.

45. Other considerations, such as international business cycles and external shocks, may play an important role in determining performance. See Garey Ramey and Valerie Ramey, "Cross-Country Evidence on the Link Between Volatility and Growth," *American Economic Review* 85:5 (1995).

46. Estimates calculated based on data from the World Bank, *World Development Indicators*, 2011.

47. In the Venezuelan case, the extent to which elections were free and fair has been contested. See for example, Hidalgo, "Hugo Chávez's 'Petro Socialism.'"

48. For a discussion of the benefits of the broad availability of political alternatives see Arend Lijphart, *Patterns of Democracy: Government Forms and Performance in Thirty-Six Countries* (New Haven, CT: Yale University Press, 1999); Barry Ames, "Approaches to the Study of Institutions in Latin American Politics," *Latin American Research Review* 34:1 (1999).

49. Mainwaring and Scully, "Conclusion: Parties and Democracy in Latin America, Common Patterns, Different Challenges," in *Building Democratic Institutions: Party Systems in Latin America*, ed. Mainwaring and Scully (Stanford, CA: Stanford University Press, 1995), 466.

50. Richard Gunther, Nikiforos P. Diamandouros, and Hans-Jürgen Puhle, *The Politics of Democratic Consolidation: Southern Europe in Comparative Perspective* (Baltimore, MD: Johns Hopkins University Press, 1995), 12.

51. Andreas Schedler, "What is Democratic Consolidation?" *Journal of Democracy* 9:2 (1998), 99.

52. Dani Rodrik, "Understanding Economic Policy Reform," *Journal of Economic Literature* 34 (1996), 9; Thomas Pepinsky, *Economic Crises and the Breakdown of Authoritarian Regimes* (New York, NY: Cambridge University Press, 2009).

53. "Trying to Make Peace with International Capital Markets," *The Economist*, March 31, 2010.

54. Banco Central de Venezuela, "El PIB de Venezuela disminuyó en el primer trimestre de 2010 con respecto a igual periodo del año anterior," *Comunicado de prensa del Banco Central de Venezuela* (May 25, 2010).

55. Instituto Nacional de Estadísticas de Bolivia, "Evolución de la demanda interna, el consumo privado y la inversión, 2000–2008," March 2010.

56. Cameron and Hershberg (eds.), *Latin America's Left Turns*.

57. "El Estado puede ser más eficiente que un privado," *La Nación*, November 30, 2003.

58. Author's interview with Dyogo Henrique de Oliveira, Brazil's vice minister of finance, November 29, 2010.

59. Author's interview with Álvaro García Hurtado, Frei's minister of the economy and Lagos's chief of staff, June 18, 2009.

60. Author's interview with Carlos Arce Macías, adviser to President Fox and Mexico's undersecretary of the economy under President Calderón, August 2008.

61. Eduardo Silva, "From Dictatorship to Democracy: The Business-State Nexus in Chile's Economic Transformation, 1975–1994," *Comparative Politics* 28:3 (1996).

62. Haggard, "Interests, Institutions, and Policy Reform."

63. Haggard and Kaufman, *The Political Economy of Democratic Transitions*.

64. Alberto Alesina, "Political Models of Macroeconomic Policy and Fiscal Reform" in *Voting for Reform: Democracy, Political Liberalization, and Economic Adjustment*, ed. Haggard and Webb (Washington, DC: World Bank, 1994), 47.

65. Ricardo Hausmann, "Will Volatility Kill Market Democracy?" *Foreign Policy* 108 (Autumn 1997).

66. "Morales mira a la constituyente," *La Razón*, June 19, 2005.

67. Catherine Conaghan, "Ecuador's Gamble: Can Correa Govern?" *Current History* 106:697 (2007), 79.

68. On indigenous rights see Articles 124 and 125 of the 1999 Constitution of the Bolivarian Republic of Venezuela. On human rights, such as the right to tertiary education and health services, see Articles 83, 84, and 85.

69. Bolivian Constitution of 2009, Part I, Title I, Chapter I, Articles 1 and 2.

70. Constitution of Ecuador of 2008, Title II, Chapter VII, Articles 71–74.

71. Javier Corrales, "Origins of Constitutions and Degrees of Presidentialism in Latin America, 1987–2009," Unpublished ms., Amherst College, November 2009.

72. Javier Corrales, "Origins of Constitutions and Degrees of Presidentialism in Latin America, 1987–2009." On the different forms of constitutional change see Zachary, Elkins, Tom Ginsburg, and Justin Blount, "Can We Trust Legislators to Write Constitutions?" Paper presented at the Annual Meeting of the Latin American Studies Association, Rio de Janeiro, Brazil, 2009.

73. In Venezuela, the decision to convene a Constitutional Assembly compelled only 37.7 percent of eligible voters to cast their vote, and the approval of the final text drew 44 percent of eligible voters.

74. "De conspiración acusa Correa a los legisladores," *El Universo de Guayaquil*, January 28, 2007.

75. "Cronología del vaivén de la consulta popular," *El Universo de Guayaquil*, March 14, 2007.

76. "El gobierno boliviano alertó sobre la posibilidad de una guerra civil," *AFP*, September 11, 2008.

77. Corte Nacional Electoral de Bolivia, *Resultados del Referendum Nacional Constituyente 2009* (Bolivia: CNEB, 2009).

78. Michael Coppedge, "Venezuela: Popular Sovereignty versus Liberal Democracy," in *Constructing Democratic Governance in Latin America*, ed. Jorge Domínguez and Michael Shifter (Baltimore, MD: Johns Hopkins University Press, 2003).

79. Brian Crisp and Gregg Johnson, "De instituciones que restringen a instituciones ausentes," in *Venezuela en transición: elecciones y democracia, 1998–2000*, ed. José Vicente Carrasquero, Thaís Maingón, and Friedrich Welsch (Caracas: Red Universitaria de Estudios Políticos de Venezuela, CDB Publicaciones, 2001).

80. Javier Corrales, "Origins of Constitutions and Degrees of Presidentialism in Latin America, 1987–2009"; Ricardo Combellas, "El proceso constituyente y la Constitución de 1999," *Politeia* (Caracas) 30:30 (January 2003).

81. Guillermo O'Donnell, "Delegative Democracy," *Journal of Democracy* 5:1 (1994).

82. Jagdish Bhagwati, Richard Brecher, and T.N. Srinivasan, "DUP Activities and Economic Theory," in *Neoclassical Political Economy*, ed. David Colander (Cambridge, MA: Ballinger, 1984).

Index